JOHN S. KNOX *Liberty University*

SOCIOLOGY IS RUDE!

A CONVERSATION ON SOCIOLOGICAL THEORY AND THOUGHT

Kendall Hunt
publishing company

MW01285324

Cover illustration and illustrations throughout interior copyright ©2019 Daniel Schallau

www.kendallhunt.com
Send all inquiries to:
4050 Westmark Drive
Dubuque, IA 52004-1840

Copyright © 2019 by Kendall Hunt Publishing Company

PAK ISBN: 978-1-7924-0623-2
ISBN 978-1-5249-8574-5

All rights reserved. No part of this publication may be reproduced,
stored in a retrieval system, or transmitted, in any form or by any means,
electronic, mechanical, photocopying, recording, or otherwise,
without the prior written permission of the copyright owner.

Published in the United States of America

Contents

CHAPTER ONE: Introduction

The Basics

Sociology, a term coined by French philosopher Auguste Comte (1798–1857) in the 19th century, is the study of human relationships, choices, and actions (both public and private). It is the subdiscipline of *behavioral sciences* that has been historically committed to investigating and understanding the relationship between the individual (the person) and his/her surrounding group (the public). The word, *sociology*, literally is a combination of the words, "companion" and "study." It offers innumerable theories and speculations regarding human social existence, which (paradoxically) has been determined in the past, and yet is still continually molded by social structures and forces in the present.

A myriad of subtopics exists within the field of *sociology* that have been (and still are) researched and theorized about by social scientists all over the world. These subtopics include social interaction, socialization, research, culture, family, symbols, race, sexuality, generations, education, religion, social stratification and differentiation, and so on—all of which will be discussed in following chapters. They all encompass human behavior, social groups, relationships, and the social forces surrounding them all.

The main goals of this textbook are to help readers learn more about the foundational theories that *sociology* rests upon (*functionalism, conflict theory, symbolic interaction*); to make sense of the tools of careful sociological research; to perceive the dramatic roles of groups and organizations in society; to comprehend the social forces connected to one's family, race, ethnicity, gender, and religion; to fathom the depths and significance of life stages and the aging process; and to work out the role, power, and influence of social institutions in all human existence.

It is important to keep in mind that critical thinking is not optional when it comes to *sociology*. Conscientious social scientists are not afraid to ask questions about social realities and consequences, no matter how uncomfortable or annoying the topics or findings. They push against oversimplified social notions, they seek to debunk false and harmful social narratives (based on compelling objective evidence), they question actions and ideas taken for granted, and they look beyond the façade to pinpoint factual social forces. Additionally, they are also open to persuasive evidence and analyses that challenge social conventions long established or promoted.

Not surprisingly, such an approach is often considered to be rude by some people in postmodern culture. Uncovering "inconvenient facts" feels for many people to be inappropriate or threatening, socially (O'Hara & Shue, 2014, p. 2). This is a very human response, though, as most become comfortable and emotionally attached to their common, day-to-day ways of life, which dangerously opens the door to compromising proper social study. Sadly, far too many sociology textbooks in postmodernity begin with biased political agenda rather than straight statistical evidence and logical conclusions. Often resting upon fallacies and opinion, they trade in scrutiny for stability.

The result is a textbook that is more promotional than analytical, and one that creates more murkiness than enlightenment regarding important social topics. True sociological studies, being knowledge and research based in principle, explore controversial problems with intellectual honesty and sincere curiosity driving scholars' efforts. Adding accepted *scientific method* to the scientific effort helps to bring social problems into better focus, offering the possibility of social improvements for more than a select few or group.

Truly, beneficial sociological study approaches social phenomena from a humble position, with respect to the varied historical perspectives that have come before on relevant topics, with a discerning eye that compares and orders these sociological points of views, and with a personal charge to be as value-free and neutral as possible when investigating sociological phenomena. Perfect objectivity and neutrality may not be possible considering the foibles of the human condition, but sufficient objectivity and neutrality is more than possible. Still, it begins with self-awareness and a trust that a blind search for truth will contribute the most to scientific thought and greater human society.

The Canon of Theoretical Approaches

Regarding sociological study, several different approaches have been posited by scholars over the years, based on fundamental assumptions about human nature and societal functions. These include the functionalist perspective, conflict theory, symbolic interaction, phenomenology, and social construction.

The *functionalist perspective* was initially established through the scholarly work of theorists like Herbert Spencer, Emilé Durkheim, and Robert Merton. This approach assumes that society is a complex system constructed of numerous interrelated forces and agents, with each part/person of the system performing a vital, needed function that contributes to the whole operation (like biological parts of an organism), which helps to maintain a sense of harmony and equilibrium within society.

The *conflict theory* perspective suggests that society consists of different groups of people completing and struggling against each other for scarce resources like food, domestic products, technology, information access, money, and power. Thus, society is constantly changing and shifting in response to social inequality and conflict (even within religious demesnes), in an overarching power struggle for social change, which Communists like Karl Marx (1818–1883), assorted liberation theologians, and radical feminists assert is inevitable and beneficial for a society mired in the Haves and Have-Nots.

The *symbolic interaction* perspective suggests that society is the end result of individuals directly and personally interacting with other individuals. This approach assumes that "reality" is shaped by individual perceptions, evaluations, and definitions. Thus, it includes face-to-face, nominal activities; it focuses upon how individuals treat, understand, and influence each other through symbols of expression and value. In religious circles, this could include the sacraments, hymnology, and iconography.

The *phenomenology* perspective suggests that reality and "truths" are very individualistic and mostly outside the realm of objective verification because of the ultrapersonal nature of religious experience. Thus, religious sources are key to meanings; but personal meanings are often nonconceptual, abstract, and/or mystical, with relevant language being more symbolic than descriptive. How the phenomenon is presented is mostly dependent upon the specific meaning given to the event by the observer, who goes through an internal process of analysis and interpretation when assigning meaning and value for phenomena.

Finally, the *social construction* perspective suggests that all social understandings, meanings, and values rest more upon a communal agreement than in mere individual whims or dictates. Thus, human beings work in coordination with each other to fashion the realities making up social life. According to Sociologist Peter Berger (1929-2017), this occurs in three stages: an externalization of cultural artifacts through initial social interaction, an objectification of the artifacts when they operate and are embraced by others not initially involved, and an internalization of the artifacts through socialization in general society. A good example of this might be the sacraments of Communion or the Eucharist, which began with Jesus and His Disciples, was adopted by other church leaders outside of Judea in the first few centuries of Christianity, and then spread across the world thousands of years later and is still taught to be sanctified and spiritually significant in Catholicism and other Christian groups.

Dynamic Sociological Investigations

All of the aforementioned social aspects can be considered "sociological facts" because they can be observed in operation; therefore, they can all be studied and analyzed, potentially leading to scientific theories, conclusions, and applications. Thus, social scientists can learn about the role of individuals and groups in society utilizing four key components of sociological investigation: *systematic studies, individual studies, societal studies,* and the *consequences of differences*.

Systematic studies focus on broader, overarching social patterns to investigate. Methodologically, this approach relies upon empirical data, and not just theory or pure logic upon which to base one's conclusions. Careful, cautious steps are taken to record and interpret social experiences and scientific observation, in an attempt to avoid bias leading to faulty conclusions. These studies can be quantitative (how many people in the study?) or qualitative in nature (features, traits, social characteristics).

As all groups are composed of individuals, social scientists will often investigate at a more personal, individual level. After all, as George Herbert Mead (1997) explained, "Our self exists in an interactive relationship with its environment" (p. 249). People have the freedom to choose and act independently of others and to make their own free choices, which is known as *agency*. Most likely, a qualitative study would be undertaken to "dive deep" in these studies.

Additionally, individuals have a tendency to "clump" together, creating a distinct, ordered social environment. Sociologists are very interested in the mechanics and forces behind one's family, high school clique, church body, city or state administrators, and so on. They want to know how economic and cultural resources are distributed and catalytic in social activities and attitudes. This would lead many sociologists to investigate using more quantitative methods to ascertain influential patterns of socialization.

Finally, sociologists are very interested in consequences of differences (especially in postmodernity). The seek to answer questions relating to how one's gender, economic status, religious beliefs, racial factors, political beliefs affect his or her social interactions and experiences. For instance, as Chaiklin (2011) notes, "In effect, one of the major sources of information about the nature of prejudice and discrimination comes from a selective population where the theoretical orientation of the researcher assumes that attitudes must change before behavior does" (p. 33). Because of the mix of the personal and the public in these types of studies, both qualitative and quantitative methods would be utilized to study social phenomenon.

Speaking of sociological phenomenon, postmodernity has asserted its own interpretation of human existence, challenging time-honored and traditionally accepted understandings of sociological realities. Succinctly, *postmodernism* has proclaimed that nothing can be known for certain, nor are there any metanarratives (grand, overarching social interpretations or conclusions). Additionally, logic is, at best, only true for a given individual or culture; therefore, truth is relative and not always the same truth for all times and all people in all situations. Thus, social life is more about choices than value systems, beliefs, and institutional absolutes.

Sociological Basics

One of the more fundamental notions in sociology is that commonsense knowledge may be accurate, but it is not always reliable. For example, are women better with babies than men? Are men better carpenters than women? Who can fly a jet airplane better? Who are the better cooks? Are men less emotional than women? Who are better at making clothing style choices?

Most answers to questions like these rest more upon popular held beliefs rather than any systematic analyses of facts. Yet, sociologists do not accept something as a social fact just because "Everyone believes that it is true." Being social scientists, any social question of interest needs to be tested, analyzed, and verified utilizing the scientific method, which will be discussed more fully in Chapter 2.

Witt (2009) states, "Commonsense knowledge, while sometimes accurate, is not always reliable, because it rests on commonly held beliefs rather than on systematic analysis of facts" (p. 8). Most people make assumptions about reality. Part of this helps people survive, but sometimes it can have negative effects. Understanding the "reality" of common sense puts some assertions into perspective as well as the ones making the commonsense assumptions. Authority should come from confirmation of facts—not from an assumed authoritative voice.

While natural science is the study of physical features of nature (e.g., biology, chemistry, geology) and how they interact and change, social science focuses on the social features of humanity, which are studied and shared in other social science fields like history, psychology, philosophy, and so on. Being one of the "social sciences," sociology depends upon a body of knowledge that has been obtained by methods based on systematic observation, surveys, interviews, demographic analyses, and so on.

The serious sociologist hopes to come up with a rock star sociological theory to finally help explain why men tend to like dogs and women like cats (or is that just a commonsense projection?). A *theory* is a set of statements that seeks to explain social problems, actions, attitudes, or behaviors in big and small communities. It is a speculation and not a fact until conclusively proven with statistical data to back it up.

For instance, some sociologists wonder if young people are likely to begin smoking if their parents smoke. Therefore, theoretically, young people smoke because their parents have modeled smoking as a socially acceptable behavior. Could this theory be true? Think about how many kids your own age you know to be smokers; how many of their parents smoke, too? Now, think about how many kids your own age who do not smoke; how many of their parents are not smokers? Can you see a pattern? How much clarity does it give to the theoretical assertion?

Regardless of your conclusions, just be aware that good theories are explanative and predictive. So, whether the question concerns smoking or attending church or child abuse or being a Communist or starting a postmodern disco, a theory seeks to explain a social phenomenon and back it up with evidence. "W" performs this way because of "X," but it will do "Y" because of "Z" is the general idea behind it. If there is no conclusive evidence, if there is no causation or correlation, then it is just an opinion, which may be true but is of little scientific value.

It is totally acceptable to use one's imagination and to ponder the social possibilities. According to Witt (2009), *social imagination* is "an awareness of the relationship between an individual and the wider society" (p. 2). Even though people exist as individuals, they are part of the whole of society and interact with others in a variety of ways—whether they perceive of it or not. This individual–group interaction starts during infancy and continues through all stages of life and in all circumstances. The quantity and quality of this relationship may vary somewhat, but it exists for all living human beings. Social imagination takes notice of this reality and fleshes out how individuals both affect and are affected by greater society.

This is a regular part of what it means to be a sociologist. First and foremost, they seek to understand how, when, and why people interact with others or their social environment. Many sociologists, though, are not content to merely know why people do what they do, socially; they want to affect a change in society, presumably for the better.

Concerning the utilization of sociological data to affect social change, two main fields are offered in sociology. The *clinical sociologist* seeks to facilitate change by altering social relationships or by restructuring social institutions. This could include family therapy, the reorganization of a medical center or a football team training program, or the remodeling of a classroom physical atmosphere to boost learning outcomes.

The *applied sociologist* seeks to yield practical (and sometimes political) applications for greater society, working with and for government commissions, anti-gang programs, antidrug and alcohol programs, poverty-relief charities, and so on. This activism is commendable as long as its basis rests upon solid sociological knowledge and not just fashionable social opinion.

So, two main things to keep in mind when it comes to applied sociology in the field or in the lab: (a) it is all about the sociological evidence and (b) it is all about the sociological evidence. A sociologist who ignores clear and compelling sociological data to promote a personal or popular agenda is no longer a social scientist, but a sophist or lobbyist who is likely creating or adding more social problems in an arena with more than enough issues (which will be discussed more fully in Chapter 11).

Sociology from Above

God, the Great Sociologist

With this in mind, another accompanying goal of this textbook is to help readers make heads and tails of the study of Sociology—from Above, from a biblical perspective. No doubt, some will challenge this approach as invalidating, but everyone has a biblical perspective that is either affirming or denying. To say that a person's beliefs invalidate proper scientific scrutiny is a self-condemning position for all human beings, logically; however, it is important to be self-aware of personal biases, to be intellectually honest in one's appraisals, and to follow proper scientific methodology—even (or especially) as a conscientious, caring Christian.

Approaching *sociology from above* requires three things: (a) utilizing sociological evidence and facts, (b) resting upon biblical evidence and facts, and (c) applying the Christian worldview virtues of truth and love. If one does this faithfully, useful and beneficial analyses are sure to follow. Of course, Sociology from Above mentality embraces one immutable idea: God is the great Sociologist, according to Scripture.

More than just the Creator, God knows humanity intimately and thoroughly—in reality, He's the Sociologist of sociologists; He's the Psychologist of psychologists; He's the Historian of all historians. He's the Teacher of all teachers. He's the Judge of all judges. He knows the hearts and minds of every man and every woman throughout human history (and the future) better than they know themselves.

In Psalm 139, King David speaks to God's grand knowledge of His children when he writes,

You have searched me, Lord, and you know me.
You know when I sit and when I rise; You perceive my thoughts from afar.
You discern my going out and my lying down; You are familiar with all my ways.
Before a word is on my tongue You, Lord, know it completely.
You hem me in behind and before, And you lay your hand upon me.

David's words on God's omniscience are dramatic and total. Like other human sociologists, God searches, He perceives, He discerns, He knows, He gathers, but unlike human sociologists, God does these actions completely in *"All [our] ways."* He is not the great Theorist; God is the great Factualist.

A pioneer in the Social Sciences in the Age of Liberalism, French Sociologist Emile Durkheim expended much scholarly effort over the years trying to understand the role of religion in society. He wrote,

If religion has given birth to all that is essential in society, it is because the idea of society is the soul of religion.

It is science, and not religion, which has taught men that things are complex and difficult to understand.

By definition, sacred beings are separated beings. That which characterizes them is that there is a break of continuity between them and the profane beings.

Sadly, although Durkheim seems to grasp the importance of God and religion in the affairs of humanity, he did not embrace the immanence of God in all people's existence. David, however, perceived the closeness and comprehension of God concerning the social workings of his own life.

David continues,

Where can I go from your Spirit? Where can I flee from your presence? . . . Your eyes saw my unformed body; all the days Ordained for me were written in your book Before one of them came to be.

For David, nothing and no one was more knowledgeable and understanding than God—

How precious to me are your thoughts, God! How vast is the sum of them! Were I to count them, they would outnumber the grains of sand—when I awake, I am still with you.

Reading through this Psalm, it is clear that David is not just impressed with God's knowledge base, though; being able to connect with God intimately was immeasurably valuable and immensely comforting in the dark, chaotic world that surrounded this shepherd king.

If I say, "Surely the darkness will hide me, and the light become night around me." Even the darkness will not be dark to you; the night will shine like the day, for darkness is as light to you.

So often, people's lives are filled with fearful "unknowables," but God understands it all. So often, people feel desperately alone, but God is present, and truly cares and reaches out to everyone. Remember, God is the great Sociologist. He knows all about and within human beings, but even more awesome is His love and desire to connect with His children. Joyfully, He knows people fully, and still wants to be with us, eternally.

Voices from the Street

God Is Bigger than My Disability

In 2015, I started my junior year of high school. As I was coming home from church after a youth group outing on September 27, 2015, I lost control of my car and crashed head-on into a tree. If the tree had hit another inch to the left, I would have been killed, instantly. The crash knocked me out and, by the grace of God, a friend from my church found me shortly after. She was able to get me medical help within a few minutes which saved my life. Once I was stabilized at the hospital, I was diagnosed with a diffuse axonal injury, which is a severe traumatic brain injury (TBI).

I remained in a coma for about a month. Shortly after waking up from my coma, I was transferred from Roanoke Carillion Children's Hospital to the Shepherd Center—a rehabilitation hospital in Atlanta, Georgia. I spent four months there. When I returned home from the hospital, I had a lot of trouble adjusting socially, at first. I was different from my preaccident self, and my friends no longer knew how to act around me. Sometimes, I still have trouble adapting to the culture around me because my disability presents me with some unique challenges.

I am affected physically by my disability. My joints often hurt, and I have difficulty with my speech. However, the effects are not just physical. I have a lot of trouble fitting in with groups of my peers. I often cannot keep up with conversations in group settings. My brain perceives things differently than most people, so I often misread signals as someone being upset with me when they are actually not. I do not like meeting new people because I am all too aware of my differences.

My disability makes me different, but it does not make me less than anyone else. I am still a contributing and functional member of society. I have regular social interactions with people, daily. I have already come much further than many doctors thought I ever would. I am almost done with my sophomore year of college, and many medical experts believed I would never graduate from high school. I have some physical limitations, but I can accomplish anything that I set my mind to. I do not process events at a normal speed, but I often have deep, worthwhile reflections when I do contemplate things. I have some problems speaking, but I have been told what I have to say is worth listening to.

A disability does not have to hold a person back. One of my all-time favorite Bible stories is the story of Moses' encounter with God and the burning bush found in Exodus 3 and 4. In this encounter, God appears to Moses in the desert and tells him that he is going to free the Israelites using Moses as his spokesman to deliver them. Moses offers quite a few reasons he is not the man for the job and suggests that God should pick someone else. His second excuse is that he is unable to speak well—an excuse I can relate to, well. Many Bible scholars believe Moses suffered from a speech impediment (Philologos, 2011). Exodus 4:11 (NASB) says, "The Lord said to him, 'Who has made man's mouth? Or who makes him mute or deaf, or seeing or blind? Is it not I, the Lord?'"

My disability does not hold me back because my God is bigger than my shortcomings. He is strong where I am weak. God made my body, and he makes it work how he chooses. I work at a Christian youth camp throughout the year called Camp Lowman. When I began working there, I was understandably nervous that my impaired speech would create problems for my ability to minister, effectively.

A primary responsibility of camp staff is to minister to campers during services. At first, I was unable to perform this duty during services because my soft voice could not be heard over the music that played during altar calls. The second time that I worked at camp, I learned what I needed to do. When I wanted to talk with a camper during the service, I led them to a little room near the back door. I still do this every camp. A camper and I will sit on the floor by the back door where it is quieter than in the big room. I listen to what they are struggling with and offer words of encouragement and support. We now refer to this spot as my "office."

Quite a few campers have shared with me on what a difference that I made in their lives working at camp. My ministry is so effective—not in spite of my disabilities, but because of them. In the moments when people are telling me what an impact, I have made on them through my story and the things they see me do, I know it is all worth it. All the pain I have and do experience(d) and all the problems that I have fitting into society no longer matter. A dear friend told me that God often uses our greatest pain to be someone else's seed of hope. My story, including my disability, is for God's glory.

It is the small actions that add up. That is how you make an impact. It turns out I do not need a normal voice or body parts that function correctly for that. It does not require much to be a thoughtful and caring person. Anyone can be kind and loving to others. Sometimes, all that someone needs is to know that people care, and my disability does not stop me from showing that I do.

Perhaps I cannot call someone on the phone, but I can send someone a small gift to let them know I am thinking about them. I can bring someone flowers on a random day, or just smile at strangers in public. My disability does not stop me from doing the little things that brighten people's lives, and these little things add up for everyone who struggles in life.

Ashley Mayhew
Junior, Social Work
Liberty University

Contributed by Ashley Mayhew. © Kendall Hunt Publishing Company

 Check out the Chapter 1 video at this link: https://www.grtep.com/

Vocabulary

Agency
Applied Sociology
Behavioral Sciences
Clinical Sociology
Common Sense
Conflict Theory
Consequences of Differences
Functionalist Perspective

Individual Studies
Phenomenology Perspective
Postmodernism
Scientific Method
Social Construction
    Perspective
Social Imagination
Societal Studies

Sociology
Sociology From Above
Symbolic Interaction
    Perspective
Systematic Studies
Theory

CHAPTER TWO: Research

The Basics

In sociology, there are a few things as important as research when it comes to seeking answers about why people think and act the way that they do in society. Sociologists are not allowed to guess or follow mere speculation about human behavior and attitudes. Thus, sociological research is undertaken both in the field—outside of the classroom in the public sphere—as well as in the clinic or laboratory to ascertain sociological truths. Of course, as with other productive research endeavors in the social sciences, the investigative locales are carefully controlled, analyzed, and observed.

It is expected and required that all sociologists utilize the scientific method to explore hypothetical problems or scenarios in society. To accomplish this, social scientists first define the problem or aspect of society to investigate. Second, they begin a review of all current and past literature regarding a particular topic. This not only assists in formulating a testable hypothesis that has not been studied, previously; it also aids in selecting a proper and productive research design to gather valuable and reliable information. Finally, sociologists draw upon the harvested data to formulate a grand conclusion on a topic and to generate ideas for future academic research regarding the matter. As Dowling and Brown (2010) remark, "It can generate ways of looking at the world that you didn't have before and that can motivate real developments in your professional practice as well as spur you on to further research activity" (p. 1).

When determining a sociological project, it is quintessential to start with big questions or ideas before beginning the research. For instance, what does the researcher want to know about society, specifically? Additionally, how will the researcher maintain value-neutrality when studying a social group with which he or she might disagree—such as when interviewing a supremacist convicted of child molestation or an inner-city pimp and drug dealer? Finally, what does the researcher hope to accomplish in studying the topic? Is the research purely for knowledge sake or does he or she plan on utilizing the evidence to promote a social agenda or cause (a.k.a., *applied sociology*)?

Related to these important questions, ten main steps in sociological research have been followed, traditionally: (a) determine your topic, (b) find out what others have already learned, (c) decide upon your study questions, (d) determine what resources you need to carry out the research, (e) ascertain if the research can cause harm to the subjects, (f) solidify the research method you will use in the project, (g) specify how you will record the data, (h) establish the significance of the gathered data, (i) come to a scholarly and appropriate conclusion about the research topic, and (j) figure out how you will share what you have learned with the scholarly community.

Once a research topic or *construct* (a social mechanism, phenomenon, or category created by society) has been chosen, sociologists employ various tools of study, one being a *concept*, which is a mental construct that represents some part of the world in a simplified form. They then clearly state, or *operationalize*, what they will be sociologically measuring in the project. They also look for a *variable*, which refers to the concept or idea or factor that changes from case to case, or a *measurement*, which is the procedure for determining the value of a variable in a specific case. Additionally, they choose a selection of society, or a *sample*, that is statistically representative of the overall population.

Sociologists rely upon various approaches of study, systematically planned and implemented, to find out more about their subjects and social research area. They might employ *qualitative research*—where information is primarily collected through individual or small groups—to collect and report data that indicates the depth of the problem. They might also focus more upon *quantitative research*, which is more numbers based or broadly demographic in nature (ethnicity, gender, age, etc.) to show the breadth of the problem. Ultimately, social scientists mostly depend upon the four main methods of existing sources, surveys, participant observation, and experiments to investigate social forces.

All of the information, called *statistics*, will be gathered, compiled, and analyzed, which can suggest patterns of sociological behaviors or attitudes in effect. These statistics are representative of the larger population and state what is average for the sample importantly for that population, in general. Concerning research statistics, investigators consider such factors as the *mean*, which is the average of all measures; the *median*, which is the halfway point in a series of numbers; and the *mode*, which is the score that occurs most often in the data.

Sociologists use these statistics to ascertain any correlations or causations experienced or observed within the research subjects. A *correlation* indicates a change in one variable that coincides with the change in another (but might not be necessarily caused by it). A causation indicates a causal link or relationship between a condition (or variable) and a particular consequence, with one event directly leading to another event. For example, there is a generally accepted correlation seen between poor people and a lack of education, and some sociologists claim that one's economic status causes one to be either more or less educated (which we will discuss later in Chapter 8).

Still, as mentioned earlier, sociologists are not to make grand presumptions about social forces without evidence to back it up. To be of scholarly or social value, sociologists (and other social scientists) need to have confidence in research findings, which is achieved through maintaining traditional standards of the scientific method. Thus, the data must be both *reliable*—demonstrating a consistency in measurement and repeatable results—and it must be *valid*—actually measuring what the project intended to measure. Without these two pillars, all research datum becomes mere political props, and hardly reflects the sociological reality of the examined phenomenon.

This pessimistic attitude can be observed within postmodern sociology (at least, in Western society), which asserts that scientific research objectivity is an impossible endeavor to achieve. Therefore, according to some sociologists, the best action that sociologists can take is move the ideas, theories, and applications of sociology into the public domain (and not just to share with other academics) to engage and dialogue with nonacademics about public issues under social scrutiny. This is called *public sociology*, and it is very fashionable in most progressive sociological circles. Still, public sociology has a residue of political partisanship about it (Collins, 2007, pp. 110-111), and although it is not wrong to investigate sociological ideas that touch upon political events, there is a danger of losing one's scientific objectivity for the sake of partisan agenda. Too often, politicos hijack sociology to achieve political goals. It is important to maintain a professional and emotional distance to what one is studying, and public sociology could potentially tread upon dangerous territory without such safeguards.

Moreover, while it may be true that there is no perfect objectivity, science has never been about operating in perfection or without error. In fact, good science allows for adjustments and alterations of scientific theory because, despite the genius and insightfulness of humanity, our perspectives are limited by our natures and our abilities. Yet, over the centuries, scientists have made amazing discoveries and advances in human understanding through careful, honest application of scientific principles of study.

Contrary to postmodern thought, there is certainly enough sufficient objectivity for social scientists to fairly and accurately study society; however, it does take effort, discipline, and purposefulness. To do so, conscientious social scientists must strive for personal neutrality in (first and foremost) allowing the facts to speak for themselves. This is also called *intellectual honesty*. Regarding which, Foster (2009) advises, "In intellectual honesty, we should be willing to study and explore the spiritual life with all the rigor and determination we would give to any field of research" (p. 3).

Additionally, social scientists must acknowledge and admit their personal biases so that they can find ways to remove themselves as much as possible from their experiments. Otherwise, they might influence or manipulate the data or inject their "scientific" conclusions with personal biases of the researcher (or their subjects) rather than evidential logic. As Loannidis (2018) puts it, "We do know that leaving research practices to serendipity, biasing influences, methodological illiteracy, and statistical innumeracy is inefficient" (p. e2005468).

Of course, it is totally acceptable for social scientists to research topics of which they care about, but they need to be more dedicated to finding the truth *as it is* rather than *as they think it should be*. Plus, although sociology is supposed to be mostly an epistemological field, there is a clear moral or ethical aspect of the social sciences.

The chief aim of most sociologists (at least, the "good ones") is to understand how and why people believe, act, and interact the way that they do, but there is also a strong component to do no wrong to those whom they study. Research ethics begins with the awareness that research can harm as well as help their subjects and related communities. As Vogt, Gardner, and Haeffele (2012) suggest, "Our responsibilities as researchers can be divided into three fairly distinct groups . . . persons being studied, other researchers, and the broader society or community" (p. 229).

To accomplish this, the American Sociological Association (ASA, 2018) has come up with several axioms to protect all parties involved in sociological investigations and experiments: (a) sociologists are to be skillful and fair-minded in their work, (b) sociologists are to disclose all of their research findings, (c) sociologists are to make their results available to other sociologists, (d) they are to get informed consent from their research subjects before they begin any experimentation—alerting them to any potential risks, (e) sociologists are to maintain the privacy and dignity of their subjects, (f) sociologists are to make sure that no research subjects are ever harmed—socially, psychologically, or physically, and (g) sociologists are to stop their research work, immediately, if they suspect their subjects are in danger.

Fundamentally, sociological research exists to help sociologists conceptualize, create, distribute, manage, collect, and properly analyze data from important sociological investigations pursued in the scholarly world. Yet, all research findings are contextual—thus, making a universal application of some research findings could be misleading or damaging. Furthermore, some research studies work well in a microsetting, but fail in a macroenvironment; some research studies can be/have been hijacked by various political groups to promote a social agenda irrelevant or unrelated to the research intentions; and some research studies have been disproven by later contemporary studies with more/better controls and designs.

One of the main goals/tenets of the scientific method is the value of scientific cynicism to ensure truthful, dependable findings (and any subsequent implications). Although such presuppositions may lead one to a skeptical attitude toward scientific inquiry, it is never wrong to challenge or recheck any scientific research studies. Doing so will only either (a) confirm or (b) debunk the previous studies, leading to a greater, more precise, more accurate understanding of the scientific question and investigation. Repeating a scientific study allows for reflection, rejection, or reaffirmation of research conclusions.

Sociology from Above

Have You Not Read . . .?

One of the joys of my life was teaching a Bible Survey class for over a decade while at George Fox University. Term after term, I walked the students carefully through each ancient sacred book (all 66 sixty-six!) in the Old and New Testaments. Our goal was to probe the depths and heights of Scripture to come to cogent conclusions about the biblical stories. I often reminded them that we were doing far more than "Sunday School" in class; we were trying to be honest, sincere seekers of truth, for God's word deserves nothing less.

It warmed my heart to look out at their faces and see an intense curiosity and drive to get to the bottom of the various biblical matters. The students may not have been aware of it, but in a great sense, we all were researchers investigating one of the most amazing tales of divinity and humanity that has ever been recounted.

As anyone who has read the Bible can attest, it is replete with marvelous, miraculous deeds that challenge scientific principles, such as Moses parting the Red Sea, Elijah being taken up in a chariot of fire, Shadrach, Meshach, and Abednego surviving the furnace of fire, Jesus' countless healings, St. Paul's divine encounter with Jesus on the road to Damascus, and so on. These are incredible moments that demand a response from readers, for they are not presented as mere metaphors, but as actual events in human history. They detail when the supernatural overlapped with the natural.

Not surprisingly, many skeptics cry, "Foul!" regarding the biblical accounts. The (in)famous Atheist Christopher Hitchens (2007) submits,

> There still remain four irreducible objections to religious faith: that it wholly misrepresents the origins of man and the cosmos, that because of this original error, it manages to combine the maximum of servility with the maximum of solipsism [only the Self can be truly known], that it is both the result and the cause of dangerous sexual repression, and that it is ultimately grounded on wish-thinking (p. 12).

In other words, in his opinion (and for others of like-minded skepticism), the aforementioned events never happened because they violated natural law and collective scientific thought. The presumption is that the Bible's stories are based more on emotion and superstition than empirical data; yet, such thinking reveals a shallow interpretation and understanding of Scripture.

By its very claims, the Bible invites scientific scrutiny, and as I tell my classes, we never have to worry about seeking truth. In fact, the Bible directs, "Ask, and it will be given to you; seek, and you will find; knock, and it will be opened to you" (Matthew 7:7). Additionally, the Apostle Paul explains, "For whatever was written in former days was written for our instruction, that through endurance and through the encouragement of the Scriptures we might have hope" (Romans 15:4). This should not be unexpected as God is Truth, the Bible proclaims (John 16:13) and he wants His followers to ". . . not love in word or talk but in deed and in truth" (1 John 3:18). Truth matters in Christianity; if false, there is no reason to follow Jesus (1 Corinthians 15:14).

Yet, the Bible's stories do fall well within the sociological methods of qualitative investigation. The Bible is *archival*, with numerous research opportunities based upon existing records such as narratives, official chronicles, cultural curriculum, poetry, biographies, letters, and public predictions. It offers multiple *case studies*, for readers to research and examine for in-depth explorations of an event, program, process, or of one or more individuals. It provides several *ethnographies*, presenting ancient studies of people and cultures in a systematic manner. Its *narratives* weave together various sequences of events, usually from one or two individuals to form a cohesive story. It follows *grounded theory*, which is basically inductive approach from which theory emerges out of systematic research—that is, "bottom up." Finally, it is *phenomenological*, embracing a qualitative approach to investigation that emphasizes consciousness and direct experience.

The Bible is not just a book of fairy tales and emotional pabulum; it makes bold claims that are backed up with a plethora of eyewitness confirmations. The book of Exodus states that all of the Hebrew children wandering in the desert observed the pillar of cloud during the day and the pillar of fire at night that led them for forty years (Exodus 13:21). The book of Daniel recounts that King Darius and all his nobles saw Daniel go in and come out of the den of lions meant to devour him (Daniel 6:16–21). Surrounded by onlookers, Jesus healed the paralyzed man of both his spiritual sins and his nonfunctioning legs (Mark 2:1–12), and after His death on the cross, over 500 people saw him alive and resurrected, just as Jesus said he would be to the Disciples (Matthew 28:6).

Most people discount the biblical stories, not because they cannot believe the supernatural accounts, but because of the convicting message of the Bible and its implications that threaten their embrace of radical individualism and provoke unpleasant feelings of guilt and remorse.

Therefore, they set their own version of a "scientific" investigation, which offers an emotional rejection of the Bible falsely presented as an empirically proper one. Regarding critics of intelligent design theory, David Berlinski (2009) asserts, "The doctrines of quantum cosmology are what they seem: biased, partial, inconclusive, and largely in the service of passionate but unexamined conviction" (p. 103). Evangelical atheists have turned scientific methodology into political methodology, sadly.

All Christian investigation of truths must not—and need not—model itself after this sloppy, scientific, secularist pattern of circular reasoning. As in mathematics, there are Christian proofs that clearly, logically, and reasonably affirm the faith. And having taught Apologetics for nearly a decade, I can comfortably say that our faith is not based on vapid or vacuous thinking or justification.

The Bible has stood the test of time for centuries. There were doubters in Adam and Eve's day, Moses' day, Elijah's day, Jeremiah's day, John the Baptist's day, Jesus' day, Peter and Paul's day, in Augustine's day, in Luther's day, in Calvin's day, in Wesley's day, in Finney's day, and into postmodernity. Still, they believed. Why? Because the Bible is explanative, predictive, and no enemy of true scientific inquiry.

Voices from the Street

The Superman-Jimmy Neutron Complex(ity)

Sociology, particularly in reference to the subset of medicine and the interactions between the primitive science of medicine, the god complexes of doctors, and the lack of understanding from patients, provides a splintered paradigm that leaves physicians shaking their heads and grabbing the nearest anti-inflammatory to treat their growing headaches. The reality of medical science is that the entire field depends on these three foundational principles: ideas, statistics, and the sheer chance to keep patients healthy and providers employed.

Not long ago, on rounds with an internal medicine/infectious disease physician, I had a unique opportunity to do a simulation experiment. The provider asked me to write her notes during rounds; however, I was to write my own "notes" on a separate interface. On one particular day, I was getting case after case correct, until the inevitable occurred—my simulation patient diagnosis was inaccurate. With grace and tact, the doctor replied, "You know Skylar, medicine can be like a science experiment in a high school biology class. There are hypothesizes, procedures, and theories; but in medicine, if your hypothesis is wrong, the patient dies!" Thankfully, this was just a simulation, but this one lesson changed so much of my paradigm regarding the medical world. The lesson was that no matter the turnout, pride can drag you down, while humility will propel you far.

Still, patients expect doctors to be God! They depend upon medical professionals to be invincible walking encyclopedias of knowledge; yet, doctors are also expected to be model citizens of charity and to be attentive to patients' every need—a "Superman meets Jimmy Neutron" kind of fantasy. More accurately, perhaps one should think of a doctor as a calculator, constantly computing statistics provided by other medical researchers. Depending on one's source, different statistics yield different courses of action.

Moreover, medical professionals are to be "steely-eyed missile men (and women)," free from any emotional sentiment (intentional or not). Facts and cutting-edge medical insights are to be our medical guides, increasing our efficiency and success rates. Succinctly, we are live and breathe statistics.

For example, considering the following:

A woman arrives at the clinic complaining of chest pain. The patient is a fifty-four-year-old, married, nonsmoker, social drinker. The patient reports a three-week history of an upper respiratory infection with some localized left-side chest pain for the past four hours.

Statistically, one would most likely concur that this patient is having a heart attack. This is based on three key points: "fifty-four-year-old," "four hours," and "left side chest pain."

Now, let's use another example with the same chief complaint:

A woman arrives at the clinic complaining of chest pain. The patient is a twenty-eight-year-old, married, nonsmoker, social drinker. The patient reports a three-week history of an upper respiratory infection with some localized left-side chest pain for the past week.

In looking at this case, the provider would think cardiovascular related first and then perform the previously set protocols to ensure the worst-case scenario is not a legitimate concern (i.e., Is this young lady having a heart attack and at risk for dying?). For the purposes of this case, all reports come back normal and, in the end, she just has chest wall tenderness from excessive coughing as a result of the disease that she reported in her recent medical history.

One can see that these are two identical chief complaints, but with two different prognoses. Both of these cases called upon the entire knowledge of the medical professionals and occurred with the same expectation of tender care. In the first case, if the doctor had misdiagnosed the heart attack, then the patient could have lived a life full of pain (or worse, premature death). In the latter case, if misdiagnosed, the patient would most likely have forgotten the encounter, entirely.

With either consult, medical professionals are changing a person's life every time that they interact with the patient. Thus, medical professionals must balance an encyclopedia of knowledge (Jimmy Neutron) and still keep a disconnected-yet-tender heart (Superman) even in the toughest of cases. Yet, sometimes a dismal diagnosis turns favorable despite the bleakness of the stats.

Every doctor has that story—the patient who died and somehow came back. In medicine, this goes by a few street names: they are called the "statistical outliers," an "act of God," or "just by sheer chance." Personally, I know that things are often not a statistical anomaly, but rather a response that the viewer does not understand, fully—thus, thought to be coincidental. Patients continue to defy the odds. A 100-year-old war veteran who smokes and drinks all day could outlive a 25-year-old triathlete. Why? No one knows. Sheer chance is all a part of the process in medicine—likely more than anyone realizes or is willing to admit.

Which is more important, partaking in feelings or actual, biological health? Sexuality and gender orientation are one subset in a long list of markers like race, occupation, age, and nutrition (among other adjustments to better provide on behalf of the patient). Even if it may not be the patient's preference to be labeled as man, old, diabetic, and so on, that separation from opinion keeps them alive and healthy. After all, patients are full of numbers, and race or gender preferences each are just that—numerical statistics, in which some numbers are significant, and others are just outliers. But patients have feelings, which matter, too; doctors must juggle this paradigm all day and struggle to make the patients "feel" comfortable while still saving their lives.

Having great knowledge like a Jimmy Neutron means nothing without the tender protection of a Superman. Even with all of these advances and the dedication of medical professionals, medicine frequently digresses to sheer chance—a simple intervention of statistical oddity or the will of God. Yet, God is the premise by which statistical anomalies become sane and through which a perspective of astronomical proportions becomes medically feasible.

Ultimately, though, medicine is not about medicine at all, but rather a moment of great humility for all parties. Providers enter the room and force out all their other personal distractions. Patients, with great fears yet full of trust and hopefulness, wait for the physician to speak news to them, even if that truth is painful to bear. Doctors are indubitably beneficial human healers (and calculators), but awful gods. No one can replace the Great Healer's diagnoses and His treatment plan. Doctors and patients need to always keep in mind that all healing—planned or not—is the careful work of a divine creator who cares about people in all situations and all conditions.

Skylar Collins

Contributed by Skylar Collins. © Kendall Hunt Publishing Company

 Check out the Chapter 2 video at this link: https://www.grtep.com/

Vocabulary

Archival	Mean	Research Data
ASA Research Standards	Median	Research Ethics
Case Studies	Measurement	Sample
Causation	Mode	Scientific Objectivity
Concept	Narratives	Scientific Theory
Consequence	Operationalize	Sociological Project
Construct	Phenomenology	Sociological Research
Correlation	Public Sociology	Statistics
Ethnographies	Qualitative Research	Validity
Grounded Theory	Quantitative Research	Value-neutrality
Intellectual Honesty	Reliability	Variable

CHAPTER THREE: Sociological Pioneers

The Basics

When considering the classical sociological theories, one must begin with the pioneering theories of sociology that originated in Europe and America in the 1800s through the early 1900s by well-known social scientists such as Comte, Spencer, Marx, Weber, Durkheim, and so on. These founders of sociology began their studies in the new social environment that blossomed after the Age of Reason and with the Enlightenment (roughly, 1685–1815 CE), wherein human beings had more personal social liberation and "rights" than ever before in history.

In the eighteenth century, an intellectual movement began in Europe, which promoted "enlightened rationality" and pushed key principles of proper living such as ethics (how to live), aesthetics (how life should look), and epistemology (what one should know). The social leaders of the day sought to move culturally away from old, superstitious, tyrannical thought begun in the Dark Ages (ca. 450–1000 CE) that was set by popular culture and antiquated religious institutions. As the philosopher Immanuel Kant (1784) wrote, "[The] Enlightenment is man's leaving his self-caused immaturity" (p. 54).

Instead, they advocated for a social milieu that attempted to systematize all fields of study, they sought to understand the magisterial role of humanity as earth's keeper and questioned the factual role of God in nature. Thus, they embraced a belief in a rational, orderly, understandable universe. There was nothing that human beings could not understand. Even God was analyzed and put in a box: no longer an eminent part of intelligent people's lives, the Deistic view of God made Him merely an ancient clockmaker in the heavens wanting to be left alone from the affairs of mankind. They also constructed a moral architecture to knowledge, trying to liberate the mind from old cultural shackles that only held people back. The ultimate goal was to gain fuller understanding so that they could become gods of their own universe.

Somewhat ironically, they also demonstrated an intense, personal spirituality, which would centuries later be seen in the sacro-egoism of postmodernity (Knox, 2016). Paradoxically, faith and ecclesiology were still important; however, Enlightenment social entrepreneurs mocked the old system and its agents, the priests. They wanted a new religious system to reign in their enlightened world, so many leaders discarded the Judeo-Christian model that had been in power for thousands of years, replacing it with a new brand of "religion," which replaced "Yahweh" with "Human," as seen in the religiosity of Comte, Jefferson, and Marx.

The emergence and development of these new human freedoms, and the sociology pioneers' investigations and theories regarding them, were also aided by the American and French Revolutions, the spread of industrialism and capitalism across the Western world, and the swift growth of urbanization in Europe's major cities.

The Pioneers of Sociology

Plato

One of the first investigators and philosophers who focused on human society was a man named, *Plato* (Greek, 427–347 BCE), the pupil of Socrates (Greek, one of the most important philosophers in all history). Plato (whose real name is "Aristocles") founded the Academy at Athens, which was operational until 529 CE. Plato is well known for his teachings, writings, dialogues, epigrams, and letters, but he is perhaps most famous for his literary work on Greek society called, *The Republic*. Within this masterpiece, Plato spells out his six basic assumptions regarding society. First, man is an organism. Second, all organisms strive to survive. Third, human beings survive in groups. Fourth, human beings are social animals. Fifth, people like to live in ordered societies. Last, this order of societies is observable and knowable. Thus, Plato's categorical approach is one of the earliest attempts at "social science."

Plato has been tied to many other philosophers and social scientists who came later in history including Hobbes, Hume, Locke, and Kant—all of whom sought to make sense of the human experience of personal reality and social interactions with other people. Many scholars throughout the centuries have lauded and honored Plato's works for being foundational to their understandings of objectivity and subjectivity, especially in Plato's "Allegory of the Cave," from *The Republic*, which presents a metaphorical tale wherein people are chained and facing a blank wall with a fire between them and people passing between them. The chained people are unable to fully perceive or discern the images projected from the fire on the wall of the cave; all they see are distorted, fantastic shadows.

Plato then explains that the philosopher is like one of the chained who has escaped and seen what is actually happening behind them. Yet, the people reject the philosopher's explanation at first and fight against seeing reality, content to remain where they are—chained and ignorant but feeling safe in their world of illusion. Eventually, the prisoners do escape, and then they see the world and the Sun, which they find hard to understand because it was nothing like they had conceived in their minds. Ultimately, Plato's message is that truth, the world, human existence itself, is often just perceptions and not reality.

Plato was kept busy in his professional life by managing and teaching at the Academy. He also traveled extensively across the Mediterranean region, possibly visiting Egypt, Italy, Sicily, and possibly even to Judea to speak with other great and important thinkers. The Church Father Ambrose (Italian, 337–397 CE), the Bishop of Milan and teacher/preacher of St. Augustine (Algerian, 354–430 CE), even suggested that Plato may have had some contact and conversation with the Jewish prophet, Jeremiah (Judean, post-650–570 BCE), but many scholars consider this to be unsubstantiated myth and incompatible with the men's historical lifetimes. Regardless, later in life, Plato also became involved in local politics at Syracuse, nearly being executed by the tyrant Dionysius (Greek, 432–367 BCE), but who instead sold Plato into slavery (Plato was later freed from a rich benefactor and forgiven, politically). The philosopher eventually returned to his tutoring in Syracuse, and purportedly died in bed, or at a wedding, or in his sleep, depending upon one's ancient sources.

Auguste Comte

One of the first sociologists to apply scientific methodology to understanding human interactions and behaviors, *Auguste Comte* (French, 1798–1857) was a popular social thinker who officially coined the term, "Sociology," in 1838. He was originally going to name his scientific approach to social science, "Social Physics," but that term was stolen (or at least already put out, publicly) by Adolphe Quetelet (Belgian, 1796–1874), who also was interested in the social sciences (particularly regarding statistics) along with astronomy and mathematics.

Regarding the history of social science, Comte suggested that there were three stages in the development of sociology. The first, a time of superstition and supernatural explanations, he called the *theological stage*, which went from the beginning of human history to the end of the Middle Ages (ca. 1530 CE) in Europe. The second, when human beings realized that society was a natural and not supernatural phenomenon, he called the *metaphysical stage*, because their assertions were largely devoid of scientific proofs. This stage focused on the social and philosophical challenges, investigations, and humanist proclamations in Europe around the time of the French Revolution (1789–1799 CE). Comte, a *positivist* (someone who believes that knowledge is based on natural phenomena and their manifestations to humanity), called his final stage, the *scientific stage*, which focused on scientific advancements and answers to social problems after the end of the Revolution and the rise and fall of Emperor Napoleon. Although considered "classical" in postmodernity, in Comte's time, the scientific contributions of scientists such as Nicolaus Copernicus (Polish, 1473–1543), Robert Boyle (English, 1627–1691), Isaac Newton (English, 1643–1727), Blaise Pascal (French, 1623–1662), Thomas Hobbes (English, 1588–1679), and John Stuart Mill (1806–1873) were still quite fashionable in Europe, with a potential for social scientific application.

Before dying on September 5, 1857 from stomach cancer, Comte published a four-volume collection called, "Systéme de Politique Positive" (1851–1854) and his final work, "La Synthése Subjective" (1856). He also began a new secular religion called the *Religion of Humanity* that was inspired by the death of his platonic love interest with Clotilde de Vaux (French, 1815–1846), and which centered upon altruism, progressive thought, and the power of human will in matters of morality and virtue. Comte's secular church is still operational today with chapels in France and Brazil.

Harriet
Martineau

One of the first female sociologists (and a prolific essayist, novelist, and journalist) was *Harriet Martineau* (British, 1802–1876). A brilliant scholar during the Victorian era (1837–1901 CE) when women were relegated in society to more domestic avenues, Martineau demonstrated a keen intellect and investigative mind in her sociological, historical, and economic writings such as *Illustrations of Political Economy* (1832), *Society in America* written in 1837, *How to Observe Morals and Manners* (1838), *Retrospect of Western Travel* (1838), *Deerbrook* (1839), *The Hour and the Man* (1841), *The Crofton Boys* (1841), *Household Education* (1848), *The History of Thirty Years' Peace, A.D. 1816–1846* (1849), *Biographical Sketches* (1869), and her most famous sociological writing, *The Positive Philosophy of Auguste Comte, Freely Translated and Condensed* (1853), which Comte himself recommended for his students to read instead of his own works. Martineau also wrote an autobiography, which was published after her death in 1876.

Martineau was interested in many facets of human society and suggested that an effective, holistic study of society was needed for proper and full scientific understanding. Thus, many of her investigations focused on topics such as domestic life, education, marriage, parenting and childcare, history, race relations, sociology, and religion. She traveled to the Middle East in 1846 to study religion and its development. Thereafter, she publicly announced her disenchantment with Unitarianism and her embrace of *atheism* (the lack of belief in the supernatural or gods), which was bolstered by her friendship with *Charles Darwin* (British, 1809–1882), the naturalist and geologist who famously theorized that all earth's species descended over the millennia from common ancestors (including human beings).

Despite the social restrictions for women in the Victorian Era, her fame and reputation grew, even internationally, and Martineau traveled to the United States to meet with various dignitaries such as former President James Madison (American, 1751–1836) and several leaders of the Abolitionist Movement, which made her unpopular in some U.S. circles; however, her "infamy" did not seem to hurt her book sales, which were higher than many other popular British writers during the 1830s.

Sadly, suffering physically from a uterine tumor discovered in 1839, Martineau continued in her writings and scholarly ruminations, although she was sometimes confined to bed because of her affliction and treatments. Still, she remained intellectually active and joined in the political action of the 1850s and 1860s, advocating for women's rights and suffrage. During this time, she thought that she might soon die, so Martineau wrote her autobiography; however, she held on for another two decades before succumbing to bronchitis on June 27, 1876.

Few individuals have been as influential or impactful in world history than the philosopher, journalist, social scientist, and historian *Karl Marx* (German, 1818–1883), the coauthor of *The Communist Manifesto* (1848). When Marx died in 1883, his best and oldest friend, Friedrich Engels (German, 1820–1895), delivered his eulogy, calling Marx the greatest living thinker in the history of mankind (although many would dispute that accolade then and now).

Born into a middle-class family in Trier, Germany, Marx grew up in an ethnically Jewish family, although he and all his family members were also baptized into the Lutheran Church in 1824. His father provided young Karl with his education until his teen years, when he entered Trier High School, which was run by liberal headmaster, Hugo Wyttenbach (German, 1767–1848), who was soon fired by government authorities (along with many others that Wyttenbach had hired at the school) for their illegal liberal indoctrination of the students. In 1835, Marx left Trier to attend two universities in Germany: *The University of Bonn* and the *University of Berlin*. Marx wanted to study philosophy and literature, but his father forced law studies upon him because he considered it a more lucrative and serious field of study. Marx and his peers enjoyed a typical collegiate social climate, but also became involved at school with politics in 1837 and with a radical group called the *Young Hegelians*.

During his law studies, he grew more serious about his studies and his writings (he finally graduated in 1841). He began composing both fiction and nonfiction, with works such as *Scorpion and Felix* (1837), *Oulanem* (1839), *The Difference Between the Democritean and Epicurean Philosophy of Nature* (1841). Marx thought about pursuing a career in academia; however, because of his involvement and activism with the Young Hegelians, the government blocked that vocational dream. Thereafter, Marx moved to Cologne, Germany (1842), and began work as a journalist for the radical newspaper, *Rheinische Zeitung*, which eventually was banned by Tsar Nicholas I (Russian, 1796–1855). Frustrated but still ready to fight for the cause of Liberalism in Europe, Marx left for Paris, France, to study the French Revolution and become an editor for yet another radical newspaper, the Deutsch-Französische Jahrbücher, which also was banned— this time by Bavarian governmental authorities. Thereafter, Marx became even more deeply interested, invested, and involved with Liberal politics and revolutionary movements.

In 1844, Marx met *Engels*, a German socialist writer, in Paris, who shared similar ideals and philosophies of life. The two men became lifelong friends and began collaborating on a systematic analysis and interpretation of political economics that would eventually evolve into the Communist movement. In fact, by 1844, Marx had outlined the general tenets of "Marxism," which Marx shared with his readers in another radical newspaper, *Vorwärts!* This newspaper was also shut down and banned by French authorities, so Marx was forced to move to Brussels, Belgium in 1845; however, the Belgian authorities forbade Marx to publish any more radical socialist writings, although Marx surreptitiously continued to dialogue with other radical, socialist exiles. In due course, Marx's writings and activism, especially during the Europe-wide Revolutions of 1848, were considered to be too dangerous by the governments of Germany, France, and Belgium, which forced Marx to flee to England in 1848, where he kept a permanent residence for the remainder of his life.

Central to Marx's economic and historical theory was the notion that world history provides a chronicle of class conflict played out between the oppressed and the oppressors. In Marx's time, he considered the bourgeoisie (the middle class) as being dominant in culture, with the government solely existing to help them out, financially, with middle-class economic interests superseding all other classes' needs. Therefore, Marx predicted a time when the proletariat (the working class) would rise in rebellion against the bourgeoisie (the middle class) and overthrow their oppressive masters. A new economic society would then be created based on a classless, beneficial society, with a temporary dictatorship set in power to reorganize production and redistribution of wealth and goods. Some countries around the world have attempted to see Marx's dreams come to reality; however, so far, no Communist or Socialist Revolution has proved successful, with most "Communist" countries eventually retreating into capitalism (such as Russia and China) when their Communism philosophy causes more harm than good.

The last years of Marx's life provided little comfort to Marx. He suffered ill health from all of his earlier (and ongoing) partying, drinking, and smoking. He stopped writing and producing, and slipped into a depression, especially after the deaths of his wife and daughter, which happened within a two-year period. Marx died *a stateless person* (a man or woman with no national citizenship from any country) of a lung abscess on March 14, 1883, and was buried in Highgate Cemetery in London, England.

Emile Durkheim

The son of a rabbi, *Emilé Durkheim* (French, 1857–1917) was one of the most influential founders of sociology and anthropology—especially regarding religion, methodology, and suicide. Durkheim is probably most famous for his penning of the term, *anomie*, which is the feeling of social powerlessness, unrest, and disorientation when a person's social influence and/or control in society is useless and ineffectual.

Although he attended a rabbinical school growing up, Durkheim rejected supernaturalism and embraced secularism in his studies, in which he displayed brilliant insight and understanding. He studied Hebrew and the Old Testament, and tried out Catholicism for a time, before settling into Agnosticism (the belief that one cannot know if God or the supernatural actually exist). In 1879, he enrolled at the École Normale Supériure and focused in the humanities—specifically in psychology and philosophy, which bored him. His college dissertation was on Charles-Louis de Secondat, also known as Baron Montesquieu (French, 1689–1755), the famous political philosopher who wrote about the need for a separation of powers in governmental affairs. Durkheim shifted his studies to ethics and sociology and began to study the works of Auguste Comte (French, 1798–1857), Herbert Spencer (British, 1820–1903), and Wilhelm Wundt (German, 1832–1920), all of whom inspired him to dig deeper into the social sciences.

He eventually passed his agrégation (a civil service exam needed to teach in public education) in 1882. After graduating, Durkheim was engaged as a teacher of philosophy at several French academies, but he left them in 1885 to study sociology at the *University of Marburg, Humboldt University of Berlin,* and *Leipzig University,* where he sharpened his scientific approach to and methodology of social science.

In his theoretical work, he asserted, first and foremost, that society is complex; therefore, social scientists needed to avoid reductionism in their theories and investigations. Things in science are usually more, not less, than they appear to be. He also concluded that *social phenomena* are "facts" and that these "facts" are external to all individuals, which made them effective guides and controls of social conduct—if one was cognizant of them. Furthermore, Durkheim suggested that a person could not explain all characteristics and behaviors of human social interactions with just psychological, biological, or religious tenets. Other powers were in play, and for Durkheim, these social forces appeared as a direct result of organization and/or individual agency.

Once he found his vocational field and specialty, Durkheim became a prolific, productive, provocative scholar. Some of his most famous works include *The Division of Labour in Society* (1893), *The Rules of Sociological Method* (1895), *Suicide* (1897), and *The Elementary Forms of the Religious Life* (1912). Not surprisingly, he rose in academic ranks to become first, a full professor (1906), and then later "Chair of Education" and still later "Chair in Education and Sociology" (1913) at the Sorbonne (also known as the University of Paris). Durkheim also held an advisory position in the government with the Ministry of Education.

Despite these achievements, Durkheim's final years were troubled with the civil strife surrounding World War I. Compounding this was the simplistic and irrational nationalism he saw overtaking France before and during the war, and the tragic loss of his son, André, in battle on the war front in 1915. Heartbroken and depressed, Durkheim died of a stroke on November 15, 1917.

Herbert
Spencer

With a strong background in mathematics and natural science, it is not surprising that *Herbert Spencer* (British, 1820–1903) was an advocate of evolutionary theory and its potential application in understanding how societies function. Chiefly a self-made and self-educated man, Spencer held several roles during his lifetime including school teacher, railway engineer, political scientist, and newspaper editor. A prolific writer and essayist, his most famous work is *The Synthetic Philosophy* (1896), which contains several volumes on biology, psychology, ethics, and social studies.

Spencer was a *Social Darwinist* who firmly believed that Darwin's "survival of the fittest" was not just an animal phenomena, but that it was also a relevant factor in human social interactions. Thus, in Spencer's mind, society evolves just as nature does in Darwinian Theory. All societies include a natural selection process, they move simple to complex, and social science (as a whole) should embrace the notion of noninterference as orchestrated social changes disrupt the natural social evolutionary process, which is quite different from applied sociology theory in postmodernism. Thus, Spencer advocated for laissez-faire economics from the government, which would achieve social progress and advancements in Western society through the natural mechanisms of Darwinism.

Spencer wrote several economic and social works including *The Proper Sphere of Government* (1843), *Social Statics* (1851), *The Principles of Psychology* (1855), *Education: Intellectual, Moral, and Physical* (1861), *Principles of Biology* (1864), and his most famous work, *The Synthetic Philosophy* (1896), which laid out his philosophical synthesis of deism and positivism (like Auguste Comte) in understanding reality and existence. An argumentative-yet-engaging man, Spencer became friend and confidant to several famous writers and thinkers of the Victorian Era like George Eliot (British, 1819–1880), Thomas Huxley (British, 1825–1895), John Stuart Mill (British, 1806–1873), and Beatrice Potter (English, 1866–1943).

Before dying of natural causes at age 83, Spencer was nominated for a Nobel Prize in Literature in 1902, invented a binding pin that would later evolve into the modern paper clip, and was one of the most well-known philosophers of the day, influencing innumerable people and movements in both England and abroad.

Booker T.
Washington

A former slave, *Booker T. Washington* (American, 1856–1915) was an influential educator, reformer, and social advocate for African American civil rights after the Civil War. Born into involuntary servitude in the late 1850s, Washington received his first educational training from his mother, who gave him an alphabet reader to study when he was nine years old (the same year as the Emancipation Proclamation—1863); thereafter, he rose early each morning to study before going out to work in the salt furnaces in Malden, West Virginia. In 1866, Washington worked as a houseboy for Viola Ruffner (American, 1820–1904), a local coal miner's wife, who allowed him to go to school briefly each day during the winter seasons. Always willing

to labor while he learned, Washington eventually found work at the *Hampton Normal Agricultural Institute* in Hampton, Virginia. The founder and headmaster of the school, *General Samuel Armstrong* (American, 1839-1893), realized Washington's academic potential, and provided a scholarship for him, which Washington gladly accepted and utilized, graduating in 1875 with a university degree.

For a time, Washington was employed as a school teacher in Malden, Virginia, and then he took some seminary classes from *Wayland Seminary* in Washington, DC for about a year. In 1879, based on the recommendation of his former mentor and friend (Armstrong), Washington was appointed as principal of the *Tuskegee Normal School* to help train freed black men hoping to become teachers. By and large, Washington founded the school, for although monies had been provided by the Alabama state government for school officials' salaries, no land or offices had yet been purchased or rented for the school. Therefore, Washington devoted much time to recruiting students and soliciting for funds, which he achieved, quickly. The school sessions were first held in a broken-down African American church in 1881, but eventually Washington bought and renovated an old mansion into an official school campus with assorted buildings and offices. By 1888, the *Tuskegee Normal School* had hundreds of students—both men and women—and other scholars were hired to assist with the black students' training including *George Washington Carver* (American, b. 1861-1943), the famous black agricultural chemist and a perfecter (but not inventor) of peanut butter.

Washington soon experienced political popularity (and some condemnation) from civic leaders in both the North and the South for his views on healing the wounds of racism in America. Unlike other radical activists' appraisals and solutions to racial inequality, Washington promoted a political philosophy of black self-help, racial solidarity, and social accommodation, which some considered to be traitorous (so W. E. B. DuBois). Perhaps based on his own personal experiences of social mobility, in a speech at an exposition in Atlanta, Georgia, in 1895, Washington suggested *The Atlanta Compromise*—the proposition that African Americans should ignore racial discrimination in America for a time, thinking that through hard work and subsequent prosperity, the white community would come to respect them and see the black people as more than just former slaves.

In Washington's view, a virtuous life would ultimately lead to social acceptance and integration of black people into American society. In his pursuits for racial equality, he met frequently with other influential social leaders such as millionaire Henry Huttleston Rogers (American, 1840-1909), Sears company owner and president Julius Rosenwald (American, 1862-1932), President Theodore Roosevelt (American, 1858-1919), and President William Howard Taft (American, 1857-1930), who all saw Washington as a reasonable (and safe) adviser on race relations.

Washington wrote several influential books including *The Story of My Life and Work* (1900), *Up From Slavery* (1901), *The Story of the Negro: The Rise of the Race From Slavery* (1909), *My Larger Education* (1911), and *The Man Farthest Down* (1912). In 1900, he also founded the *National Negro Business League* (NNBL) to assist African American businesses, to aid in their financial development, and to counter restrictive discriminatory financial laws against African Americans. Washington earned honorary degrees from both *Harvard University* and *Dartmouth College* before dying on November 14, 1915 from complications of Bright's disease or hypertension.

Considered by many to be the founding father of sociology, *Max Weber* (German, 1864–1920) was a trained lawyer who used his keen intellect and brilliant analysis to study economics and sociology. Weber focused much of his work upon capitalism, bureaucracies, and scientific methodology in the social sciences, although there is not much that he did not investigate and comment upon in sociology—few scholars had (or have) offered as much on so many subfields within sociology as Weber did during his lifetime.

M a x
W e b e r

He enjoyed great academic and vocational success in Germany, which led him to rise quickly in scholarly ranks, receiving an appointment to be the Chair of National Economy and Finance in Freiburg in 1895, and becoming a full professor and Chair of the National Economy and Finance at the *University of Heidelberg* in 1897. Weber experienced some emotional setbacks, however, after the death of his father that year. He lapsed into a depression and then suffered a nervous breakdown, which kept him from working for five years. Although Weber slowly returned to academia in 1903 (but not lecturing again until after World War I ended), he produced many of his sociological contributions as a private scholar between the height of his mental illness and his death.

Regarding his theories of sociology, Weber asserted that sociology is a comprehensive science focused on social action. Thus, some people interact in society using *zweckrational acts*, where the goal and means are rationally chosen. Others choose *wertrational acts*, where the goal is not necessarily rational, but the means are logical. Some embrace *affective acts*, which are anchored in the emotional state of actor, but some settle on *traditional acts*, which are guided by customary habit of thought and the "eternal yesterday."

Weber was also concerned about scientific methodology in the social sciences, suggesting, like Durkheim, that sociologists should do their best to set aside personal, private values in their scientific analyses, owning and adjusting their methodology to correct for subjectivity and bias. Weber also asserted that sociology, as a scientific study, should embrace axiological neutrality, making sociology a value-free endeavor—describing, analyzing, and explaining how society operates and not judging or pushing society to a desired outcome.

Like others, Weber was a serious writer, with his most famous work being *The Protestant Ethic and the Spirit of Capitalism* (1905); however, not many of his writings made it to book form during his lifetime, although he did write and publish *Economy and Society* (1922), *The Vocation Lectures* (1919), and *The Sociology of Religion* (1920). He was popular and well-read within German academia, though, because most of his essays starred in German scholarly journals eagerly read mostly by German scholars.

J a n e
A d a m s

The last years of Weber's life were busy, but not as socially successful as earlier in his life. He helped found the Liberal German Democratic Party in 1918, ran for a seat in Parliament in 1919 but failed, provided advice for the committee drafting the Weimar Constitution in 1919, and sadly died of the Spanish Flu in his mid-fifties on June 14, 1920.

Nicknamed the "mother of social work," *Jane Addams* (American, 1860–1935) was a feminist, sociologist, political activist, reformer, and social worker in Chicago, Illinois, and later throughout the United States. She graduated with a bachelor's degree from *Rockford Female*

Seminary (later changed to *Rockford College for Women*) and pondered a career in medicine; however, poor health from a congenital disorder made her reconsider her vocational options. During an overseas trip to Europe, Addams visited the slums of London and a settlement house (an inner-city center providing needed social services to the poor and needy) called, *Toynbee Hall*, which inspired her to start a similar project in Chicago to help improve life for the poorest people suffering in the slums of industrial Chicago.

Consequently, in 1889, *Hull House* was founded by Addams and her friend, Ellen Gates Starr (American, 1859-1940). The pair leased the home built by Charles Hull and began their philanthropic enterprise to directly meet the needs of the underprivileged in the surrounding community. Their efforts began modestly, but soon their classes and clubs enrolled thousands of people each week, with building improvements and additions being added year after year to Hull House—including an art gallery and studio, a gymnasium with a swimming pool, a public kitchen, a library, a book bindery, several boarding rooms, and even an employment office.

Due to Addams' and Hull House's social success, she was invited to take on greater civil responsibilities, and so she joined or led such groups as Chicago's Board of Education, the School Management Committee, the Chicago School of Civics and Philanthropy, the National Conference of Charities and Corrections, the Women's International League for Peace and Freedom, and she guest-lectured at the *University of Wisconsin*, *The Hague* (in Holland), and other venues in America and abroad. With such social opportunities and influence thrust upon her, she also became an ardent proponent and voice for women's suffrage and civic pacifism.

She authored several books including *Democracy and Social Ethics* (1902), *The Spirit of Youth and the City Streets* (1909), *Newer Ideals of Peace* (1907), *The Long Road of Women's Memory* (1916), *Peace and Bread in Time of War* (1922), and *The Excellent Becomes the Permanent* (1932). A political protestor during World War I, Addams was severely criticized at home and in the press for being unpatriotic; however, she found work as an assistant to (the future) President Herbert Hoover (American, 1874-1964) arranging food relief packages to be sent to women and children of the Central Powers overseas. Addams eventually was awarded the Nobel Peace Prize in 1931, which was the first time that any sociologist (male or female) had ever received that prestigious award. She suffered a heart attack in 1926, from which she never fully recovered, and Addams' doctors discovered cancer during an operation in 1935, the same year that she died.

One of the most influential African American political activists, *W. E. B. DuBois* (American, 1868-1963) was a prolific writer, scholar, and journalist in post-Civil War America. A child prodigy, he graduated valedictorian from *Great Barrington High School* and went on to receive a BA from *Fisk University*, another BA from *Harvard University*, and eventually became the first African American to earn a PhD from *Harvard University*. His doctoral dissertation was entitled, "The Suppression of the African Slave Trade in America," and was soon published in book form (1896) by Harvard University Press. Thereafter, he taught at several universities including *Wilberforce University*, the *University of Pennsylvania*, and *Atlanta University*. He also acted as editor for the Niagara Movement's magazines—the *Moon* and *The Horizon*—as well as editor for the National Association for the Advancement of Colored People's (NAACP) magazine, *The Crisis*.

W.E.B. DuBois

In his fight for black civil rights, DuBois advocated for immediate social and legal equality between blacks and whites, equal access to classical higher education for all blacks, and the ending of institutional racism and segregation in America. He helped found the *NAACP* along with William M. Trotter (American, 1872-1934) at the *Niagara Movement* (1905-1910) in New

York. Although the two groups made significant progress in the pursuit of black equality in American society, DuBois was unhappy with the internal compromises allowed within the movement to his radical political interpretations and remedies by other social movement leaders like Trotter and Booker T. Washington (American, 1856-1915), who suggested a more amicable, passive healing of social wounds in America. DuBois eventually left the NAACP, which he considered to be ineffective and counterproductive in achieving comprehensive civil rights for blacks in America.

Despite these challenges, DuBois continued to use his scholarship and writing to advance his political dreams for African Americans (and all Africans abroad). He is famous for authoring such works as *The Philadelphia Negro* (1899), *The Souls of Black Folk* (1903), *Black Reconstruction in America* (1935), and his essay, "The Need for an Encyclopedia of the Negro" (1945). Later in life, DuBois joined in the peace movement during the *Cold War* (1945-1991 CE) between America and the Soviet Union. He ran for a senatorial position as a Socialist in 1950 and lost, which put him in the sights of the Federal Bureau of Investigation (FBI), who considered him a subversive, dangerous, political agent. DuBois confirmed their fears when he officially declared himself a Communist in 1961 (after the State Department took away his passport), renounced his citizenship, and moved to Accra, Ghana.

In his final years, DuBois accepted editorship of the *Africana Encyclopedia*, which he hoped would provide a complete and inspiring collection of positive African American stories and social/scientific contributions by all black people in human history. Although DuBois never saw his dream of an encyclopedia of black people written by black people come to fruition, three volumes of the *Encyclopedia Africana* were finally published in the 1970s and 1980s under editors Henry Louis Gates, Jr. (American, b. 1950) and Kwame Anthony Appiah (British-Ghanaian, b. 1954). DuBois died on August 27, 1963, at age 95, one day before Rev. Martin Luther King, Jr's (1929-1968) famous "I Have a Dream" speech in Washington, DC.

Sociology from Above

The Four Main Sacro-States of Christianity

Historical records have detailed the religious affiliation, participation, and power throughout the Western world and into its spheres of influence. Although there have been exceptions to societal acquiescence and obligation to religious involvement throughout the centuries, the general pattern has been one of overall adherence (voluntary or forced) to the church institution in the Western world (Gill, 2003). As Heelas, Woodhead, Seel, Szerszynski, and Tusting (2005) put it, Christians have enjoyed a ". . . life lived in terms of external or 'objective' roles, duties and obligations" (p. 2). Organized religion, specifically Christianity, has been traditionally accepted by Western society as good and beneficial to society for centuries; however, it was not always so, and it may not be so, presently.

With this in mind, four main expressions of Christianity—what I term sacro-theism, sacro-communalism, sacro-clericalism, and sacro-egoism—are proposed and explained. All of these approaches to religion are differentiated in terms of being based in different forms of authority. *Sacro-theism* relates to where primary authority is given to direct revelation/calling(s) from God in people's lives, *sacro-communalism* focuses on nondenominational, noninstitutional, unofficial religious beliefs (including the family or small groups), *sacro-clericalism* centers on ecclesiastical hierarchy and institutions, and *sacro-egoism* concentrates on the ultimate authority of the individual in spiritual matters. They all have their historical origins in Christianity, but they are not ancient ruins of the past; rather, they are still present in the modern religious world in varying intensity and manifestation.

The Historical Presence of Sacro-Theism

The origins of the Christian community began with the belief that God, through Jesus Christ, his son and comember of the Trinity, directly revealed themselves to humanity (sacro-theism) in order to provide a way to heal the problem of human sin and separation from God. Through Jesus, God imparted to his Disciples ". . . the way, the truth, and the life" (John 14:6, NIV), and they listened and obeyed—God was their ultimate authority and his words and commands superseded all else. The Holy Spirit, too, directly revealed its will to the believers then (and some say now). Sacro-theism, as with the other sacro-states, is not just a first-century approach to Christianity; it is evident in other historical periods of Western civilization such as in the mystical movement in 13th-century Germany.

Therefore, anyone who gives primary authority to mystical encounters and directly perceived revelation from God is a sacro-theist. Schleiermacher, known as the "Father of Modern Liberal Theology" (Gerrish, 1984, p. xi), considered religion and Christianity to be ". . . the distinctly human awareness of something infinite beyond the self on whom the self is dependent for everything" (Olson, 1999, p. 544). Many Christian movements focused on the words, beliefs, and practices of these men and women who claimed to have experienced the gift of theophany.

The Historical Presence of Sacro-Communalism

Sacro-communalism focuses on nondenominational and noninstitutional group beliefs. In the first century, not far removed from the presence of Jesus on the earth, early Christians established the foundations of what it meant to be a follower of Christ, to be a "Christian." People, like Paul the Apostle and other early church leaders, sought to spread the word of Christ and of his eminent return. This was not a new understanding of faith, but "rather the fulfillment of the promises made to Israel . . . through the resurrection of Jesus, the age of the Messiah had dawned" (Gonzalez, 1985, p. 27).

Luke, the traditional author of Acts, claims,

All the believers were one in heart and mind. No one claimed that any of his possessions was his own, but they shared everything they had. With great power the apostles continued to testify to the resurrection of the Lord Jesus, and much grace was upon them all. There were no needy persons among them. For from time to time those who owned lands or houses sold them, brought the money from the sales and put it at the apostles' feet, and it was distributed to anyone as he had need (Acts 4:32–35, NIV).

If sacro-communalism focuses on the belief system(s) of the lay community operating without instruction from an institution or religious hierarchy, then the first sacro-communalism period lasted for three centuries, roughly from 35 CE until the legalization of Christianity by *Constantine* in 325 CE, with Christians facing persecution from both Jewish and pagan authorities as well as internal threats from heresy and doctrinal challenges. Of course, any modern-day spirituality or religion that exists outside of institutional control or influence and utilizes a local community in its particular worship of God/the Divine could also be considered to be sacro-communal. Yet, sacro-communalism can quickly transform into sacro-clericalism when enough followers officially organize and expand their movement.

The Historical Presence of Sacro-Clericalism

As the Christian faith in the first centuries after Jesus' departure matured, religious thought developed into an institutional approach. This *sacro-clericalism* period, from the legalization of Christianity until the nineteenth century, is defined by the development of an official church hierarchy, construction of church buildings, the acceptance of common creeds and doctrinal positions, and the definition and development of denominational movements—all detailing what it meant to be a Christian, at least legitimately and corporately. Soon monastic orders, religious movements, and nationalistic religiosity became integral to becoming a Christian.

Sacro-clericalism can be seen in this form of legal-rational authority summarized by Weber

(1964) when he states, "It is a declaration of confidence in and dedication to a prophet or of the authority of a structured institution" (p. 194). This manifested itself in regular attendance, obedience to denominational codes, and fidelity to specific religious movements.

According to Gonzalez (1985), during the *Golden Age of Medieval Christianity*, "Christendom most nearly approached the ideal of being 'one flock, under one shepherd'" (p. 261). McGrath (1997) claims, "By the fifth century, Christianity had begun to establish itself securely in the Mediterranean region. Holding the title of a Christian required being under the authority of the Church." This is the essence of sacro-clericalism—spiritual acquiescence to an ecclesiastical body.

The Historical Presence of Sacro-Egoism

Nonetheless, as theological thought changed, specifically after the advent of liberalism in the nineteenth century, a change began to take place in the religious world. Religious attitudes and prioritization seem to begin shifting from sacro-clericalism, where authority is given to the church and its representatives, to *sacro-egoism*, where the individual assumes greatest authority.

The role of the individual, the self, was elevated more than ever before and self-reliance was glamorized, epitomized, and utilized in society—even in postmodernity. Liberal theologians like Schleiermacher, Ritschl, and Tillich ". . . sought to anchor that faith in common human experience and interpret it in ways that made sense within the modern worldview" (McGrath, 1998, p. 233).

Though first a subtle and infrequent occurrence, more and more the authority and centrality of the Church began to lose ground to the prominence of the individual. Culturally, the expression of religion and Christianity encountered ". . . a turn towards life lived by reference to one's own subjective experiences (relational as much as individualistic)" (Heelas et al., 2005, p. 2). Leaning on one's own understanding became an asset, not a detriment, to religious life and approval. According to Heelas et al. (2005), "The subjectivities of each individual become a, if not the, unique source of significance, meaning and authority" (p. 3-4).

Starks and Robinson (2007) comment that modernists ". . . see individuals and not a deity as the ultimate arbiters of moral authority and hold to a largely individually directed universe" (p. 32). This sacro-egoism reveals itself through a radical authority/priority of the self, an antagonism or ambivalence to religious institutionalism, a personal or pragmatic commitment to the spiritual journey, and an openness to and toleration of nontraditional beliefs and practices.

Currently, this shift can be observed in a variety of ways as mentioned earlier, most visibly in lowered membership and attendance numbers. This situation has been attributed to poor religious offerings, to a modern emphasis on the secular world, to ineffective participation and devotion of believers worldwide, or to the will of God—in some religious circles (Hatcher, 2005).

While all these may be partially true, the danger is making a synecdoche of the products of decline and overestimating their importance and influence in religion. Christian society has never operated out of a vacuum. Furseth and Repstad (2006) state, "It is simply not true that individuals invent their own world-view in a void" (p. 124). From its earliest beginnings, this religious movement has interacted closely with culture, as did its founder. Thus, this interaction ". . . is two-way: Christianity both influences and is influenced by culture" (McGrath, 1998, p. 9).

Conclusion

Beyond these descriptions, it is very likely that some people may exercise a mix of the sacro-states in their understanding and appreciation to religion and spirituality. They may be sacro-egoistical when it comes to which Bible version that they read, but sacro-clerical when it comes to their belief on the Sacraments. They may be sacro-theistic and frequently hear the voice of God by themselves as they pray, but they still perceive a need to continue their fellowship with other believers at church. They may be born into a sacro-communal lifestyle (due to the biological limitations of being an infant and child), but then shift into radical sacro-communalism when they go away to college and join a club or fellowship group.

Today, all over the United States and in the Westernized world, people continue to approach the sacred in a variety of ways—some in older, more time-honored fashion, and others with a radical edge. Moreover, one's freedom quotient rises exponentially in life as time goes by. Some people clearly act upon this freedom to shirk the bonds between them and the church; others cling dearly to the church as an old, trusted, valuable friend.

The timeline of the Christian church shows an intertwining, evolving story of mysticism, individualism, community, and institutionalism, but what is clear is that the sacro-states are not static states—they are apt to change because people (and greater society) change in their perspectives and needs, historically.

The Sage from the Stage

Distinguished Perspectives: The Disciplines of Sociology and History in Modern Society

The relationship between sociology and history is among the most fascinating to consider. In many ways, the work of several sociologists in the field of history connects the two disciplines; yet, a core difference remains. Modern sociology begins with current society being its focal point and then, if they do look at history at all, sociologists work their way backward through history to reveal cultural flaws or inconsistencies, rationalizing the notion that society is moving toward a dystopian future. In equal isolation, historians (as a rule) believe their craft dictates that evaluation begins at the complete opposite end: from the past and moving forward to the present. The historian Marc Bloch best summed up both dilemmas when he famously stated, "Misunderstanding of the present is the inevitable consequence of ignorance of the past. But a man may wear himself out just as fruitlessly in seeking to understand the past, if he is totally ignorant of the present" (Bloch, 1953, p. 43).

While the study of society and social phenomenon goes back centuries to the Renaissance, a recognizable change occurred in the nineteenth century. Following the *French Revolution*, the first sociologists claimed to see a brighter future for Europe arising from the cultural and political rubble. In France, the works of Auguste Comte represented the distinct formation of sociology. His propensity to see order out of chaos and progress from instability, led him to claim sociology was a bright, new science that could keep European civilization moving forward, despite the revolutionary fervor still permeating Europe. Comte's personal life, born to conservative monarchists but personally espousing liberal republican and socialist views, clearly mirrored the broader questions troubling French society in the nineteenth century (Chambliss, 1954, pp. 392–395). The evident contradiction between society and progress, one requiring stability and order and the other requiring innovation and change, presented the most extensive predicament that Comte attempted to address in his groundbreaking works, *Positive Polity* and *Positive Philosophy*.

This initial bond between nascent sociology and the newly minted positivism ingrained in nineteenth century intellectuals a concrete belief that statistical, metaphysical data and quantitative research would provide the order that society craved while also revealing the path forward. It is important to note that Karl Marx was among those most attracted to such activity even as he undermined key notions of the young field. As such, many sociological models and philosophy incorporated Marxist teachings on economic materialism and collective progressivism.

Progressive scholar Herbert Spencer also contributed to the early framing of sociology by adding new cultural and social analysis. Spencer advocated for sociology within the context of "bettering society." His thesis advocated synthesizing studies to further progress, even advocating more freedom in society, including universal suffrage. Sociology, he believed, could be the discipline that brought all other academic fields together. However, his ideas remained tainted by the great pseudoscience of *Social Darwinism* as he embraced a concept of "survival of the fittest," where Darwinian evolutionary theory applied to society as a whole. As a "Structural Functionalist," Spencer saw progress toward a "more perfect" society in order to promote "more perfect" human beings, as the two were both organically connected (Laluddin, 2016, pp. 8–26). Widely read, Spencer's ideas remained at the forefront of early sociology, but some have since rejected his tendency toward "natural order" arguments and racial ideologies.

Certainly, there is value to categorizing and ordering information. However, these three individuals mark both vital, credentialed developments in the sociological discipline and early pitfalls, which still haunt the field despite current trends to the contrary. In perspective, consider Emile Durkheim, who, in searching for a philosophy of science that maintained ethics, turned to sociology in order to differentiate between what "is" and what "ought to be." Durkheim engaged with the philosophers of the Enlightenment, Kant, and Hume, in order to establish a firm basis for a new code of conduct that was traditional in nature, but inclusive in its intention (Miller, 1996, pp. 1–3).

For him, sociology was a tool to determine the worth of new ideas through experimentation, inquiry, and analysis. His 1897 work on *Suicide* became a defining moment in the furthering of sociology as a science. Durkheim's "cautious optimism" sought the conclusion of any scientific study to affirm, not threaten humanity (pp. 1–3). His humanity was moral and cultural but also individualist rejecting base commercialism for cultural abundance.

While Durkheim sought to quantify society's "collective consciousness," Max Weber saw sociology as a means to establishing a better methodology in his historical analysis. Building off his studies at the University of Berlin, under famed historian Leopold von Ranke, Weber not only incorporated sociological theory into his historical analysis, he contributed back into the field of sociology in essays forming the basis of his theories (such as *Legitimate Rulership*) on the state monopolizing the use of coercive force. His "Three Forms of Rulership" (legal, traditional, and charismatic) remains an important theoretical piece in current sociological studies on authority (Bruun & Whimster, 2012, pp. xi–xii).

As an historian, Weber became famous for his establishment of the "Protestant Work-Ethic" during the Reformation as a cause of the Industrial Age. While Weber's ideas have since been scrutinized, and many of his observations are questioned by historians and sociologists alike. His overall analysis remains a striking example of how to combine the fields of history and sociology.

As the discipline of sociology progressed and its forms increased, later generations began to glean certain work from earlier sociologists and discard the material they disliked. An outstanding example of this is Harriet Martineau. As one of the first female sociologists, Martineau converted concepts from Comte (such as the "law of progress") and others, yet ultimately sought to uphold cultural values in the face of growing class strife. Her views on the necessity for proper education and equality in educational standards across class and gender lines remained focal points guiding her social analysis. Her fight against slavery and institutional exploitation ultimately led her to believe that the individual owed it to themselves to be educated enough to stop exploitation.

Far from fanning victimhood, Martineau looked to social science to provide security for individuals who resisted the system and prevented themselves from becoming victims through education and compassion. As one biographer wrote, "Whether it was political economy, mesmerism, positivism, or scientific socialism, the security, prediction and promise of science were the goals. Harriet Martineau was never an advocate of scientific socialism; had she been born a little later in another place she might well have been" (Webb, 1960, pp. 365-366).

In truth, we are always limited in our view and approach. Statistical data tends to reveal an artificial ranking of information, creating a dichotomy into realms of important and unimportant. The statistical data that a study leaves out becomes as telling as what is included. While no study can focus on everything, dangers exist in limiting one's range, lest later researchers discover errors, holes, missed stanzas, blanks, or socially constructed ideas that they judge manipulative. Being marked in a future textbook's footnote as a past error is a fate to which both sociologist and historians commonly fall victim.

As one historian turned sociologist observed about the famed Renaissance historian Jacob Burkhardt: "Writing over a hundred and fifty years ago, Burckhardt viewed the Renaissance as a modern culture created by a modern society. Today, it looks rather more archaic" (Burke, 2014, p. 1). Indeed, long ago the prophet Daniel similarly warned the Babylonians: an entire kingdom was doomed to fall based upon faulty weights and measurements (Daniel 5:25-28).

We see the same among our examples in sociology, as, for instance, many writers still debate Weber's contributions to both history and sociology (Gregory, 2012, p. 241). It behooves the modern sociologist to seek to avoid weights, numbers, and measurements based solely upon apparent value. Balancing modern tendencies and requirements with contextual analysis of historical phenomenon produce an intrinsic and authoritative form of sociology, which will remain relevant far beyond its original intention. We hereby acknowledge that there remains a useful connection between history and sociology as disciplines. If there were none, then there would never have been so much crossover between the two disciplines despite their distinguished perspectives.

Dr. Benjamin Esswein, PhD
Assistant Professor of History
Liberty University

Contributed by Dr. Benjamin Esswein. © Kendall Hunt Publishing Company

 Check out the Chapter 3 video at this link: https://www.grtep.com/

Vocabulary

Abolitionist Movement
Academy at Athens
Aesthetics
Affective Acts
Africana Encyclopedia
Age of Reason
Allegory of the Cave
American Civil War
American Revolution
Anomie
Atheism
The Atlanta Compromise
Axiological Neutrality
Bourgeoisie
The Communist Manifesto
Dark Ages
Deism
French Revolution
Enlightened Rationality

The Enlightenment
Epistemology
Ethics
Evolutionary Theory
Hull House
Liberalism
Marxism
Metaphysical Stage
Middle Ages
Moral Architecture
"Mother of Social Work"
NAACP
NNBL
Positivism
Proletariat
Religion of Humanity
The Renaissance
The Republic
Sacro-Clericalism

Sacro-Communalism
Sacro-Egoism
Sacro-Theism
Scientific Stage
Social Darwinism
Social Phenomenon
Social Physics
Social Work
Sociology
Suffrage
Theological Stage
Traditional Acts
Tuskegee Norma
   School
Unitarianism
Victorian Era
Wertrational
Young Hegelians
Zweckrational

CHAPTER FOUR: Culture

The Basics

Culture is the totality of human shared language, knowledge, material objects, and behavior. Although society is above culture, neither society nor culture can exist without each other. Culture shapes people's activities, people's perceptions and interpretations, and how they feel about life's journey.

For instance, from its colonial beginnings, the United States has valued individualism and personal freedoms above all else. There is a plethora of historical and sociological evidence to back this up, and this sociological aspect is easily observed in American culture in its movies, music, clothing, art, political movements, and so on. Sherman (1998) writes, "The folkloric film [and this can also include other forms of entertainment media] covers a wide range of traditional behavior, from rituals, ceremonies, folk art and material culture to games, sayings, and songs, and to the lore of various people bounded by ethnicity, age, gender, family, occupation, recreation, religion and region" (p. 63).

Of course, what is fashionable in the United States is not necessarily true in other places across the globe. One could say that Japan values collective harmony, Britain values sensibility and peaceful order, Russia values strong leadership, and France values paternalism (or maternalism). While facets of these qualities are no doubt found in every country in the world, they are emphasized to such a great degree that people cannot doubt their significance, sociologically.

In 1984, Kohls asserted that the *key American values* were (a) personal control over the environment, (b) change is good, (c) time and its control is important, (d) equality and egalitarianism, (e) individualism and privacy, (f) self-help, (g) competition and free enterprise, (h) future orientation, (i) action or work orientation, (j) informality, (k) directness or honesty, (l) practicality and efficiency, and (m) materialism and acquisitiveness (pp. 4–17). Although many of these values have remained the same in the United States, clearly some have shifted in their prioritization or have been removed/ replaced with others more relevant to postmodern culture, such as personal identity or access to personal-use technologies.

With some variance, the elements of culture include symbols, language, values, and norms. *Symbols* are anything that carries a particular meaning recognized by people who share a culture. *Language* is a system of symbols that allows people to communicate with each other. *Values* are culturally defined standards that people use to decide what is good and beautiful in society. *Norms* are rules and expectations by which society guides the behavior of its members.

People also find themselves being herded or migrating into social groups common to the characteristics of their audience. For instance, in most Western societies, one can encounter *high*, *low*, and *popular cultures*. *High culture* typically includes forms and ways of existence associated with the economic elite and the dominant subculture. *Low culture* includes forms and ways of existence associated with the economically struggling and stagnate. Similar but less tied to socioeconomic status, *popular culture* is usually associated with the masses or the mob, consumer goods and products, and nebulous and vacuous trends and public fads.

Despite the diversity in human societies, all cultural operation includes both material and nonmaterial cultural operation. The *material world* refers to physical or technological aspects of normal human existence, which includes food, housing, consumer goods, and the raw materials to

make them. The *nonmaterial world* refers to other ways of using material objects, and also to human customs, ideas, expressions, beliefs, knowledge, philosophies, ways of communication, and so on.

While these cultural aspects seem commonplace and expected for those who have grown up with them as a daily aspect of life, stepping into foreign cultures can cause some people to feel confused, dazed, and uncertain. Sociologically, there is no way of life that is "natural" to humanity. People use their brains and personal resources to adapt to the environments that they encounter (or move into) in their life journeys.

Occasionally, though, the experience is overwhelming; this is called *culture shock*, which is a personal disorientation when experiencing or encompassed in an unfamiliar way of life. In many ways, animals have easier coping mechanisms for the unexpected as their behavior is strongly determined by instinct. For human beings, though, the intellectual or the emotional can outweigh or outmatch any human instincts that might exist in areas of sexuality, attachment, and aggression.

Considering that over seven billion people live on the planet, currently, it should not be surprising that great diversity exists within and outside all societies and cultures. With so many people, the statistical impact of the variety of public social forces in effect that are coupled with personal individual choices in society is tremendous. Added to this complex cultural reality are *subcultures*, which are segments of society that share distinctive patterns of mores, folkways, and values that differ from a larger pattern in society.

There also exist *countercultures*, which are specific subcultures that deliberately oppose certain aspect of the traditional, larger culture. Hollander (2018) notes,

> Heartfelt critiques of the alleged inauthenticity of American society and culture were another prominent theme of the countercultural critique on society. All these sentiments converged in a diffuse discontent with what was seen as the deeply rooted, ineradicable corruption of American society that was the key to the specific critiques of its domestic institutions and foreign policies (p. 25).

For such attitudes and actions, people can receive *sanctions*, which are rewards or punishments that encourage conformity to cultural norms. There can be *mores or taboos*, which are norms that are widely observed and that have great moral significance. There are *folkways*, which are norms for routine or casual interaction between people; there is *shame*, which concerns a personal and painful sense that others are disapproving of you; and there is *guilt*, which is the negative judgment that people make of themselves.

Between (and within each) cultures, not everyone enjoys or embraces diversity with open arms. Many people see these differences as a threat or perversion, leading to ethnocentrism, cultural relativism, and/or cultural wars. *Ethnocentrism* is the practice of judging another culture or person by the standards of one's own culture or personal values. Most people exhibit this practice although they may not be fully aware of it; nevertheless, it still can lead to social conflict. Opposing this is the practice of *cultural relativism*, which is the act of judging a culture by its own standards. This is more difficult as it requires both self-awareness and an openness to unfamiliar values and norms.

As previously mentioned, cultural encounters create diverse responses depending upon one's location and culture. Because of the limited human perspective, cultural battles can ensue when the ideal (norms and values aspired to) do not match up with the real (norms and values actually practiced). These *cultural wars*, with their factional points of dissension and division, occur quite frequently in mainstream culture (such as the current social and political battles between the conservatives and the progressives in postmodern American culture).

Such warfare is hardly anything new in human history and existence. Every era, every people group, every society has dealt with culture and its impact upon people's lives. *Cultural change* is a constant in all societies, usually slow and incremental in the wearing, tearing, and reweaving of the social fabric, but sometimes it can be quite rapid and dramatic, as the great technological advancements have produced in greater Western society since the turn of the century.

More than ever before, human beings have the ability to inquire and engage with other people, cultures, and societies across the globe through the Internet and through faster and more affordable transportation and communication options. This has led to increased *cultural diffusion*, when different groups share material and nonmaterial culture with each other; to *cultural leveling*, when cultures once distinct become increasingly similar to one another (think about the same restaurants that you can visit in each state, coast-to-coast).

Occasionally, though, *cultural imperialism* has occurred, which is the imposition of one culture upon another through mass media and consumer product dominance (think McDonalds, Levi's blue jeans, and American Rock-n-Roll). According to Ritzer (2018), in latter modernity and postmodernity, everyday social interactions have come to resemble and demonstrate the structure and obtuse, perfunctory interactions of fast-food restaurants like McDonalds (pp. 14–16).

This new postmodern reality has transcended national borders, which leads many sociologists to speculate over an emerging *global culture*, where the increased flow of trade, people, investments, technology, culture, and ideas have become more integrated and interdependent than ever before in human history. The effects of this worldwide cultural shift involve economics, politics, technology, natural resources on the grandest of scales. As Franklin, Lury, and Stacey (2000) remark,

Frequently assumed to condense some of the key changes that characterise contemporary sociality, globalisation in much recent social theory refers to a set of processes that are said to be transforming the social world at an unprecedented speed. Globalising processes have been seen as indicative of a shrinking of the world through new technologies and mobilities, and the speeding up of processes no longer inhibited by national boundaries or by geographical locatedness (p. 2)

Many people have lauded the change, pointing to the tremendous flow of goods, information, and people that are shared, daily; others, though, are less affirming, pointing to the uneven flow of those same goods, information, and people. Even more recently, several countries have seen *anti-globalization movements* arise, pushing back against the homogenization of cultures and accusing various nations of abuses and exploitations (which will be discussed more fully in Chapter 13).

Sociology from Above

Egyptian Culture versus the Culture of God

One of the more hotly contested items of debate in American culture concerns the Ten Commandments (also called the Decalogue). For thousands of years, followers of God (especially those of Jewish and Christian persuasions) have lauded and lifted God's ten rules of righteous living that were given to Moses directly for God's people to follow. In the past 50 years, however, the Decalogue's preeminence as universal codes of conduct have been challenged in culture and the courts by nonbelievers who find their restrictions irrelevant and irritating.

For instance, in his book, *The God Delusion* (2006), Richard Dawkins writes, "The political power of America's Ten Commandment tablet-toters is especially regrettable in that great republic whose constitution, after all, was drawn up by men of the Enlightenment in explicitly secular terms." Dawkins finds the Commandments to be contemptible and absurd, adding four of his own that are more relevant in postmodern society—(a) Enjoy your sex life, (b) do not discriminate on the basis of sex, race, or species, (c) do not indoctrinate your children except regarding proper scientific methodology, and (d) think about life in the grand scale and not just in your own timeline (p. 300). He even goes on to write (with remarkable misunderstanding of the core beliefs of Christianity and Judaism) that people can reject the Ten Commandments because "There is improved education and, in particular, the increased understanding that each of us shares a common humanity with members of other races and the other sex—both deeply unbiblical ideas that come from biological science, especially evolution" (p. 308).

With him being an "evangelical" atheist, one could understand why Dawkins would reject the first four commandments that focus so much on God, but somehow, he finds his own commandments to be more socially valuable than God's do not murder, do not steal, do not bear false witness, do not commit adultery, do not covet, and be respectful to your parents. Even disregarding Dawkins' great reductionism and volitional obtuseness concerning the Christian piety of the founding fathers (besides, perhaps, Thomas Jefferson or Benjamin Franklin), one is hard-pressed to see how Dawkins' myopic contributions offer more unifying societal benefits than the Bible's overarching commandments.

Still, Dawkins is not alone. In his own book, *God Is Not Great* (2007), Christopher Hitchens offers the critique, "But however little one thinks of the Jewish tradition, it is surely insulting to the people of Moses to imagine that they had come this far under the impression that murder, adultery, theft, and perjury were permissible" (ebook, pp. 184–185). For Hitchens, there is no doubt that the Ten Commandments ". . . is a man-made product of the alleged time and place. . ." (ebook, p. 185). He may be half-right in this assertion, as the Ten Commandments are a response to the culture that the Hebrew people had lived in for hundreds of years. Furthermore, the title of his book might also be half-right in that all other religions besides the Judeo-Christian faiths are based on false gods and false promises, which has brought calamity and confusion to human beings since prehistoric times. Yet, there is much more to the Ten Commandments than doubters like Dawkins and Hitchens comprehend.

Many scholars have made claim that the Decalogue is simply a borrowed form of an ancient legal document called, a *suzerain treaty*. According to Meredith Kline (2019), "In the Ancient Near East, treaties between kinds was common. These were treaties drawn up among equals and mostly outlined agreements to honor each other's boundaries, to maintain trade relations, and return run-away slaves" (online). The Ten Commandments is simply one of these, borrowed by Moses, to order and maintain a new Hebrew society.

While this theory is certainly a possibility (or just an anachronistic scholarly projection), some focus so much on the form of *the Ten Commandments* that they miss the overall countercultural substance of God's instructions on how to have a healthy relationship with Him and each other, despite their poor socialization in Egypt as slaves. He has brought them out of Egypt (Exodus 20:2) into a new community of faith with Him. With a new community comes a new set of cultural expectations.

For example, as mentioned earlier, the first four commandments deal directly with the Hebrew people's understanding and obligations to God. Exodus 20:3–8 make some gigantic demands concerning Yahweh: (a) they cannot have any other gods that usurp His position as God, (b) they cannot make idols of any earthly creature or feature, (c) they cannot misuse His name as a curse or to confuse, and (d) they must remember to honor God's creation of them and nature by taking a day off from work.

These first four commandments fly in the face of hundreds of years of Egyptian socialization and culture for the Hebrew people. First, the chief god in Egypt was the Pharaoh, who was the absolute religious lord for the Egyptians. He was not subject to common limitations as other human leaders; he did not work for the community—they only supported him; he was linked with the Nile flooding, fertility, bountiful agricultural harvests; he was omniscient and therefore the law in all things. It was said that justice was what the pharaoh loved, and evil was what he hated. The first commandment said that the Hebrew people could no longer worship or laud the Pharaoh as the supreme cosmic ruler any longer.

Second, all historians and archeologists concur that ancient Egypt was polytheistic for most of its existence. The *Egyptian pantheon* was huge, with more than 2,000 major or minor gods. The Egyptian religious milieu included several cults using prehistoric creatures and hybrid animal deities such as Horus the falcon god, Anubis the jackal god, and so on. The second commandment prohibited this practice and belief, which must have challenged their centuries-old socialization and trainings.

Third, God's people were not to use God's name in vain. Yahweh was God in person, not some inanimate object or force of nature. In the sixteenth century, BCE, the Egyptian religious priests would have proclaimed pharaoh to be the reincarnation of Osiris, the father of Horus, until he died, and another prince took his father's place. Of course, unlike the flawed pharaohs, Yahweh actually was the God by whose dealings one lives, the father and mother of all people, alone by himself, and without an equal. God was the one, true deity of the universe and He was associated with all His children—not just for one city or tribe. Therefore, God's people needed to respect His position over them and their responsibilities as His image-bearers.

Furthermore, after the good times ended in Egypt under their appointed ruler, Joseph (son of Jacob), the new pharaoh felt threatened by the Hebrews' numbers and previous powers and changed the Egyptian state's relationship with them to one of cruel subservience. They lost all independence, all cultural identity, and were put to work building the cities, monuments, and tombs for a false god in a foreign land—just as was promised to Abraham centuries before ("Know for certain that for four hundred years your descendants will be strangers in a country not their own and that they will be enslaved and mistreated there" Genesis 15:13).

The fourth commandment, therefore, was a command of release from God, who cared about their welfare, and ultimately wanted only the best for them. They still were under God's control and management, but unlike their previous Pharaonic masters, God knew their limits and what was necessary to be physically, psychologically, and spiritually healthy. Ironically, because of their former socialization that had been drilled into them (and fears for survival), God had to order them not to work on their day off, which still might be true of God's followers today.

The last six commandments were also linked to the emancipation of the Hebrew people who had never had so much personal autonomy and free community interactions. Of course, life under Egyptian rule and culture had taught them to be selfish, bitter, and coldhearted. So, God gave them a path to follow for charity, peace, and compassion—starting with their family, their parents.

They were to honor their father and mother (verse 12), whom they may have not known before as slaves. They were not to take the life of another innocent person for personal gain (verse 13). They were to respect the personal boundaries of other people's families and belongings (verses 14–15). They were to not lie about other people for personal gain (verse 16). Last, they were to resist the human compulsion of jealousy and coveting (verse 17), which may have been a regular part of their former austere, grim existence as slaves.

The Ten Commandments were not mere ethical codes of political control for Moses to wield over Hebrew society. They were a lifeline of resocialization to rescue God's people from slavery, sorrow, and pain, which is a common thread interwoven throughout the Old and New Testaments. Many like Dawkins and Hitchens claim that the Decalogue is no longer relevant in our radically individualistic postmodern society; yet, not all scholars concur with their dour conclusions (Berlinski, 2009). God's instructions still ring true for those hoping and striving to have the healthiest relationship with God, their creator, and with those around them, their brothers and sisters in Christ.

The Sage from the Stage

The Christian Response to Culture: Rejection, Adoption, Creativity

If a society is an ordered community of people, culture is what enriches that community with meaning. Andy Crouch (2013) defines culture as "what we make of the world," suggesting two aspects of the word, "make" (p. 23). First and most visibly, culture is what humans make or create which includes customs, rituals, foodways, dwellings, clothing, art, music, and so on. Culture is also how humans make sense of the world—how we make meaning out of the world around us. These two aspects of the word are linked in that "We make *sense* of the world by making *something* of the world" (p. 24). Culture gives meaning and reflects meaning in society.

This broad definition of culture encompasses more specific categories such as high culture, pop culture, and ethnic culture. More importantly, it is built upon that fundamental element of what it means to be human, to be created in the image of God. The human impulse to create—whether things or meaning—is a reflection of the Creator himself.

Culture is also cumulative, building on what has come before and arising within an existing context. In other words, culture is part of a story that is already in progress (p. 26). Where does Christianity fit into that story and how might believers respond to their cultural context? The history of Christianity can help twenty-first century believers answer these questions. Since the birth of the church, Christians have responded to their cultural context in a variety of ways. These include rejecting elements of the existing culture, adopting or adapting elements of the existing culture, and creating something new to enhance or replace elements of the existing culture.

The most evident cultural response of the first Christians was to reject the paganism of the Greco-Roman world. Their refusal to participate in traditional religious practices and their insistence on loyalty to Christ over Caesar led directly to persecution and, often, martyrdom. Even more radical was their spiritual egalitarianism as described by the Apostle Paul. "There is neither Jew nor Gentile, neither slave nor free, nor is there male and female, for you are all one in Christ Jesus" (Galatians 3:28). This passage not only suggests the rejection of traditional categories, but it also subverts the existing social structure and transcends ethnic identity, all defining features of the existing Greco-Roman culture. Christian rejection of this culture was most famously expressed by Tertullian when he asked. "What indeed has Athens to do with Jerusalem?" with Athens representing Greek thought and tradition and Jerusalem representing Christianity (*City of God*, book XL).

Once Rome officially accepted Christianity in the fourth century, cultural rejection by Christians became less extreme with thinkers like Augustine favoring instead the adoption of useful elements of the existing culture, appropriating them for the use of the church (*City of God*, book XL). Although Augustine's concern was primarily related to learning and ideas, the impulse for appropriation extended to other aspects of culture as well. The history of the early church is replete with examples of Roman cultural influence. Early Christian church buildings were modeled after the basilica, a type of Roman public building. The chief high priest of Roman religion was known as *Pontifex Maximus*, from which derived pontifex or pontiff and was applied to bishops, particularly the bishop of Rome. The organizational structure of the church mirrored that of the Roman Empire in many respects. For example, provinces were grouped into a unit known as a diocese for administrative purposes, an organizational feature adopted by the institutional church. And, of course, *Latin* became the official language of the church just as it had been the official language of the Roman Empire.

After the fall of Rome, cultural adoption increasingly extended to include Germanic culture, much of which has followed Western Christianity down to the present. Perhaps the most lasting example of such adoption is in the calendar which identifies months of the year and days of the week from both Roman and Germanic traditions. For example, July and August are named for two Roman rulers, Julius Caesar and Caesar Augustus. Germanic examples include Wednesday, from Woden's Day, and Thursday or Thor's Day, both named for Germanic gods. Other Germanic practices are reflected in common holiday traditions such as the decoration of trees to celebrate Christmas.

Even while some aspects of the existing culture were rejected and others were adopted or appropriated, early Christians began to create culture as well. Perhaps the most profound example of cultural creativity is the New Testament itself. By the end of the second century, Christians had accepted as authoritative most of the writings that would form the New Testament and all twenty-seven texts were affirmed in the fourth century. After careful vetting and debating, the Church reached a cultural consensus, the product of which would form the basis of the Christian faith from that time to the present. Added to this immense contribution is the development of a sophisticated theology (though not without controversy) through a series of church councils and the writings of the early Church Fathers. Articulating difficult doctrines such as the Trinity and the deity of Jesus Christ represents an enormous cultural achievement.

As late antiquity gave way to the early Middle Ages, other forms of cultural creativity emerged. Sincere believers who sought new means for expressing intense religious devotion in a culturally identifiable way founded monasteries. Until the rise of the university in the thirteenth century, these monasteries preserved Christian cultural heritage through the laborious task of copying manuscripts in their scriptoria. Although they removed themselves from the mainstream of medieval life, monks and nuns were not so much rejecting the culture as separating themselves from it in order to focus on a religious life without distraction. In the process, they created a new kind of culture, one that at least theoretically embraced a kind of social equality since the monastic lifestyle did not permit possessions. Women also participated in monasticism, opening up an avenue of cultural creativity that otherwise would not be available to them for centuries to come.

Often mistakenly identified as the *Dark Ages*, the Christian Middle Ages yielded astounding examples of cultural creativity. In addition to the flourishing of monastic life, other examples include illuminated manuscripts, a new style of architecture we now call Gothic, and a new institution of learning called the university.

The era of the Reformation further demonstrates the complex interaction of Christians with their cultural context including rejection, adoption, and creativity. The *Protestant Reformation* launched by Martin Luther was, by definition, a rejection of the existing Roman Catholic culture. The theological question of salvation was the impetus, but the rejection grew to encompass other aspects of theology, religious observance, and even the organization of family life. Ironically, the movement also rejected one of the most profound vehicles of creativity, monasticism.

In spite of this revolutionary spirit, reformers still managed to adopt elements of the existing culture. Even while Protestants rejected the authority Catholic Church, they continued to operate in the context of an alternate official state church. Though they espoused the "priesthood of believers," which denied the mediating function of priests, Protestants maintained a clear distinction between clergy and laity that in many ways mirrored the traditional church.

What is most notable, however, is the cultural creativity that emerged from the *Reformation*. The availability of printing led to the creation of mass communication; vernacular translations of the Bible resulted in the standardization of languages; congregational singing yielded new forms of music; and wherever the Reformation spread, it sparked a burst of theological creativity.

This pattern of rejection, adoption, and cultural creation is evident through the Great Awakening of the eighteenth century, the expansion of world missions in the nineteenth century, and the rise of modern evangelicalism in the twentieth century. Christian opposition to culture is well known today as is evidenced in the so-called culture wars. There are also plenty of examples of adoption or appropriation of culture, bringing what are deemed the most useful aspects the existing culture into the service of the church. What seems to have received less attention is cultural creativity. With more attention to this kind of cultural response, one can only imagine what new aspects of culture might be created and how such cultural creativity might enrich society by reflecting biblical teaching and furthering the gospel.

Donna Davis Donald
Assistant Professor of History
Liberty University

Contributed by Donna Davis Donald. © Kendall Hunt Publishing Company

 Check out the Chapter 4 video at this link: https://www.grtep.com/

Vocabulary

Anti-Globalism Movements
Christian Culture
Christian Middle Ages
Counter-cultures
Cultural Change
Cultural Creativity
Cultural Diffusion
Cultural Imperialism
Cultural Leveling
Cultural Relativism
Culture
Culture Shock
Culture Wars
Dawkins' Four
    Commandments
The Decalogue

Diocese
The Egyptian Pantheon
Ethnocentrism
Evangelical Atheism
Folkways
Global Culture
Guilt
High Culture
Individualism
Key American Values
Language
Low Culture
Material World
Monasticism
Mores
Non-Material World

Norms
Pontifex Maximus
Popular Culture
Protestant Reformation
Relativism
Roman Culture
Sanctions
Shame
Subcultures
Suzerain Treaty
Symbols
Taboos
The Ten Commandments
Values

CHAPTER FIVE: Socialization

The Basics

Regarding socialization, understanding how we have come to believe and behave as we do in society is crucial in getting along with others. Socialization is "the life-long process through which people learn the attitudes, values, and behaviors appropriate for members of a particular culture" (Witt, 2009, p. 67). Knowing why people behave like they do is instrumental in stopping assumptions that often lead to judgmentalism or unnecessary condemnation. As an American born in the 1960s, I recognize that my worldview is not the same as people born in the 1990s. They know little about the Cold War or life before computers. Of course, they may have a more optimistic and less frightening attitude toward international politics because of a friendlier social climate of globalization.

All social interactions involve exchanges between two or more individuals. In sociology, these interactions can be studied in dyads (2), triads (3), or in larger social groups. Sociologists focus much upon social language in action. People's perceptions and responses are very important. In fact, our interactions with people are shaped by our perception of their position in society relative to our own. This reality is shaped by perceptions, evaluations, and definitions.

There are four basic types of social interactions. There is exchange, cooperation, conflict, and competition. A social interaction of *exchange* occurs when people do something for other people with the express purpose of receiving a reward or return. In this regard, they are being mostly self-serving.

A social interaction of *cooperation* occurs when people act together to promote common interests or to achieve shared goals. In this way, it is utilitarian or altruistic. Other forms of social interactions include *conflict*, which happens when people or groups have incompatible values or when rewards and resources are limited. *Competition* is another social interaction and is a form of conflict in which individuals or groups can fight within agreed-upon rules such as the stark market.

Sociologist Herbert Blumer (1900–1987) suggested that meaning arises out of social interaction. People act toward things according to the meaning given to them. Blumer called this *symbolic interaction*, which is the interaction that is mediated by the use of symbols. These symbols act as a stimulus and provoke responses regarding human behavior and attitudes. Everyone goes through an internal process of analysis and interpretation to assign meaning to these symbols.

Dramaturgical sociology suggests that human interaction is comparable to the role of actors in a theater, says sociologist Erving Goffman (1922–1982). It is an attempt to present ourselves to others so that they will see us as we wish to be seen.

In a similar vein, *impression management* deals with how people act toward each other. With *frontstage behavior*, we act as we do when we know that others are watching or aware of us. In *backstage behavior*, we act as we do when we think that no one is looking.

All social interaction rest upon communication. One form of communication is *nonverbal*. This refers to any communication transmitted from person-to-person in symbols other than language. This could include gestures, which are movements of the body, or personal posture, which is how people hold themselves and their bodies. This communication can include body language, facial expressions, and emotional responses such as fear, security, happiness, anger, surprise, and boredom.

When people communicate, many need an area surrounding them that is employed (consciously or unconsciously) to convey meaning. This is called *personal space*. The levels of distance of personal space depend upon how well or not that person knows another. If they are on intimate terms with the person, there might be contact within 18 in. If one knows a person fairly well, it might be 18 in. to 4 ft. If it is just a social connection, it would be 4–12 ft. And if it is a distant public acquaintance, it is typically beyond 12 ft.

Many times, when we interact with each other, we construct our performances to idealize our intentions. We show people what we want to believe about ourselves and about what we want to be. Sometimes we make mistakes; this leads to embarrassment, which is discomfort resulting from failed actions.

Kindly, many people help others save face when they make mistakes. This is called *tact*. Abraham Lincoln said that "Tact is the ability to describe others as they see themselves." This helps us maintain good relationships with each other.

Sometimes, our interactions are humorous. Humor is the product of reality construction. It stems from a contrast between two different realities and arises from contradiction, ambiguity, and double meanings. Often, it allows expression of a personal opinion without seriousness or threat to other people.

There are two different types of humor: conventional and unconventional. *Conventional humor* is what people expect to happen or to hear in a regular or expected situation. *Unconventional humor* violates cultural patterns and creates a moment of incongruence that people find amusing. Many comedians play upon every day rules of interaction to create their jokes. This is called *ethnomethodology*, and is a term coined by sociologist Harold Garfinkel (1911–2011). Many behavior patterns are taken for granted; often, these patterns are not noticed until they are disrupted.

With this in mind, many comedians rely upon *breaching experiments* to provoke their audience. Breaching experiments involve behavior scenarios in which the researcher refuses to share the basic assumptions of the situation and the experiment; so, the viewer does not know what to expect. Thus, jokes are like mini-breaching experiments and the comedian is like an ethnomethodologist.

Time and television have shown that, in modernity and postmodernity, breaking norms is funny for most people. Rules are not funny; pushing boundaries is exciting, though, because it is just playfully deviating in an accepted form.

Sometimes jokes are not funny, which is painful to endure. Part of this comes from when the joke is no longer unexpected. Sometimes, a joke loses its effect because there is no context or cultural capital left in what the comedian is saying.

In all social interactions, there is a structure that surrounds the relationship and this structure is predictable. Thus, in our relationships, we can observe different statuses, social roles, groups, networks, virtual worlds, and social institutions. Many public interactions demonstrate stability despite changes in the interactors. This makes human activity more efficient and it creates steadfast boundaries, although it does restrict personal freedom. When it is excessive, our social interactions may cause social change.

Social status refers to the social position that an individual occupies at work, at home, in school, and with friends. Social status also refers to any of a full range of socially defined positions within a large group or society. This could include your boss, your mom, your dad, a social secretary, a joker, or a friend. This is part of typical normal human social identity. Social statuses define who and what people are in relationship to other people. A *status set* is all of the statuses that a person holds at a given time. Each status has related roles, though.

People receive an *ascribed status* at birth, which is given without regard to a person's unique talents or characteristics. Later on, people can attain an *achieved status*, which comes about by a person's own efforts and personal abilities.

Over everything is a master status; this is the status that dominates all the other statuses for a person. It floods up all other aspects of a person's identity. For instance, you could say that Dr. Knox is a professor; this might be my master status. The term, *master status*, was coined by sociologist Everett Hughes (1897–1983) in the 1940s.

A person's social role refers to the behavior expected of someone who holds a particular status. An individual's performance in this role varies person-to-person and he or she might have multiple roles for that status. So, the difference between status and role is that a role is what a doctor does, and the status is what the doctor is. One could be a Hollywood actor with a role that is the expected behavior attached to that position. Thus, actors are supposed to entertain, not educate.

The reality of status and role is that people occupy them in different ways and at different times, and they sometimes conflict with each other. *Role conflict* occurs when incompatible expectations arise from two or social positions held by the same person. *Role strain* occurs when the same social position imposes conflicting demands and expectations. A *role exit* is the process of disengagement from a role that is central to one's self-identity in order to establish a new role

in identity. So, basically, people are pulled with role conflicts, they experience tension with role strain, and they seek escape with *role exits*.

It seems logical that the older one gets, the more likely that a person will gain new statuses—both ascribed and achieved. This is definitely true in my case; in the past 52 years, I have become aware of several social positions that were given to me by others or created by my own merits. Regarding ascribed statuses, those ". . . assigned to a person [me] without regard for the person's unique talents or characteristics," at birth, I was given the statuses of being newborn, male, Caucasian, a Southerner from Virginia, and cute/cuddly. I had no choice in society concerning these social attributes; I have only been able to change the cute and cuddly status over the years, but the rest were out of my control.

Concerning my ascribed statuses, there is not much I do to maintain them, although some technically I have lost. I am now officially "middle-aged," which takes away my baby status although my wife says that sometimes she thought she had three babies to deal with at home. Too much food, not enough exercise, and our friend gravity have helped dissipate the cuteness status. I do not plan on having a sex-change operation nor will I be undergoing any genetic alterations, so I will keep the male status throughout my life. Similarly, I will always be a Caucasian at the genetic level—not much anyone can do to physically change that fact. As for my cultural label of "Southerner," it all depends if you think that moving to the North changes you somehow and negates your place of birth. My parents still insisted we were Southerners, not Yankees, even though we lived in Oregon for a few decades.

Supplementing these ascribed statuses, I have added some achieved statuses to my social position: college educated, technical illustrator, loving husband/father, A-level racquetball player, published writer, guitarist, sociology/history/religion instructor, among others. To maintain these achieved statuses, I have taken nearly 30 years of education courses to increase my knowledge level of particular subjects and taking more classes is very likely (my wife calls me a professional student).

For my illustrator status, I take on part-time paid projects to keep my skills sharp despite working in a different field, mainly. I actively work on building up my relationship with my wife and sons by reading parental/spouse wisdom literature, by setting aside quality time to spend with each of them, and by keeping them at the top of my priorities list. I spend a few hours a month playing my guitar, although in the past I played more for church groups, and so on. As an instructor of history/religion, besides the years of education, I read as much as possible about these fields in my spare time.

Sociology from Above

God's Holy Socialization

For countless generations, people have used the term, "holiness," to both describe God and as a standard for His believers to follow in life. Unfortunately, the definition of holiness has come to mean innumerable things—not all of which find their basis in scripture. Too often, holiness has centered more around human priorities and actions (a.k.a., works righteousness) rather than Godly ones, as seen in the bible.

Yet, despite the variegated interpretations and approaches to the idea of holiness, Leviticus 11:44 clearly states, "For I am the LORD who brought you out of the land of Egypt, to be your God; you shall, therefore, be holy, as I am holy." As delivered, holiness is not just a suggestion; it is a commandment on personal socialization from God, and because of that reality, it is incumbent upon all believers to seek a truer understanding of what it means to be holy today, especially in the new dangerous era of postmodernism.

Reading through the Hebrew and Greek Scriptures, it is impossible to ignore how often holiness is referenced, promoted, and/or mandated for God's followers. As previously mentioned, Israel, God's chosen people, were instructed time and time again to be holy as God is holy. In fact, the Hebrew word for holy is "Qadosh," which means radiance, separation, or purity. Thus, holiness is not just a legal matter; it included an injunction to integrate into the socialization of God's community. Furthermore, it also contains attributes of action, protection, righteousness, and exclusivity—all characteristics of God, as described in the Scriptures.

Not just an Old Testament tenet, the New Testament writers also admonish Christians to conform to the biblical standard of holiness. 1 Peter 1:15 states, "But as he who called you is holy, be holy yourselves in ALL your conduct." In their writings, these men directly and indirectly pushed for holiness as they discussed being set apart from the world—morally, ethically, and spiritually. Moreover, for the disciples and apostles, being holy also means being faithful, blameless, loving, and obedient to God—qualities they observed in Jesus Christ during His ministry on earth.

Not surprisingly, with all these notions embedded in the concept of holiness, it is easy to become overwhelmed with trying to conform all activities and attitudes to God's standard of holiness. All of the aforementioned requirements of holiness are an important part of its definition, but none alone are sufficient to define what it means to be holy. Thus, it is advisable to approach holiness in a holistic way (ironically) in order to gain a fuller and more productive understanding of holiness.

The most dangerous tactic that some followers have embraced throughout history is to myopically promote one aspect of holiness as THE quintessential manifestation of holiness while ignoring all the other characteristics of holiness. By making the part the whole (also known as "synecdoche"), the balance of understanding holiness is lost. Moreover, too often, holiness is narrowly defined merely in terms of behavior alone, when it should also focus on believers' relationships with each other and the lost.

In reality, a person is not holy because of his or her actions; people are holy because of their relationship with God through Jesus Christ. As one of my former seminary professors put it, holiness (or sanctification) is "the dynamic relationship between God and His followers" (Dr. Larry Shelton, 2002). It is a recognition that humanity is flawed, but God is not. It is a desire to separate from the evil of the world to the good of the divine in order to find true peace, true purification of the heart, mind, and soul. Finally, it is a synthesis of belief and action in the life of the believer that leads to a deeper, more meaningful reconciliation with God.

This understanding may sound complicated, but it is not. Ultimately, holiness comes down to a personal social transformation wherein the believer is no longer serving sin but embracing God and His ways. It is being lovingly obedient to Yahweh (the Covenant name of God)—not only because it is "commanded," but because it is a good, healthy, and wise way to maintain and cultivate one's relationship with the Creator/Redeemer (2 Samuel 22:31).

All believers are adopted children of God through our brother and sisterhood with Jesus Christ. Striving for holiness, then, is just a healthy expression of appreciation for our Father, and a request to get as close to God as possible—just like His Son. To put it in simpler terms, holiness is moving closer to God through a covenantal relationship in Jesus Christ.

Outside of this concept or relationship, being holy has little meaning. Therefore, reading the biblical exhortation to "Be holy for I am holy" (1 Peter 1:16), a fuller understanding can be observed. Being holy is not just an obscure list of do's and don'ts; being holy removes the stumbling blocks that prevent us from moving closer to the divine source of love, power, and salvation in our relationship with God.

Still, holiness has come to have some bad connotations in the postmodern era. In many circles (Christian and nonbeliever alike), piety and holiness are synonymous with snobbery and elitism. In reality, though, holiness is the humble admission that our sinful ways are not His good ways; therefore, we need to reflect Him more. With that healthy attitude, believers can experience and share their deep affection with God, each other, and to the world who needs love now more than ever.

We are called to be holy as God is holy. Yet, making the part the whole and picking one aspect of holiness to focus on might be a practical and efficient way of exercising one's faith, but Christianity is not about pragmatism or expediency. It is about shining in the darkness; it is about discarding all that hurts our relationship with God; it is about submitting to the Lordship of Jesus Christ and rejecting our own self-righteousness and self-deification.

Holiness needs to be sought after in its entirety, and the why of being holy is just as important (if not more) than the how, because striving for holiness allows a closer and less encumbered communion with God, the Father—and truly, nothing else in society is as important as our relationship with Him who created and saved us.

Voices from the Street

Remarks and Responses to SOCI 200 Employment Survey

Dear Dr. Knox,

Thanks for inviting me to provide some personal input regarding the employment survey that you have students do in your Intro to Sociology class. I took the survey myself this morning and being the owner of the business, it is a little different for me, but I tried to answer from both perspectives.

You asked what I look for in a prospective employee as the owner/hirer:

Before the interview even starts, I think about these factors:

1. Have they been loyal—did they stay in a single job or career field for a decent length of time?
2. Have they ever been fired or asked to leave? For what reason?
3. Is the resume or application complete and purposeful?
4. Do they meet the minimum qualifications for the position?
   a. This is relevant because if they do not, do they still give me a reason to interview them (this is a strong indicator of an "A-Player" and good employee potential)?

During the interview itself, I ask about these questions:

1. Do they talk about their accomplishments?
   a. True A-Players naturally talk about where they started and how far they got to for an employer.
      i. "Business sales were at _____, but when I started working there, I changed two tactics, which increased their overall sales some 11% over the first four months and maintained an 8% increase overall."
      ii. "I started at John's Garage as a *cleanup and car porter*; I was there for over three years. Now, I am applying for your master level tech position."
2. Are they able to articulate well in a given hypothetical scenario?
3. Can they think on their feet?
   a. Trying to keep it Godly, but this is the "B.S. factor"—can they swing it?

4. Are they always looking for something better or are they generally content in their work?
5. Can they find an answer to a problem at all costs?
   a. Too many people give up or hope someone else will carry the torch.
6. Do they seem to work well with others?
7. One of the most important questions: *Have they ever been terminated?*

After the interview, I reflect upon these realities:

The biggest indicator that I have made a great hire is whether or not their current employer tries to get them to stay. For my best hires, I have had to kick out more money or sign bigger bonuses for them to seal the deal.

My worst hires have been released without a counteroffer or a delay. It is not a good sign if their current employer does not want them around anymore. Also, nearly every employee that I have terminated was previously terminated elsewhere. There are a few exceptions in this category. Some say, "I hated the job," "I refused to change," and so on.

One ex-employee lost his driver's license for medical reasons at age 20, but he did not tell me about it until it was suspended. Ultimately, he lost his driver's license due to unsubmitted diabetes paperwork. Although he is still eligible for rehire, I had to let him go for a minimum of at least ninety days because there had to be a separation due to his negligence and the danger that he put the team in, working there in that condition.

Please do not take this critically, but I noticed maybe two questions that I suggest tweaking: For question 2, I recommend adding "Skilled Trade Journeyman" as a selection. Globally, there is a shortage of skilled, trained individuals. Several of my friends are CAD designers, but not technically "engineers" as they are not fully stamped. The skills trades may not require a college degree, but they end up doing alright from hours of on-the-job training and self-study to get to a place that a person is able to excel in their field. Personally, I am a "Master Certified Auto Technician," and I will keep that vocational endorsement for life. At my current job, I wear many hats and I am still just as much a technician, but I am a manager and "cheerleader," as well.

For question 10, I recommend adding "Loyalty" as a selection. I feel that loyalty is one of the biggest areas that is lacking in the younger workforce (especially with the millennials). I know this also reflects my leadership ability, but I see that some employees will embrace my policies more wholeheartedly than others. The loyalty and devotion to the work mission is paramount in most professional arenas. Sadly, I have seen far too many millennials who lack any true loyalty.

I hope that this helps! My wife is scanning the documents that I filled out and I will e-mail it back to you, soon.

Regards.

Stephen Konyndyk, Owner
Endurance Auto Repair and Tire
Lynchburg, Virginia

Contributed by Stephen Konyndyk. © Kendall Hunt Publishing Company

Check out the Chapter 5 video at this link: https://www.grtep.com/

Vocabulary

Achieved Status
Ascribed Status
Backstage Behavior
Breaching Experiments
Conflict Interactions
Competition Interactions
Conventional Humor
Cooperation Interactions
Cultural Capital
Dramaturgical Sociology
Dyads
Embarrassment
Employment Factors

Ethnomethodology
Exchange Interactions
Front Stage Behavior
Holiness
Impression Management
Master Status
Nonverbal
Personal Space
"Qadosh"
Role Conflict
Role Exit
Role Strain
Sanctification

Social Status
Socialization
Social Interaction
Social Role
Social Transformation
Status Set
Symbolic Interaction
Symbols
Synecdoche
Tact
Triads
Unconventional Humor

CHAPTER SIX: Family

The Basics

Few social institutions have more influence and power over the lives of individuals and groups than that of the family unit. *Family* is traditionally defined as a social unit of people related through marriage, birth, and or adoption. They reside together in sanctioned relationships, they engage in economic cooperation, and engage in proper sexual relationships between members. They are committed, they have love attachments, reproduction or procreation is part of their relationship, and they engage in child-rearing together.

White, Klein, and Martin (2015, p. 13) provide four theories on family theory that seem to suggest a universality of the social group named, "a family." These four theories are relatively general, so there are no absolute parameters—such as specific duration, number of intergenerations or biological/romantic relationships between members, or linkage to a bigger kinship system. For example, a *patrilocal kinship* has the wife residing with the husband and his social group; a *matrilocal kinship* has the husband moving with the wife to live with her family of origin. No doubt, there are pros and cons for each approach, and surely personality types and psychological factors are key parts of any decision on marital residence.

This is not just an American phenomenon, though. There seem to be examples of these four theories found in other non-Western cultures. For instance, in China, people are married and take care of children until they reach adulthood; some households include children, parents, as well as grandparents (or great grandparents); cultural rules and taboos exist for the health of members within this social group; and innumerable manifestations of the Chinese family unit are found in all cities and villages in all regions across China. This would suggest a universality to the four theories offered by White and Klein.

That being said (and as mentioned earlier), the boundaries of what constitutes the life of a family is somewhat murky. In some regions of America, children stay with the parents well into their late 20s or early 30s; in other parts of the world, children leave as soon as they reach legal adulthood. Furthermore, in America, the proximity or frequency of intergenerational contact varies greatly. Some adult children see their parents daily or weekly; other situations stretch into the months or years; having grandparents living with their adult children seems more the exception than the norm in America, presently.

Some might consider the functionalist perspective to be the sole lens for family life; however, family mechanics are far less monolithic but still allow for adjustments and adaptation to occur to regain/maintain/retain harmony and unity within the group. If the family unit is likened to an organism (Witt, 2009, p. 13), then one could expect deviations to naturally occur as parents and children grow older and experience different complications, consequences, and social contexts to emerge. A middle-aged parent may suddenly find their teenager pregnant, which would set about a chain of events and interactions previously unneeded and unattempted. Similarly, a 30-year-old child could lose both aged parents, leading to an unexpected and unprepared future. Thus, certain ages bring with them certain risks and realities, which automatically elicit change and/or deviant behaviors (Hiedemann, Sukhomlinova, & O' Rand, 1998, p. 229).

Whatever the case, for family stability to continue (in the functionalist perspective), any deviance needs to be addressed and then adopted or abandoned based on its value, which may relate to symbolic interactionism. If allowed, the deviance is integrated into the family system and into any nonfamily institutional activities, too (White et al., 2015, p. 117). Thus, although deviance may have individualist origins, its value and place within the family social system is determined by its relative value and benefit to both the individual and the collective, which sounds a bit like rational choice theory.

Within family relationships (especially with the inclusion of stepfamilies), a variety of expectations can be found; some stepfamilies are merely considered "close relatives" while others make no distinctions between children from a bloodline or remarriage; some families employ a hierarchical governance—others are more laissez-faire. In America, some people honor and promote their family system of lineage (like the Mormons or some Asians); others could not tell you much about their family line or history beyond their grandparents. A simple Google Scholar search proves that there are many additional and/or specific family theories in Eastern cultures. Ultimately, how much or how little these theories are in play in a particular non-Western culture could be determined by utilizing the empirical fit, testability, contextualization, and practical utility for each family structure.

In postmodernity, though, it is clear that the definition of *family* has changed. With all the legal and cultural transformation in the past decade, perhaps the easiest definition of family in America (for better or worse) is to call it a primary group of people who form a cooperative economic unit. Of course, this is an embrace of reductionism that overlooks the complex overarching needs and functions of members that are typically found within all families. An abdication or skewing of familial roles may seem revolutionary or noble, but the reality is that men, women, and children have needed certain permanent social components to thrive or even to survive in society. In the healthiest of families, husbands and wives take care of each other—physically, emotionally, and economically; and parents love, raise, and protect their children.

In regard to that, one of the biggest familial parameters or taboos is that of *incest*. Historically and universally, there has been a prohibition of sexual relationships and marriage between close kinsmen. This is done or enforced for various reasons. First, it is not biologically healthy for family members to marry other family members. Many blood disorders and genetic abnormalities occur when the bloodlines are too closely tied. Second, besides any physical harm, though, the emotional or psychological damage done in incest cannot be understated. So, although one can marry a second cousin with a reasonable degree of confidence that no health issues will occur for any offspring, marrying or having deviant sexual liaisons with first cousins, half siblings, or one's parents are not allowed, wisely. Ultimately, any deviation is integrated into family norms when the deviation has a positive effect for all members of the family unit—or rejected if the family unit cohesion is dissolving.

All social groups, like the family, include hierarchies of power. In the United States, there is much variance regarding social power and access to resources and decision-making for the family. If the family embraces *patriarchy*, men hold the most social power; if it is a *matriarchy*, women hold the most social power; but in many families in America and all over the world, *egalitarianism*, where husbands and wives share the power, is embraced; one could also make the case that in some millennial families, especially, children hold the power, which amounts to *anarchy*, where no one holds any power (Lehman, 2019, online).

Sociologists also look at the family structure's place in society and categorize family social circles in two ways: there is the *nuclear family*, which is one married couple residing together with any children they might have together, or there might be an *extended family*, with a network of parents, children, and relatives that they come into contact with, occasionally.

Family and marriage seem to be in a never-ending cycle in society. Parents marry, have children, and then those children go on to marry other people. Historically, there have been numerous marriage parameters placed upon people regarding whom they can marry or be coupled with, in society. Common factors permitting or prohibiting marital unions include age, gender, religion, race, ethnicity, economics, and so on. Marriages are typically made with exogamy or endogamy in mind. Exogamy is the selection of a permanent life partner outside one's social group; endogamy is the selection of a permanent life partner inside one's social group. The final judgment is undecided as to which one is more common (just ask Romeo and Juliet).

Within the family system, various kinship agreements exist (or are adhered to) in deciding who can marry whom, when, where, and so on. *Kinship systems* decide how property is passed on for older generations to younger generations, they decide where the family should reside, they decide how social power inside the family will be distributed, they decide the appropriate number of marriage partners, and often they even decide who is permitted to marry whom.

Marriage and Divorce

For millennia, in the countless cultures across the globe, marriage has been the central foundation of family life. Ostensibly, people enter into marriage commitments for emotional fulfillment, social stability, and personal security; and contrary to current shallow postmodern myopia, monogamy has been the standard form, with marriage restricted to an exclusive relationship between husband and wife.

Four's company

That being said, in some countries and cultures, one can find other marriage agreements in place. Polygamy has been allowed (even in the Bible), which is multiple marriage partners. Additionally, *polygamy* is the marriage of one husband to multiple wives, and *polyandry* is the marriage of one wife to multiple husbands. Very few cultures or communities allow for *polyamory*, which is a romantically open relationship between all the members of a social group or clique of people (Klesse, 2006, p. 566). These are exceptions, of course, but an exception is not the norm or always socially accepted.

Regarding marital statistics, the age of marriage has risen sharply in the past fifty years. In 1977, the average age of marriage was twenty-one for women and twenty-three for men. In 2010, the average age of marriage for women was twenty-seven and the average age for men was twenty-nine. This is dramatically different than in 1955, when the average age of a female to get married was twenty and the average age of a man to get married was twenty-two.

Various reasons can be seen to contribute to this phenomenon. The most likely factor for changes in female marital age would be the empowerment that women have gained since the civil rights movement in the sexual revolution of the 1960s. More than ever before in American history, women have greater social power and access to personal resources. Whereas before the 1960s, women were expected to stay at home and do more of the domestic chores and duties while the men worked outside the home, now more women are working in the paid labor force than ever before in American history.

Compared to their grandmothers, women in postmodernity enjoy far more independence and autonomy in society. For men, besides fewer women being open or inviting of exclusive, closed marriages, there are fewer social stigmas for men in remaining bachelors and focusing more on their careers and recreational lives than in previous decades. Still, some men are mocked for being in their 30s and still living in their parents' basement, which seems indicative of stunted social development (Bentley & McCallum, 2019, online).

The shift in age of marriage also corresponds to a shift in parenting age. Although the term has been around for a couple of decades, many millennial couples are referred to as *DINKs*, which means "Double-Income-No-Kids." Currently, American families are smaller than their parents or grandparents' families, having fewer children and children more closely spaced in age. Married couples make up a smaller proportion of households in America, with single parent, post-childbearing couples, and LGTBQ couples on the increase. Finally, there are more female-headed households than any time before in American history.

My friends at home.

Me in my basement abode.

Regarding the LGTBQ movement, *homosexuality* or being *gay* refers to people who are sexually attracted to members of their own sex. According to the 2000 U.S. Census Bureau's "Family

Research Report," around 3%–4% of people within the United States embrace the homosexual lifestyle. Although the current social trend in America is more approving and permissive of the gay lifestyle, most other non-Western cultures consider the practice to be an anomaly and one to be avoided. This is based on several conclusions: (a) it threatens the biological function of the traditional family structure, (b) it violates many religious dogmas and scriptural prohibitions, (c) it is associated with other socially unsanctioned activities long considered taboo, and (d) gay identification is often originated in physical or sexual abuse and emotional neglect or abandonment.

Since the removal of homosexuality as a mental illness from the *Diagnostic and Statistical Manual of Mental Disorders* (DSM) in 1973 (Drescher, 2012), attitudes began to change about the LGBTQ lifestyle in many U.S. institutions and public forums. As of 1987, all references to homosexuality were completely removed from the DSM. According to Burton (2015), "Today, the standard of psychotherapy in the U.S. and Europe is gay affirmative psychotherapy, which encourages gay people to accept their sexual orientation" (online).

Not everyone agrees with the progressive facilitation of the LGBTQ lifestyle, though, as nothing has changed medically about homosexuality. As Sorba (2007) notes, "Dishonesty and intimidation had won the day for the same-gender sex movement, and when activists publicly claim that this [1973] vote was a scientific decision, they hide three years of deceit and intimidation" (online).

Only about 35% of American Psychological Association members voted "Yes" to remove homosexuality as a mental illness. Thus, the decision to change the LGBTQ classification was mostly a political one, stemming from intense LGBTQ activism, lobbying, and some say intimidation. Add to this, the AIDs epidemic of the 1980s and 1990s brought into question the validity of assumptions that same-sex coupling was natural, healthy, and a safe social relationship.

Currently in America, the LGBTQ movement has made great political bounds; however, it still finds great resistance from Middle America and conservative churches, who point to biblical texts that clearly outlaw the practice as being immoral and unhealthy. Although more liberal churches are trying to find middle ground on the issue, "Considering the effect and seriousness of the early church's witness regarding sexuality, it is hard to imagine any scenario in which the nature of marriage and sexuality would be considered an 'agree to disagree' issue for the earliest Christians" (Wax, 2019, online). As with other social issues, homosexuality shows no signs of ceasing to be a divisive issue in a society not absent of other fractured and dysfunctional social environments.

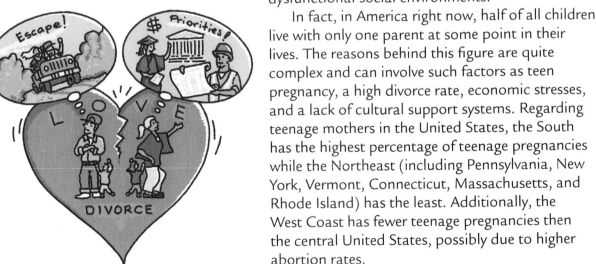

In fact, in America right now, half of all children live with only one parent at some point in their lives. The reasons behind this figure are quite complex and can involve such factors as teen pregnancy, a high divorce rate, economic stresses, and a lack of cultural support systems. Regarding teenage mothers in the United States, the South has the highest percentage of teenage pregnancies while the Northeast (including Pennsylvania, New York, Vermont, Connecticut, Massachusetts, and Rhode Island) has the least. Additionally, the West Coast has fewer teenage pregnancies then the central United States, possibly due to higher abortion rates.

Living together is also very common now among single people in American and European society. This *cohabitation* occurs when two people live together in a sustained a committed relationship, but without any legal or binding vows or agreements. In fact, three times as many unmarried couples live together now than in the 1970s. Unfortunately, cohabitation is only a short-term fix for many/most people. Plus, the divorce statistics for people who cohabitate is rather high (Rosenfeld & Roesler, 2019, p. 43).

Speaking of divorce, the United States leads the world in the divorce rate. Although death used to be the typical major cause of early family disruption, as of late, divorce has now taken over that spot, statistically. Nearly 20,000,000 people have divorced but not remarried, currently. The American divorce rate used to be higher in the 1970s and 1980s, but it has declined, recently. Still, since 1960, the divorce rate has doubled. The marriage rate is 8.4 per thousand people; the divorce rate is 4.0 per thousand people.

For people claiming to be "Christian," another factor of divorce is church attendance and gender (to a small degree). Half of all divorces occur to people who do not attend weekly church services; however, if people do attend, men only have a 32% chance of getting a divorce while women have a 41% chance of getting a divorce. Nondenominational churches members have the highest divorce rate at 34%, Baptists come in second at 29%, Episcopalians are third at 28%, Pentecostals are fourth at 28%, Methodists are at 26%, Presbyterians are at 23%, and, perhaps because of their liturgical sacramental understanding of marriage, Catholics and Lutherans have only a 21% chance of getting divorced.

Sociology from Above

Three Reasons to Marry for Love

It is no secret that in our post-Christian world, societal mores are changing in all aspects of life—not least of which is that of marriage, perhaps the oldest social institution of them all. Some sources (www.prb.org) suggest that 108 billion people have lived on the earth since life began, and no one would doubt that marriage was an important event for the majority of those people.

Unfortunately, historians and sociologists do not have an exhaustive reservoir of cultural data to examine regarding marriage throughout history. Yet, all too often, without any evidence to back it up, one can read assertions like, "For most of human history, marriage wasn't a very romantic institution. It was more akin to a business deal between men, the bride in question had very few rights or other options" (people.howstuffworks.com), and "When love entered the picture as the reason to marry, dissolutions became more commonplace" (www.psychologytoday.com). Proclamations like these only add confusion to the matter and blame the disease on the medicine.

Reading through a well-intentioned, completely simplistic article in *Psychology Today* entitled, "Three Reasons Why You Shouldn't Marry for Love" (Gadoua, 2013), it is evident that modern people are resisting the traditional understanding and incentives for marriage, opting for a more pragmatic and self-serving agenda. Considering the radically individualistic, sacro-egoistical spirit of the age, it is not surprising; however, the illogical and shallow argumentation is evident.

The article begins with the (incorrect) axiom of "But if you really think about it, love is a luxury." My computer dictionary defines a *luxury* as "an inessential, desirable item that is expensive or difficult to obtain," but if love comes from within a person's heart and mind, then its expression and application costs nothing monetarily or materially. Children are the best example of loving without cost or condition. They freely dispense love to all around them—be it a parent or pet or toy or stick or whatever—because it is in their intrinsic nature to love and be loved.

The author, Gadoua, continues on to say, "When you marry for love, it generally means you have all—or at least most—of your other needs met (like food, shelter, warmth, etc)." Speaking from personal experience, I had few, not all, of my personal needs met when I fell in love with my wife-to-be and asked her to marry me. We wed without a steady job or income for either of us, with more bills than money to pay, with a long-term journey of working and struggling to survive. Yet, we felt (and still do) that all we really needed was a deep love to sustain us. Twenty-one years later, I will still marry my love, even knowing the inconveniences and sacrifices that we have made to be together.

According to the article, however, "In our attempt to make marriage stronger by raising the bar to meet our higher love and romance needs, we have seriously weakened the institution. These are both highly changeable emotions: When love wanes, the marriage gets shaky; when the romance stops, the nuptials die." The mistake in this evaluation is the author's confusion between "love" and "romance."

In C. S. Lewis' book, *The Four Loves*, Lewis presents the basic types of love demonstrated in humanity: Storge or natural affection, Philia or friendship, Eros or romance, and Agape or Charity, which is the highest, selfless form of all loves. Each one of these kinds of love has a different goal and implementation, and by working together, can bring harmony and health to any relationship. The problem is if one embraces or exhibits only one of these in a marriage or intimate relationship; then, the union will be strained, which the article misses in its conclusions on marriage.

Instead, Gadoua offers, "People whose primary reason to marry is other than love—such as to have children with someone they believed would be a good co-parent, to have financial security, or for companionship—generally have longer and perhaps better marriages because their choices are made for a defined purpose." Of course, the author offers no evidence or statistics to back up this jaw-dropping advice. She just concludes with "I'm not saying love shouldn't be on the list of things that need to be in your relationship, but it doesn't need to be number one (and perhaps shouldn't be)."

For the Christian, though, love is the number one key for all lifestyles and life choices. In Matthew 22, when asked what the greatest commandment of the law was, Jesus responded, "Love the Lord your God with all your heart and all your mind . . . And the second is like it: 'Love your neighbor as yourself.'" Such advice negates the self-focused pragmatic guidance of the aforementioned psychology article.

Wisdom and love from above begin with someone else outside of us—God—and then embraces everyone else, spouses included. This amatory advice is seen in other Biblical passages. 1 John 4:7–12 states,

Dear friends, let us love one another, for love comes from God. Everyone who loves has been born of God and knows God. Whoever does not love does not know God, because

God is love. This is how God showed his love among us: He sent his one and only Son into the world that we might live through him. This is love: not that we loved God, but that he loved us and sent his Son as an atoning sacrifice for our sins. Dear friends, since God so loved us, we also ought to love one another. No one has ever seen God; but if we love one another, God lives in us and his love is made complete in us.

In simplifying marriage to a mere social contract present to provide mental peace and physical comfort alone, Gadoua has missed the holistic nature and divine origins of love, which begins in and is sustained through actions without absolute certainty of reaping benefits for oneself.

Marriages do not fold because husbands and wives are kind, affectionate, unselfish, and understanding with each other. Unions end because of personal selfishness and hatred, because of an unwillingness to submit to God's ethical designs for love and relationships. Gadoua places the focus on what one can get from the marriage; God places the focus on what one can give to the marriage. It is doubtful that any marriage would end if spouses simply and devotedly followed Paul's advice in 1 Corinthians 13:

Love is patient, love is kind. It does not envy, it does not boast, it is not proud. It does not dishonor others, it is not self-seeking, it is not easily angered, it keeps no record of wrongs. Love does not delight in evil but rejoices with the truth. It always protects, always trusts, always hopes, always perseveres.

Thus, I end with my own three reasons why you must marry for love.

1. God is love.
2. Love is the only force that can fully heal emotional, psychological, and spiritual wounds.
3. Love is the only force that is eternal, leaving behind a legacy that influences others for good.

Gadoua's article reminds me of the book of Ecclesiastes, with its emphasis on life without God (and His love) and in the center—vanity, vanity—a chasing after the wind. Instead, let us follow God's lead in our relationships and in marriage, which, after all, is just a glimpse of the joy to be had for all God's children in the eternity of Heaven.

The Sage from the Stage

But Children Matter

Scripture is very clear that children matter to God, as evidenced by passages such as Psalm 127:3–5, where God says, "Behold, children are a heritage from the LORD, the fruit of the womb a reward. Like arrows in the hand of a warrior are the children of one's youth. Blessed is the man who fills his quiver with them! He shall not be put to shame when he speaks with his enemies in the gate" (ESV). Additionally, Jesus became angry about the treatment of children on at least one occasion in Scripture. In Mark 10:13–16, Jesus states,

> And they were bringing children to Him that He might touch them, and the disciples rebuked them. But when Jesus saw it, He was indignant and said to them, "Let the children come to me; do not hinder them, for to such belongs the kingdom of God. Truly, I say to you, whoever does not receive the kingdom of God like a child shall not enter it." And He took them in His arms and blessed them, laying His hands on them.

By studying Old Testament history, one can easily see the value that was placed on children, as demonstrated in Exodus, Leviticus, and Deuteronomy. There is little in these books directly on parenting, but much is presented on the notion that children are to be participants in a loving, caring faith community (Richards, 1988, p. 18). The church has a role to play in the development of children, and it is much more than the presentation of a simple lesson in Sunday school each week. The children's ministry volunteer assists in a child's cognitive, social, and spiritual development. Although communities today may look nothing like those of the Old Testament, the role of the church community in ministering to children is certainly implied in the Old Testament.

In Old Testament times, the communities of which children were a part played a key role in their development. According to May, "Moses' instructions in Deuteronomy were given to the whole faith community. Parents and children were to talk about and live out God's commands and keep their feasts in the home. Yet, they would also gather for corporate celebrations of the feasts and observe other families in the community living God's laws" (May, 2005, pp. 165–166).

One has to wonder how much of the downward spiral of morality in society today can be attributed to the lack of ministry to children in the church and the church's lessening influence on society, which is almost exclusively done by children's ministry volunteers. Is the church engaged in truly aiding children's cognitive development and helping them think about the decisions they are making and decisions they will need to make in the future?

For example, Old Testament history does not provide readers with the exact role of the faith community in the life of the Old Testament prophet, Daniel. Although he is most famous for his experience in the lion's den, his ability to think and morally take a stand for what was right reveals someone who was the product of not only a solid parental foundation, but also a strong faith community. When he was taken into Babylonian captivity and offered the king's food and wine, which was forbidden by Jewish culture, Daniel refused.

The scriptures record Daniel's response to the King's offer in Daniel 1:8: "But Daniel resolved not to defile himself with the royal food and wine, and he asked the chief official for permission not to defile himself this way." This resolve that Daniel displayed did not just happen on its own; it was something that had been cultivated in Daniel, beginning with a personal relationship with God and then developed in him through the faith community.

At some point, Daniel had been trained to think proactively and he was able to be decisive and righteous in his decision. Daniel knew where the boundaries were, and he had (evidently) made a decision in advance that he was not going to displease God—even if it meant the loss of his life. The scriptures do not depict an individual who had to take time to contemplate this decision; it manifested from the overflow of who he was as a person. This resolve from Daniel also appears in the account of the lion's den in Daniel 6:1–28.

An interesting component of Daniel's development is the social aspect of the resolve that Daniel displayed along with his friends Shadrach, Meshach, and Abednego. Although Daniel's friends appear to have benefited from a strong foundation like Daniel, readers can observe the contagious nature of the resolve that Daniel displayed in Chapter 1. Daniel's influence on his friends represents another important impact of children's ministry and the volunteers ministering within the church community.

When children are well socialized, they may bond with others who have a similar resolve and are willing to be used by God to increase the level of determination and commitment to Christ in others, just as Daniel's three friends would later do in Daniel Chapter 6. From this account, it looks as though this occurred for Daniel and his friends. With Daniel, it is obvious that his spiritual development also affected the cognitive and social aspects of his life, which is something every children's ministry volunteer needs to comprehend. The impact being made in the cognitive, social, and spiritual realms within a child is significant.

George Barna "stresses the importance of children's ministry by contending that lifelong moral views are largely in place by adolescence. 'What you believe at age thirteen is pretty much what you're going to die believing'" (Kennedy, 2004, online). Research compiled by his Barna Group shows that children between the ages 5 and 13 have a 32% probability of accepting Jesus Christ as their Savior. That likelihood drops to 4% for teenagers between the ages 14 and 18, and ticks back up to 6% for adults older than eighteen.

Although Proverbs 22:6 speaks to the parents' role of training children, the church also has a responsibility to come alongside parents to aid them in the spiritual development of their children. If children are truly being trained up in the way they should go, then there should be more fruit of the training than what is often observed.

According to Kinnaman and Hawkins (2011), reporting on a 2011 Barna nationwide survey, "59 percent of young people with a Christian background report that they had or have 'dropped out of attending church, after going regularly'" (p. 23). No one made these students leave the church, but with statistics this elevated, there must be numerous reasons these students did not remain plugged into a local church. It is also possible that many of the 59% who left the church did not have a personal relationship with Christ to begin with, thus increasing the number of those who navigated their way through church ministries only to eventually leave the church altogether. The question here is, does this reveal something about the quality or lack of quality of children's ministry volunteer that churches are developing?

For many of these students, it is likely that there may not have been a strong relational connection to either a children's ministry pastor or volunteer during this time, and, if there was a connection, it may have been with a low-impact children's ministry volunteer (meaning a volunteer who lacked the calling, training, or even passion to fulfill this important ministry role). Regardless, one could deduce that children may not be getting ministered to in a way that impacts them enough to cause them to want to remain connected to the local church.

Since the responsibility to spiritually prepare children lies in part with the church as previously mentioned, this survey is revealing, as some of the 1,000 participants were likely nonbelievers. Once again, parents bear the primary responsibility for the spiritual development of their children, but when considering Proverbs 22:6, "Train up a child in the way he should go; even when he is old he will not depart from it," one can surmise that even the best parent does not have all the answers for the spiritual development of their children.

The church, if allowed by the parent, can come alongside the parent and provide great support in this important effort. Testimonies are available that speak to the success of children's ministry volunteers in their partnership with parents in raising spiritually strong children.

Children's church support is also likely to impact their spiritual formation because one's connection to God is developed and maintained through reciprocal spiritual support within the church community, and one's perception of God is influenced by those relationships. In fact, prior research has found significant correlations between adults' spirituality and the quality of their relationships with other people in the church, and limited research with adolescents has also linked positive spiritual development to intimate and intentional relationships with a church youth pastor (Crosby & Smith, 2015, pp. 243–254).

Dr. Kenny Warren
Faculty Support Coordinator
Liberty University

Contributed by Dr. Kenny Warren. © Kendall Hunt Publishing Company

 Check out the Chapter 6 video at this link: https://www.grtep.com/

Vocabulary

Agape
Anarchy
APA 1973 Vote
Average Marriage Age
Biblical Idea of Love
Child Abuse
Child Development
Christian Divorce Rate
Civil Rights Movement
Cohabitation
DINKs
Divorce
Egalitarianism
Eros
Extended Family

Homosexuality
Husbands
Incest
Intergenerational Contact
Kinship Systems
Lewis' Four Loves
LGBTQ
Luxury
Marriage
Matriarchy
Matrilocal Kinship
Nuclear Family
Parental Responsibility
Patriarchy
Patrilocal Kinship

Philia
Polyamory
Polyandry
Polygamy
Postmodern Family
Scriptural Boundaries
Single-Parent Households
Spiritual Development
Storge
Teen Mothers
Traditional Family
Wives

CHAPTER SEVEN: Religion

The Basics

History tells us that all religion springs from specific social contexts (which may also include the supernatural realm) and with unique and profound differences from community to community and era to era. Typically, it begins with one individual's attention and efforts to find answers to the transcendent questions in life: are there extranatural forces/realities in the universe, how did human life begin, and what is our ultimate purpose in life? If productive and popular, the individual's belief system then becomes formalized in a community, with associated beliefs and attitudes being shared and promoted within and sometimes outside of the community. As the faith system matures, it is celebrated in practices, rites, behavior, and moral codes.

All of the aforementioned events can be considered "sociological facts;" therefore, they can all be studied and analyzed, potentially leading to scientific theories, conclusions, and applications. Social scientists can learn much about the role of individuals and groups in society, the importance of family and ethnic promotion of religion, how life stages and ages influence our views on religion, and come to better understand the roles, power, and impact of religious institutions upon daily life and culture in America and abroad.

Why Study Religion, Scientifically?

Considering that sociology is the study of human interaction, agency, and consequences, studying the topic can help in understanding why society operates as it does. This, in turn, can help promote peaceful existence between all people regardless of their culture. The fact of the matter is that, regarding all world religions and faiths, innumerable social forces, forms of socialization, examples of deviance are in action, socially.

Through investigating and analyzing the various religious forces in play in the world today (and in the past), sociology can help people to be more proactive and not just reactive in their responses to and conclusions of religious people in life. Whether it be composed by Plato or Philo, the aphorism, "Be kind, for everyone you meet is fighting a hard battle," rings true, and sociology can help in relating to people, both gently and ethically.

A scientific study of religion that utilizes both quantitative and qualitative methodology can enlighten the academy on why people are presently and historically religious, despite the secularization of postmodernity. An authentic scientific study (and not just cloaked, politically charged, applied sociology) can answer many questions about the current religious scene in the United States. A dwindling church membership, less participation in religious ceremonies, few clergy and ministerial candidates, and a general malaise or indifference regarding religious matters are provocative, sociologically (Fuller, 2001). Studying the sociology of religion might explain what is causing this change, whether it can or will be reversed, and help scholars (and pastors) make predictions of religious life in America 50 years hence.

The Existence and Relevance of Religion

This is an often mystifying and complex topic, and one that has been around for millennia. Although many sociologists in postmodernity consider religious belief to be a social construct alone, history shows that billions of people have—in every era of human existence and every cultural/ethnic milieu on the earth since recorded time began—constantly and committedly believed in a greater, transcendent realm that exists outside of the known world.

Despite the postmodern push for existentialism that suggests each person is a free and responsible agent determining their own path of development through acts of the will, people seem to be born with a natural desire to understand how they came to be a conscious individual, to understand for what reason they exist, and to have a relationship with a divine figure or figures greater than themselves who cares. Many people have even suggested that religious beliefs are instinctual in human beings. Religion provides answers for these vexing existentialist questions.

Existentialism, on the other hand, only provides self-centeredness, which typically leads to depression, desperation, and dilemma. As philosopher Jean-Paul Sartre stated, "Every existing thing is born without reason, prolongs itself out of weakness, and dies by change." Philosopher Albert Camus asserted, "He who despairs of the human condition is a coward, but he who has hope for it is a fool." These are hardly inspirational messages for most people struggling in life.

Additionally, each turn of the century or millennium advent seems to bring with it a utopian promise of lasting happiness and ultimate creature comfort; however, perfect prosperity produced through human efforts rarely remains. People still feel want; people still live in conflict and fear; people still feel life should be better, somehow. Religious belief explains and pragmatically satisfies these feelings and needs.

Various sociologists have attempted to explain religion's mass embrace in human history in controversial ways. According to Émile Durkheim, all religions are based on interpretations of the sacred, nonworldly realm; Karl Marx proclaimed that religion was merely an illusion, an opiate to control the masses; and Max Weber asserted that religion could only be understood in subjective fashion (Christiano, Swatos, & Kivisto, 2016, p. 4).

More contemporary atheistic scholars such as Richard Dawkins and Christopher Hitchens have moved judgment on religiosity to more condemning grounds. For them, it encapsulates the beliefs of the stupid, the superstitious, and the gullible; however, many theologians and apologists (and simple lay believers) have challenged their assertions as being both superficial and myopic. People believe in God because it provides something that secularization, atheism, and humanism do not. Moreover, most religious faiths are explanative and predictive, which helps people get through the choppy waters of human existence, which is still relevant in postmodernity.

Three Common Theoretical Approaches

Sociological theories abound when it comes to diagnoses and prediction for religion in the West and the world. Steve Bruce (2002) states, "There are very clear signs that the mainstream Christian churches are losing their doctrinal and behavioral distinctiveness" (p. 227), Bryan Wilson (2003) wrote, "Secular agencies have taken over functions once fulfilled by religion" (p. 67). Sean McCloud (2007) attests, "The mainstream Protestant denominations that have numerically dominated the American landscape have dramatically declined" (p. 296). Nearly 40 years ago, Peter Berger (1969) concluded, "The religious legitimations of the world have lost their plausibility—not only for a few intellectuals and other marginal individuals—but for broad masses of entire societies" (p. 156).

Few doubt that a religious paradigm shift has occurred in the past 20 years, and this leads sociologists to ask key questions like, what is causing this change? Will it be reversed in the near future? What will "church" be like when the boomers, busters, and GenX are gone? What will religious life be like in the West in 50 years?

Secularization Theory

In the Western world today, it is not difficult to find a multitude of articles, books, and television reports (either scholarly or popular) discussing the future and nature of religion in contemporary modern culture. A recent Gallup poll (2008) in America indicates that "Two-thirds of Americans think religion is losing its influence on U.S., life, a sharp jump from just three years ago when Americans were nearly evenly split in the question" (Saad, 2008, online).

As a key proponent of secularization theory, Bryan Wilson suggested, "It is simply taken as fact that religion—seen as a way of thinking, as the performance of particular practices, and as the institutionalization and organization of these patterns of thought and action—has lost influence in both England and the United States in particular, as it has in other western societies" (Wilson, 1966, p. 11). Religiosity has moved within the control of the individual and been removed from institutional rule. He stated, "The impact of religion on the operation of society, once great, is now negligible, and this change has been determined by technical, economic, and political factors. Religion becomes privatized" (Wilson, 1979, p. 277).

Steve Bruce suggests that with the secularization and modernization of the West comes a growing uselessness and irrelevance of religion in greater society. In his opinion, there are "irreversible" trends and thus, the importance of religion and Christianity will wane in several places where it used to reign. Thus, the current spirituality and religiosity in the West is just ". . . the last gasp and whimper of concern with the sacred in the West, an inconsequential dabbling that is doomed to disappear almost as quickly as it appeared" (Heelas, Woodhead, Seel, Szerszynski, & Tusting, 2005, p. 2).

In postmodernity (in the West), the religious institution can no longer overtly "force" people to conform to traditional religious mores because of the personal liberties gained in the last century from historical, political, or scientific advancements. As such, "Religion is manifestly a social artifact, but it retains that mark of simultaneous representation, objectively and subjectively, that is found at the very core of sociology itself; in the sense that society is represented both as an objective entity and as something that exists only in the minds of men" (Wilson, 1979, p. 268).

As an "artifact" of the past, the usefulness, commitment, and rationale for religion are seemingly waning in Western society. Wilson (1982) stated, "Whereas religion once entered into the very texture of community life, in modern society it operates in interstitial places in the system" (p. 155). Furseth and Repstad (2006) add, "For Wilson, secularization means that the social functions of religion are undermined" (p. 84), leading to diminishing social importance.

In society, rationality and functionality are quintessential in its operation and many of the old values have been replaced in the modern world with secularization.

Whereas, in the community, the individual's duties were underwritten by conceptions of morality which was ultimately derived from supernatural sources, or which had reference to supernatural goals, in the society, duties and role performances are ultimately justified by the demands of a rational structure, in which skills are trained and competences certificated; roles are assigned and coordinated; rewards are computed; and times are measured and allocated (Wilson, 1982, pp. 155–156).

Based on some sociological investigations, Wilson's conclusions could be plausible. Wilson (1966) stated,

The Churches have increasingly faced the circumstance in which the authoritative will of God has made less and less impact on men in a society where social and legal control have become increasingly separate from religious control, and where men cease in large measure voluntarily to put themselves under the guidance of ecclesiastics (p. 86).

However, his ideas fail to fully answer the questions of revival, resurgence, and renewal movements that seek a total lifestyle change in accordance to biblical principles, not to mention the existence of megachurches that are by no means "interstitial" or insignificant. People are still going to church despite the growing secular options to find spiritual sustenance without the aid, control, or observation of religious institutions. Thus, Wilson's assertions fail to explain why, in some locations around the world, strong religious movements are developing wherein community social integration occurs ". . . based on commitment, conformity, and close community, [and] is one of many securing a foothold in society and among this younger generation" (Flory & Miller, 2007, p. 113).

Wilson, himself, admitted to the limitation of making his assumption a universal theory. He stated, "New religious movements are phenomena that tax existing conceptual apparatus" (Wilson, 1990, p. 204). The complex nature of religion and the dynamic attachments believers have toward their faiths show the weaknesses of such exclusive, moribund theories.

Moreover, Wilson's suggestion to their existence is one that correlates religiosity with security and possibly superstition or self-preservation. He claimed, "Salvation is the commodity in which all religions deal, whether it is release from witches, illness, disgrace, bad luck, early death, punishment after death, or damnation to recurrent lives of misery" (Wilson, 1990, p. 206).

Religious life in the Western world has undergone a dramatic change in the last two centuries. Whereas earlier the religious institutions held an enormous degree of influence and control in the lives of their parishioners, currently, modernization and secularization has removed this power and placed it into the hands of the parishioners, themselves. This, potentially and observably, means that people can and will exercise their religious beliefs outside of the public sphere. The question remains, though, to what degree and to what measure.

Rational Choice Theory

Succinctly, rational choice theory asserts that religious groups flourish if they have something to offer believers in regard to personal benefits and/or rewards. Thus, people are involved in religions or attend church services to get something or to find relevance in personal matters. Although some scholars (Bruce, 2002) have suggested that secularization inescapably leads to a moribund state of religiosity, others (Finke & Stark, 1992) claim that people are merely discarding the old form of American religion, but not the substance. For instance, liberal churches historically flounder not because of their orthodoxy, but because of their watered-down offerings.

Still, one can see great evidence in American religious culture that 50s-styled churches are passé and full of more elderly members. GenX'ers and Millennials seem to be seeking for doctrine "with teeth that sinks to the bone" before they commit (Flory & Miller, 2007). Additionally, American religiosity is quite individualistic compared to 30 years ago, which goes along with the rational choice theory assertions of a personal, marketing approach to belief.

Yet, rational choice theory is not without some intrinsic problems. First, it is insulting to people, presuming motivation that is somewhat flaky and narcissistic. Second, it ignores why people all over the world are religious despite the dangers of maintaining their belief surrounding them. Last, it ignores contrary evidence showing that diverse choices do not always lead to an increase in participation. Oregon has a completely open religious market, but it is one of the least-churched states in the United States (I have witnessed this, personally, living there for nearly 40 years).

Good sociological theories, if they are to be applied in macrofashion, need to function in both macro- and microsocial climates. It is not certain that rational choice theory does that (or secularization theory), which is just more proof of why the academic world needs more ongoing scientific study of religion—along with a purist study that first begins with scientific methodology and does not immediately jump to an applied sociology conclusion, with its political and tribal murkiness, which is offered in far too many sociological textbooks today.

The Spiritual Revolution (the Subjectivists)

The school of scholars whose approach follows a relativist or personalized approach to understanding religious life, represented by scholars like Charles Taylor, Paul Heelas, and Linda Woodhead, takes a broader, more inclusive attitude than the secularization theorists (Gill, 2003, p. 204). Religion and spirituality are not headed in one direction, and especially not in a direction toward destruction or dissolution, per se. Instead, Woodhead et al. (2002) offer, "Unilateral theories of religious decline are increasingly being abandoned in favor of more nuanced 'mappings' of religion and secularity and the factors which explain them" (p. 11).

People are just as spiritual as before—in the modern age, they are merely expressing their faiths in nonstandard forms. Substantiating this concept, Paul Heelas and Linda Woodhead suggest, "The West is currently experiencing both secularization (with regard to life-as forms of religion) and sacralization (with regard to subjective-life forms of spirituality)" (Heelas et al., 2005, pp. 9–10).

Taylor states, "What is new is that this kind of self-orientation seems to have become a mass phenomenon" (Taylor, p. 80). Finally, Roof claims, "The suppliers in this new spiritual marketplace are themselves diverse: some are specialists in turning old, dying churches into places that are coming alive again" (Roof, 1999, p. 109). For the subjectivists, the new world is not one devoid of spiritual expression and religious faith— it is exactly the opposite. There are more opportunities to worship, more options of faith all over the Western world.

As with secularization theory, there are some problems with the subjectivist/spiritual revolution assertions. In regard to an abandonment of traditional Christian religiosity, the statistics do not strongly support it. Alternative spirituality practices may eclipse Christianity, if trends continue, by the year 3050 CE, presuming that no resurgence or revival occurs in the West between now and then. Additionally, the embrace of alternative spirituality practices is in the extreme minority, with perhaps 1% of the population affirming these practices to have religious value.

Finally, the spiritual revolution assumes that personal spirituality always dominates over organized religion, but across the globe, there are many different regions where traditional, corporate religion is promoted and adored by non-Western believers. Some of the biggest churches, worldwide, are outside of the United States and Europe. In this regard, the spiritual revolution contention is somewhat ethnocentric and cultural myopic in its perceptions of religious trends.

Religious Epistemology and Research Methods

Since this prompt focuses on the "How do we know," it involves epistemology, the study of knowledge, and how human beings can distinguish that which is justified belief from mere personal opinion. It is the methodology of sorting, defining, and valuing of "the facts." Moreover, it is a complex issue, especially when it comes to religion and supernatural assertions, which reside in murky waters of faith and fantastic (but possibly true) facts.

The reality of epistemological studies is more of a dynamic than an "either/or" matter. On one end of the spectrum is the *objective*, which carries with it an absoluteness and easy verifiability. On the other end of the spectrum is the *subjective*, with its foundation of personal observation, analysis, and interpretation, which often lays outside empirical verification. In the middle is the *intersubjective*, which is more communal, vacillatory, but substantively verifiable—to a degree.

For example, that Jesus of Nazareth lived is a mostly accepted historical fact; however, that Jesus' deity was shown to Peter, James, and John on the Mount of Transfiguration (Matthew 17:1–13) could be more of a subjective matter as only those four men saw it and the experience could not be (or was not) repeated. Jesus' fame as an amazing teacher and popular healer of sorts lies within the realm of the intersubjective, though, depending upon what people groups mean by "great teacher" and "healer."

In practice, the verification of religious truths by most people utilizes all three approaches, typically. Still, the Bible speaks of faith being the hope of (supernatural) things unseen and without evidence (Hebrews 11:1). So, for many people, in all the different faith groups, their religious beliefs and truths are empirically unprovable and dependent upon what they personally and sometimes collectively agree upon concerning a religious figure, supernatural event, or doctrine. For instance, did Moses receive the Decalogue (the Ten Commandments) directly from God; did Muhammed receive the Quranic message directly from the archangel Gabriel; did Joseph Smith receive the golden plates from the Angel Moroni; does God answer prayer?

Specifically, sociologists of religion rely upon empirical and statistical data, collected both quantitatively and qualitatively, to investigate various theories of religion (from the mundane to the phenomenal) and to determine their validity and significance. The four main methods of study include experiments, surveys, participant observation, and a survey of existing scholarly sources on the topic(s).

First, the sociology researcher could employ exploratory research to investigate religious phenomena or praxis, although he/she needs to always maintain an awareness that research can be harmful to the subjects studied, if not done with great care (and abiding by the American Sociological Association guidelines for sociological research). Second, sociologists of religion can utilize surveys (a bank of quantitative and qualitative questions) to form a deeper or broader perspective on religious thought and praxis from his/her respondents. Third, social scientists might try to personally observe the sociological phenomena in action and in the field; this sometimes includes case studies and ethnographies.

Finally, wise sociologists know that others have probably investigated their topic of interest (at least to some degree), which can be found in the plethora of primary and secondary sources available from books and academic journal articles. There is no need to reinvent the wheel, as the axiom goes; as Newton said, we all stand on the shoulders of other scientists who went before us. Historical analysis is there for those who are willing to comb through the archives to find it.

Sociology from Above

Human Agency and Christ's Redemption

From the dawn of history, human beings have demonstrated a unique propensity among earthly creatures to exercise free will in their daily decisions and actions. People may have natural instincts, but we are not necessarily slaves to them.

All people, all individuals, operate independently regarding their attitudes, actions, and interpretations. In sociology, this is called, *agency*, and it has been affirmed throughout the ages.

The Greek philosopher Epictetus wrote, "You may fetter my leg, but Zeus himself cannot get the better of my free will."

The great theologian Augustine of Hippo wrote, "There is no sin unless through a man's own will, and hence the reward when we do right things also of our own will."

The infamous author of *The Prince*, Niccolo Machiavelli claimed, "God is not willing to do everything, and thus take away our free will and that share of glory which belongs to us."

The pugnacious Reformer Martin Luther explained, "The very name, Free-will, was odious to all the Fathers. I, for my part, admit that God gave to mankind a free will, but the question is, whether this same freedom be in our power and strength, or no?"

Later, Sociologist George Herbert Mead diagnosed, "Our self exists in an interactive relationship with its environment." Additionally, as part-time apologist and full-time novelist C.S. Lewis put it, "The sin of men and of angels, was rendered possible by the fact that God gave us free will."

The evangelical Atheist Richard Dawkins admits, "I am very comfortable with the idea that we can override biology with free will" and inspirational speaker Sean Covey proclaims, "You are free to choose what you want to make of your life. It's called free agency or free will, and it's your birthright."

The Bible, too, is replete with stories, teachings, and admonitions discussing this exercise of personal freedom. From Genesis to Revelation, one does not need to read too deeply to encounter the biographical stories of biblical characters making choices and experiencing the fruits (sweet and sour) of their decisions.
The seeds of human agency began with Adam and Eve, the first human couple on Earth. Genesis 2:15-17 state,

The Lord God took the man and put him in the Garden of Eden to work it and take care of it. And the Lord God commanded the man, "You are *free* to eat from any tree in the garden; but you must not eat from the tree of the knowledge of good and evil, for if you eat from it, you will certainly die" (Genesis 2:15–17).

Despite this clear and ominous warning of God, Eve also displayed her own ability to make autonomous choices (separate from Adam and God)—

When the woman saw that the fruit of the tree was good for food and pleasing to the eye, and also desirable for gaining wisdom, she *took some and ate it*. She also gave some to her husband, who was with her, and he ate it. Then, the eyes of both of them were opened, and they realized they were naked; so, they sewed fig leaves together and made coverings for themselves (Genesis 3:6–7).

Agency is a human trait that gives all men and all women the right to choose as they will, regardless of consequences and common sense. This freedom is not a product of a fallen nature; the human ability of free choice existed in the Garden of Eden before the Fall. The reality is that based on the biblical texts, sometimes people choose wisely; other times, they come to lament their decisions, which the biblical texts clearly affirm.

Thus, agency can be seen in Cain's slaying of Abel, in Job's mournful resolution to wait for God's explanation for his tribulations, in Abraham's faithful migration from Mesopotamia to Canaan, in Hagar's choice to return to a potentially abusive tent, in Jacob's willingness to work seven more years to gain Rachel's hand, in Joseph's decision not to slay his wicked brothers who had earlier sold him into slavery, in Samson's blinding vanity and suicidal final mission, in King Saul's decision to disobey God, in King David's decision to commit adultery and murder, in Esther's courageous unbeckoned approach to King Xerxes to save her people, in Jeremiah's decision to stand bravely before the Temple sharing God's warning of exile, in Jonah's escape of his prophetical duties to Nineveh, in John the Baptist's passionate but politically incorrect warning to Israel (and her leaders) to repent, in the Disciples' abandonment of their nets to follow a fisher of men, in the Apostles' unwillingness to worship a crazed despot, and in the early church's willingness to sacrifice their social security to share the light of eternal security with those in spiritual darkness.

The Bible presents a checkered account of the darkest and most desperate corners of human pursuits, which seems to go on forever, without an end in sight some 2,000 years later. This leads many to an existentialist crisis, provoking the famed Renaissance artist Michelangelo to lament, "I live in sin, to kill myself I live; no longer my life my own, but sin's; my good is given to me by heaven, my evil by myself, by my free will, of which I am deprived."

Yet, the Gospel suggests a greater understanding of human agency fulfilled and perfected in the Son of God, Jesus Christ (and faithfully reflected in the loving submission of His followers, the church). No greater example of human agency can be seen than in the person and power of Jesus of Nazareth, who knew no sin, who was a teacher and preacher beyond compare, who could heal the lame and blind with a touch of his hand (or robe), who could command and cast out evil spirits with just a simple command—"Go!"—whose heart for humanity encompassed all brothers and sisters from all ages, and who willingly gave up His life that all may have everlasting life. He was the ultimate man of action and agency, choosing to fully obey God in life.

The Apostle Paul speaks of the incomparable Son of God in Colossians and writes,

For He rescued us from the domain of darkness and transferred us to the kingdom of His beloved Son, in whom we have redemption, the forgiveness of sins. He is the image of the invisible God, the firstborn of all creation. For by Him all things were created, *both* in the heavens and on earth, visible and invisible, whether thrones or dominions or rulers or authorities—all things have been created through Him and for Him. He is before all things, and in Him all things hold together. He is also head of the body, the church; and He is the beginning, the firstborn from the dead, so that He Himself will come to have first place in everything (Colossians 1:13–18).

Despite the inevitable lethal repercussions for fallen people exercising free agency, the path of a stumbling humanity does not have to end inescapably in death. As the Apostle John proclaimed long ago,

This is the message we have heard from Him and announce to you, that God is Light, and in Him there is no darkness at all. If we say that we have fellowship with Him and *yet* walk in the darkness, we lie and do not practice the truth; but if we walk in the Light as He Himself is in the Light, we have fellowship with one another, and the blood of Jesus His Son cleanses us from all sin (1 John 1:5–7).

The beauty of the Gospel story is that human beings are still allowed to exercise their free will, their personal agency—in a display of personal strength, wisdom, and courage—just as Jesus did over 2,000 years ago.

Jesus could have chosen a life of hedonism and carnality, but He did not—He submitted to the Word of God. He could have set Himself up as the ultimate ruler of the world, but He did not—He chose instead to be a servant of the Lord. He could have been a rebel, a doubter of God and His goodness, but He did not—He humbly trusted in His loving, righteous Father in Heaven.

Freedom is a gift, but nowhere near as precious a gift as choosing a life in God through Jesus Christ.

The Sage from the Stage

Commitment and the Christian Church

Several years ago, our aging refrigerator became a "Can't-No-More" refrigerator. My wife and I picked out a brand-new replacement with a bottom freezer and we anxiously awaited the delivery day. The day when the truck pulled into our driveway, two 20-something guys dressed in their uniforms and appliance straps walked up to our doorstep, and then announced their long-awaited arrival.

They immediately set to work. When the installation was complete, I had to sign some papers. I was asked if we were considering the extended warranty, and I informed them that the appliance actually belongs to the Methodist Church across the street, that this was their parsonage, and that I would have to pass that decision on to them.

Our conversation drifted to the topic of the "Church." One of the young men, Justin, said that he believed in God but added that he very seldom attended church services. I asked him his reasons and he mentioned that he just did not think it was necessary in life, that church services were really not his sort of thing, and that he was certain that his belief in God was not dependent upon something so superficial as attendance. We continued to chat about such things, and it was clear that while he was open to the idea of having a relationship with God, he just did not see how attending "church" had any relevance for his experience.

Justin was a tall and strong young man, and made a living delivering heavy appliances. I asked him if he lifted weights to keep himself in shape and he said that he did, when he had the time. "Do you have a membership in a particular gym or at the YMCA or somewhere like that" I asked? "Oh sure," Justin replied, "I just don't get there very often because of work." I heartily agreed with that and jokingly continued, stating that I wish there was a gym membership out there that would get me in shape without me having to go there and work out. Justin laughed and nodded his head in accord.

As we walked out of the house, down the ramp and into the garage, I then became a little more serious and I said, "Justin, as unrealistic as it is to think that by merely belonging to a gym would help get me into shape, so it is to imagine that I can adequately grow in my relationship to God apart from a community of believers called the church."

I wonder how many "Justins" are out there. How many others sincerely desire a closer relationship with God and yet find no significance or meaning in the covenant community called "church"?

As North American postmodern society moves closer and closer to radical individualism, there are incalculable effects upon the values, ethics, and norms that once defined our culture. All truth has become relative, tolerance is the superlative value (with exclusion to those who are identified as intolerant), narcissism has surpassed altruism, personal choice is becoming a treasured dogma, individual rights have superseded community consciousness, and trust in organizations and institutions is rapidly diminishing, just to name a few.

Michael Mascolo, Professor of psychology at Merrimack College, notes than in Western culture (especially after the Civil Rights Movement), "Large groups of people began to lose faith in public institutions such as government, religion, community values, public virtue, objectivity, shared conceptions of taste, and so forth. As a result, a morality of individual rights flourished" (2016, online).

More and more, people are growing less and less inclined to answer to anyone or anything for the decisions they make, the actions they take, or the lifestyle they live. Without some form of external authority, radical individualism begins to spin out of control. As Mascolo (2016) concludes, "If we all have the right to our own personal morality, then 'the right to choose freely' easily degenerates into 'If it's freely chosen, then it's all right'" (online).

You might now be wondering what all this has to do with Justin. I would be gravely mistaken to say that Justin personified all of the earlier characteristics of radical individualism; yet, I cannot help but wonder if he were moving about his faith "under the influence" of a societal shift that is happening even beyond his cognizance.

What I can say is that folks like Justin seem to struggle with the value and significance of not only belonging to, but participating in, the community called "the church." As people privately internalize and individualize their faith, it becomes superfluous as to whether they publicly commit to a church fellowship. But there is a not so subtle danger lurking amid the isolated experience of one's personal expression of faith. Perhaps E. Stanley Jones frames this danger best when he said, "Christianity that doesn't begin with the individual, doesn't begin. And Christianity that ends with the individual, ends" (Dough, 1994).

If I could chat with my likeable appliance delivery man again, I would like to point out to him that belonging to the family of God is neither inconsequential nor something to be casually ignored. The person who says, "I do not really need the church," or, "I do not really care for the body of Christ," has failed to take into account the witness of Jesus Christ toward the Church.

The Church is so important to God that Jesus died on the cross for it. Christ loved the Church and gave His life for it (Ephesians 5:25). The Bible calls the Church, the "bride of Christ" and the "body of Christ"! With that in mind, how could we ever imagine us saying,

Jesus, I love You . . . but I dislike that for which You gave Your life!
Jesus, I love and respect You . . . but I don't respect what You love!
Jesus, I honor You . . . but I don't honor Your bride!
Jesus, I accept You . . . but I don't accept Your body!

I often hear, "I'm all for Jesus . . . but I can take or leave the church." How can you say you are all in favor of Jesus Christ and not be all in favor of what Jesus is all in favor about, the Church? The Bible says to love the fellowship of believers (1 Peter 2:17b, Acts 2:42). Our fellowship is not optional or inconsequential; it is essential.

I would also accentuate the witness of Scripture regarding the Church. The Bible says a Christian without a church home is like an organ without a body (1 Corinthians 12:12-21), a sheep without a flock (John 10:11-16), or a child without a family (Ephesians 2:19). It is an unnatural state. Scripture clearly states that God's unchanging plan has always been to adopt us into His own family by sending Jesus Christ to die for us (Ephesians 1:5). To say we have no part in the Church is to say we have no interest in the Family of God. Such a position stands against the very plan that God has for humanity.

Furthermore, I would share the witness of my own experience. Committing to the fellowship is not only essential, critical, and indispensable, but committing to the fellowship is practical. It identifies me as a genuine believer. It surrounds me a spiritual support family. It gives me a place to use my gifts. It provides for the much-needed spiritual accountability. It brings encouragement to others. It affords protection from the enemy. It increases my effectiveness in sharing in Christ's mission to the world. My own experience has unequivocally demonstrated that I cannot be the follower of Jesus that God intends for me to be apart from the church.

The Christian life is more than just a commitment to Christ; it also includes a commitment to other Christians. The first commitment results in salvation, the second commitment results in fellowship. Community requires commitment. Can I truly be the best follower of Jesus I can be apart from the Church?

And then there is one final thought for my fellow believer, Justin. It regards the compass needle of truth. There are some things we can only know if God reveals them.

The Harvard University seal of "arms" was introduced in 1643 and has gone through a number of revisions. Originally, it was a shield, three books and the word *Veritas,* which is Latin for "truth." Interestingly, two of the three books were face up while the third book was face down. The books were depicted this way to symbolize humanity's abilities to examine and discover (the two faced up books) as well as the limits of human reason and the need for God's revelation (the book placed face down). Around the 1920s, some rascal changed the seal to depict all three books face up, representing the belief that there is no limit to human reasoning and God's revelation is no longer needed—an ironic commentary on the present world.

This, of course, stands in stark contrast to the message of Scripture. Consider what the Apostle Paul wrote in Ephesians 3:10, "Through followers of Jesus like yourselves gathered in churches, this extraordinary plan of God is becoming known and talked about even among the angels!" (The Message). Have you come to realize that when you became a Christian, you were swept up into God's eternal plan? God's plan is to accomplish His will, through Christ, and His Church—not only in temporal time, but for eternity! The Church is a "figure" of what God has planned forever. The extraordinary plan of God is made manifest both in heaven and on earth, through the Church! That is God's vision.

Meanwhile, back at the church, we are arguing about what music to sing. Meanwhile, back at the church, we are upset when the preacher speaks too long. Meanwhile, back at the church, we are becoming all riled up because of the budget, and the color of the carpet, and the flavor of soup. Paul says the church is worth living for and the church is worth dying for; and we often say, it is not even worth showing up for, today. I will go if it is not too inconvenient. I will go if there is nothing better going on. I will go if there is some special program, and we miss the vision God has for the Church—that in the Church His majesty is revered.

When one looks through a telescope by the wrong end, they are left with a distorted view of the world. I am afraid that is so often the case when it comes to our perception of the Church. Maybe it is time to consider turning the telescope around and perceiving our world from the Divine perspective.

Pastor Brian Cook
Brookhill Wesleyan Church
Forest, Virginia

Contributed by Pastor Brian Cook. © Kendall Hunt Publishing Company

 Check out the Chapter 7 video at this link: https://www.grtep.com/

Vocabulary

Biblical Authority
Christian Commitment
The Church
Church Membership
Existentialism
The Fellowship
GenX Religiosity
The Gospel Message
The Intersubjective
Liberal Churches
Millennial Religiosity
The Objective
Open Religious Markets
Personal Benefits

Personal Freedoms
Personal Relevance
Privatization of Religion
The Profane
Radical Individualism
Rational Choice Theory
Religion
Religious Agency
Religious Epistemology
Religious Institutionalism
Religious Paradigm Shift
Religious Verification
Religiosity
Renewal

Resurgence
Revival
The Sacred
Science of Religion
Secularization
Secularization Theory
Sociology of Religion
The Spiritual Revolution
Spirituality
The Subjective
Subjectivism
Traditional Churches
Truth

CHAPTER EIGHT: Stratification

The Basics

Simply, *social stratification* is the classification of persons into groups based on shared socioeconomic conditions such as wealth or power. As Witt (2009) states, "Ever since people first began to speculate about the nature of human society, they have focused on the differences between individuals and groups within society" (p. 216).

In stratification, groupings are vertical, based on social position or status superiority, and often include a criterion of economy, honor, and education. From top to bottom, distribution of goods and monies is based on perceptions of right, authority, or stereotypes.

Most societies create ranks that place people into categories, influencing every part of human existence (for better or for worse). Some categories and ranks come with comforts and luxuries; others are more Spartan and austere. Although many politicians promise a utopian community where no one suffers and no one acts as "lord of the manor," the reality is that inequality is found in all societies and all economic systems. The axioms that it takes money to make money and that inequality begets more inequality are evidentially true, historically. Access is all about having the right social "key" to scare goods and resources.

There are *four main principles of social stratification*. First, the stratification is a significant trait of society—not simply a reflection of individual differences. Second, the stratification carries over from past generations to future generations. Third, it is universally recognized, but still with some variance. Fourth, it carries with it some inequalities but also manifestations of personal or group beliefs, too.

Throughout history and in cultures all over the globe, common social systems or groupings have been observed. Some cultures, such as India or in China, have a *caste system*, which is locked, hereditary, and ontologically divisive. Some countries, such as France and England, have utilized the idea of estates to order political bodies and differentiate their social classes. *Slavery*, too, has been a severe form of inescapable stratification that has its roots deep within every

continent, every race, every culture, and every people group. To be a slave is to be the property of another human being, without rights or self-autonomy. Incredibly, according to the *Global Slavery Index* (2018), some 40 million people in the world today are living in a form of slavery.

The fourth system is that of *class*, which brings with it the social dimensions of wealth, prestige, and power (or a lack, thereof). For instance, in Western society, there have been three main classes. The *upper class* includes individuals with considerable wealth in regard to personal property, real estate, stocks, bonds, or money. The *middle class* is the largest class in the United States, and includes people between the upper and worker classes, such as professionals and businessmen. The *lower class* includes individuals with the least amount of education and with the most employment problems.

In most Western societies, a huge rift exists between the classes. For instance, in 2003, the 13,000 richest families in the United States had the same income as the 20 million poorest people. Even more, the richest 1% of the U.S. population owned as much property and goods as 96% of all other Americans' combined holdings. Sociologists (and economists) find questions on how much the richest person in the United States made in 2019, how many people are currently in the American middle-class, and what are the salary ranges for each socioeconomic class to be intriguing, at the least.

Johnny Winstar
TheRealJohnnyWinstar

I'm thinking about running for Prez.

#wannabeprez #superioritis #windbag

♡ 250K   3:45 AM - March 1, 2019

One of the most important factors in predicting future earnings for people relates to their family background. Sociological studies have shown that men from families with high incomes tend to make more money than families with low incomes. One can conclude that financial and social success is more about being born into a wealthy family than simply personal ambition or hard work. Succinctly, money and wealth open doors to occupations, lifestyles, education, housing, and legal protections.

This presents sociologists with some underclass realities. First, being in the lower classes severely hampers one's social life and chances of betterment. Second, although there are different types of poverty, *absolute poverty* occurs when people fall below the federally defined subsistence level. Third, most impoverished do not have access or money to acquire the resources they need to meet their basic necessities in life.

A central factor of being impoverished is the inability to escape from one's socioeconomic circle, which concerns *social mobility*—the ability to change one's social position. As Semuels (2016) writes, "It's not an exaggeration: It is getting harder to move up in America. Those who make very little money in their first jobs will probably still be making very little decades later, and those who start off making middle-class wages have similarly limited paths" (online). Mobility influences many social aspects including the growth of large corporations, an increased standard of living, an increase of urbanization, the development of advanced technologies, and the maintenance of the split labor market.

The *split labor market*, an economic theory suggested by Edna Bonacich in the 1970s, is a virtual community where people compete for jobs and their resources. Bonacich (1972) wrote, "The central hypothesis is that ethnic antagonism first germinates in a labor market split along ethnic lines" (p. 549). Bonacich theorized that some jobs afford upward mobility while others do not. This creates a job market split between the manual laborers and other white-collar workers. Moreover, this created greater obstacles for the minorities including the disabled and the aged.

Aging and Society

Although the elderly are often ridiculed or mocked, everyone on earth ends up in the same chronological situation. It is the master status that overshadows everything else, eventually. Due to the demographic percentage of elderly people, it is akin to a subordinate group like the minorities; however, being old is all-encompassing, socially.

Despite the commonalities of aging, not every society or culture treats the elderly the same. Eastern cultures like Japan, China, and Tibet idealize the elderly. Worshipping youth, some Western cultures (such as America, Britain, or Europe, in general) either mock or ignore the elderly, as a normal part of life. Being labeled, "old," has a major impact on how others see them, on how the elderly see themselves, and issues in many negative stereotypes and social responses.

Currently, across the globe, some 7% of the world's population are 65 years or older, amounting to some 453 million elderly people. In America, one in five people are 65 years or older (2016). Not surprisingly, with the latest medical advancements, safer and healthier social environments, and a booming elderly demographic group, many people disagree that age 65 should even be considered "old" anymore.

There are so many elderly people that they even created a medical field to assist them: *gerontology*, which is the study of the sociological and psychological aspects of aging and the problem of the aged. It relies heavily upon sociological and psychological principles and theories along with anthropology, physical education, counseling, and medicine.

There are three main perspectives on aging: disengagement theory, activity theory, and age discrimination. *Disengagement theory* suggests that society and the aging mutually sever many of their previous relationships and joint activities. *Activity theory* asserts that elderly people who remain active and socially involved will be well adjusted and healthier, physically and psychologically. As the writer Gabriel Garcia Márquez wrote, "It is not true that people stop pursuing dreams because they grow old, they grow old because they stop pursuing dreams."

The final perspective concerns *age discrimination*, which is unfair treatment and prejudice based solely upon a person's age (young or old). Another name for this is ageism, which, according to Butler (1969), is any attitude, action, or institutional structure that subordinates a person or group because of his or her age, or any assignment of roles in society purely on the basis of age.

This is definitely evident in American society, where television, movies, and real life actually do mirror themselves in regard to the all-too-common stereotypic, negative attitudes regarding older adults. Many younger people fallaciously have the perception that the elderly are helpless, that they all are dependent upon support agencies, and, compared to other age groups, are the least healthy and alert.

Ageism is nothing more than patronizing bigotry. As with racism and sexism, ageism is unfair and irrational discrimination, which promotes future prejudice and fearfulness.

Essentially, it says to the vast majority of the elderly, "You are poor, lonely, weak, incompetent, ineffectual, and no longer terribly bright."

With this negative attitude, ageists avoid the elderly on an individual level, discriminate against them in terms of jobs and duties, deride and mock them for their beliefs and behaviors, and even promote their removal from society (Emanuel et al., 2016). Such vilification typically fosters the dehumanizing belief that older people are a drain on society and therefore need to be removed.

At places of employment, the elderly are often the first to be part of any company "downsizing," they are passed over for promotions and raises, they are considered to be too unsightly and unattractive to be part of a marketing team, and they find themselves often ignored and placated within a work team.

Still, some employers recognize the benefit that older employees bring to companies:

As one expert points out, 50+ workers, including boomers, differ from their younger counterparts in that they are more likely to have remained with one organization longer. Employees who are able to work in organizations for long periods of time are more likely than short-term employees to accumulate job-specific critical knowledge about business operations (Sauer, 2007, p. 8).

Within the healthcare system, the elderly are treated as hypochondriacs, patronized and bullied, and underdiagnosed or overmedicated. They frequently find themselves marginalized regarding their own health decisions and worse yet, too often presumed to be okay with a "Do not resuscitate" order. As Wand, Peisah, Draper, Jones, and Brodaty (2016) note, "The determination of rationality is subjective and influenced by one's personal view of ageing, older people, and the psychological effects of disability and chronic disease" (p. 2).

Although many people do lack personal character or compassion for people like the elderly, other reasons might be in play in eliciting ageism attitudes. These might include a fear of death, which is often observed in Western culture's art and music where "old age" is portrayed as being synonymous with death, itself. Additionally, the unrelenting cultural emphasis on adolescence drives a youth culture that too often tramples over the elderly, socially. Also, Americans are (in)famous for their Puritanical work ethic that can inadvertently shame those no longer as productive as they once were in life.

There are far too many myths of aging that are based more on insecurities than realities. For instance, to be old is not necessarily to be sick. Some old dogs can still learn new tricks (if they want to). Older people often recover from illness faster than younger people (because they allow themselves time to rest). Genes doom us all—not just the elderly. Finally, the elderly usually do more than just pull their own weight in their own social circles.

One of my favorite poems, *When you are old* (1893), was written by William Butler Yeats to his sweetheart, Gonne, when they both were in their 20s. It speaks of the poet's hopes and dreams of living out his life with her by his side (which did not happen, actually; she ended up marrying someone else). Still, Yeats opens the door to his heart a crack so that readers can see the depth and height of his love for his Gonne.

> When you are old and grey and full of sleep,
> And nodding by the fire, take down this book,
> And slowly read, and dream of the soft look
> Your eyes had once, and of their shadows deep;
> How many loved your moments of glad grace,
> And loved your beauty with love false or true,
> But one man loved the pilgrim soul in you,
> And loved the sorrows of your changing face;
>
> And bending down beside the glowing bars,
> Murmur, a little sadly, how love fled
> And paced upon the mountains overhead
> And hid his face amid a crowd of stars.

The poem shows Yeats' genius despite his age. Although it is hard for most young people to understand, to be old is a grand thing: to have lived and loved and laughed longer than most around them. Old age brings wisdom and hope because it is built upon a perspective of personal evidence and experience. So, remember this (because I will probably forget it soon enough): wrinkles and gray hair and squeaky joints and age spots are not ugly; they are the telltale signs of a beautiful, well-worn life.

Sociology from Above

Cultivating Christian Community in a World of Conflict

Teaching on the Bible and Church History, each year I am invariably asked by curious students, "What is your denomination?" Eyebrows are raised when I respond, "I consider myself a first-century Christian." True, I was sprinkled in a Presbyterian Church, saved in a Southern Baptist Church, indoctrinated in a Conservative Baptist Church, liturgicalized in an Evangelical Lutheran Church, and settled in a nondenominational church, but I long to be part of the original church of Jesus Christ, the one started by Him and His Disciples/Apostles 2,000 years ago.

I sometimes wonder if people just want to know my church background in order to (a) affirm their own church tradition or (b) dismiss any theological proclamations or biblical interpretations that I might say in class. The long-standing problem with denominationalism is that it sets up believers to promote their founders' take on God, Jesus, salvation, security, and so on, over another's. I will admit having my own biases against other different churchgoers. Too often, I have felt pity for their silly adherence to the ways of man when my church, *the real Church*, had the straight scoop and God's right ear, which is pretty pharisaical of me.

The problem was that as I read the Bible, studied Church History, and listened to my church leaders explain our spiritual superiority to others, I began to perceive that even though the other churches were leaning too much upon the ways of man, my church was just as bad. How could we be so condemning of the Catholics because of their belief in Mary's Immaculate Conception or the Nazarenes because of their assertion that Jesus never drank alcoholic wine or the Methodists because of their view that one could attain Christian perfection when double predestination is never explicitly mentioned in Scripture, either?

Reading through 1 Corinthians (TNIV), it is evident that Paul and the early church encountered similar problems. In Chapter 4, Paul writes, "Now, brothers and sisters, I have applied these things to myself and Apollos for your benefit, so that you may learn from us the meaning of the saying, 'Do not go beyond what is written.' Then you will not be puffed up in being a follower of one of us over against the other. For who makes you different from anyone else?" The only thing superior about a Christian is his or her savior—all Christians, all humans, have the same sinful nature pushing us away from God and each other. Thus, denominational, racial, or ethnic snootiness comes across like a man in a lifeboat mocking another man for his misfortune in the very same lifeboat.

Luther, Calvin, Wesley, Finney, Moody, Barth, Graham, John Paul II, Piper, Warren and the like were/are great Christian thinkers who help us get deeper to the truth of God's plan, but none of their writings are canonized biblical texts. More importantly, none of them are our savior and redeemer. Belief in their messages does not save us from our sins. That role is reserved for Jesus alone. As Paul says in 2 Corinthians 4, "For we do not preach ourselves, but Jesus Christ as Lord, and ourselves as your servants for Jesus' sake." Embracing these people's understandings of God is not necessarily a sin unless one puts Calvin's words or Bell's or one's own words ahead of Christ's.

Such behavior is what got humanity in trouble at the dawn of humanity in the Garden of Eden. Similarly, "Did God really say . . . ?" is the oft-said mantra these days that is quickly followed by a different Gospel, "which is really no Gospel at all" (Galatians 1).

Our society allows for much religious freedom and choice, which is a wonderful gift, but a gift with consequences, good or bad. The flesh craves self-empowerment, self-indulgence, and the easy road. Thus, we can pick a theologian that tickles our ears, strokes our egos, or satisfies our cravings for power and vengeance, but is that really the Way that pulled so many people to God out of the world of Paganism and godlessness 2,000 years ago? If we deconstruct the road to salvation paved by Jesus (who is God), how can any other paths built with human wisdom and purposes get us there, no matter how superior or creative or self-empowering?

Being a Christian means loving God and others sincerely and purposefully, submitting to His story—not advancing ours, acknowledging our personal weaknesses and our need for each other. God wants us to be happy in Him but understanding that requires being unified in love and mercy and truth with our human brothers and sisters. Paul speaks of this Godly reality in Galatians 3:26–28, which is just as relevant today as it was 2,000 years ago: "So in Christ Jesus you are all children of God through faith, for all of you who were baptized into Christ have clothed yourselves with Christ. There is neither Jew nor Gentile, neither slave nor free, neither male nor female, for you are all one in Christ Jesus."

In Christ, personal identity does not reside in our race. It does not reside in our ethnicity. It does not reside in our gender. It does not reside in our socioeconomic status. Only God in Jesus Christ matters. Far too many people focus on the inferior when they should have their eyes fixed on the superior, who transcends all things and helps them do the same.

Preelection, politicians always claim that they will unite the country if elected, yet they never do, but Jesus can bring people together in love and has done since the Church began. The question is whether we are going to join with Him in uniting the world or resist loving each other as Christ loves us. Unified, the Church exploded across the Mediterranean region. Divided, the Church has imploded and diminished in stature and effectiveness. Perhaps the time has come to shift the focus back to Jesus, with whom all things are possible.

When the Apostles shared the Good News in Jerusalem (the Book of Acts tells us), it was to a diverse and divided group of people from all parts of the known world. Still, the message of God's love in Christ struck home for the inhabitants of Jerusalem that day:

> Utterly amazed, they asked: "Aren't all these who are speaking Galileans? Then how is it that each of us hears them in our native language? Parthians, Medes and Elamites; residents of Mesopotamia, Judea and Cappadocia, Pontus and Asia, Phrygia and Pamphylia, Egypt and the parts of Libya near Cyrene; visitors from Rome (both Jews and converts to Judaism); Cretans and Arabs—we hear them declaring the wonders of God in our own tongues!" Amazed and perplexed, they asked one another, "What does this mean?" (Acts 2:7–12).

Succinctly, it meant that Christ's ambassadors were risking everything to reach out to people who had been alienated and living in the dark for too long. Some 2,000 years later, the same social reality faces Christians in Western society. People are hurting, people are angry, and people need the Light of Christ to show them the way back to God.

Voices from the Street

Choosing Sides

As one of three remaining kids, I feigned disinterest at the pending humiliation of being picked last. The captain—maybe three years my senior—looked us over skeptically and, gesturing to the kid next to me, declared, "We'll take him . . . and you can have the last two." That was it. The low point of my athletic career. I was not just a lesser competitor—my co-loser and I were more valuable to that captain as opponents. I do not recall if we won. I cannot even remember whether it was baseball or kickball that day, but I will never forget that moment and the accompanying feeling of humiliation. To be sure, I was grounded enough that I did not allow it to define anything about my self-worth, but I recognized that Captain Kid did not care about me because he had no use for me (I simply thought of him as a "jerk"). I was embarrassed, and I knew that I did not want to treat others that way.

Sports can be understood as a subcategory of play—unnecessary in terms of basic survival, but on another level, contributing to human flourishing in ways that are difficult to define. From a Christian perspective, sports should never be allowed to justify—let alone foster—sinful attitudes and behavior. The New Testament command to "love one another" is central to biblical teaching, and this, along with the fruit of the Spirit, should be part of any Christian's ethic as he or she participates in sports.

As anyone who has participated on any level understands, sports can be a seedbed for some of the attitudes that the Apostle Paul labels, the "desires of the flesh," such as "enmity, strife, jealousy, fits of anger, rivalries, dissensions, divisions, envy" (Galatians 5:20-21 ESV). Paul contrasts this list with what he calls the "fruit of the Spirit," which includes "love, joy, peace, patience, kindness, goodness, faithfulness, gentleness, self-control" (Galatians 5:22-23 ESV).

It is difficult to see how contemporary sports can be more conducive to the former list that the latter. One might say that many a game conceived in the spirit of good intentions has quickly given birth to the desires of the flesh—as sadly evidenced by the notorious behavior of some overzealous parents at kids' sports in recent years.

The New Testament makes clear that the genuineness or our faith in Christ is expressed through our transformed relationships within our social structures. One is to love God and love others by denying oneself and regarding others as more important. If lived out, this ethic would transform many organizational and social structures (including not a few churches), and certainly could redeem sports to their proper place in human experience.

One of the most common laments I hear from college athletes is how the pressure to perform in order to win—to earn playing time or just to keep their scholarship—has taken the fun out of their sport. This highlights the most fundamental question in the definition and expression of sport: is sport and end in itself, or is it a means to another end?

At the two extremes of the continuum might be a child jumping rope and singing along for the sheer joy of doing it or it could be a professional quarterback trying to prove he is worth his multimillion-dollar contract by winning the Super Bowl. One could say that the girl is playing, while the quarterback is working, but there is a mix of the two that can be difficult to discern.

After growing bored with skipping, the girl might add interest by counting the numbers of skips she can do without missing. Later, her brother may join her in a contest to see who can skip the most times. She may join a jump-roping club that introduces rules and organizational principles, and soon be traveling the country, to increasingly challenging competitions—until she gets burned out and quits, because it is no longer fun. This kind of scenario plays out in children's lives all around the country. With the addition of rules, organization and competition, the risk of undermining the intrinsic value of sports increases.

The well-being of participants (including how they interact with teammates and opponents) is a powerful part of the potential positive or negative value of sports. Since most sports involve teams, the social dynamic usually plays a significant—if not dominating—role in the experience for participants. The dynamics of relationships formed within a sporting context can transfer beyond the field of play, for both good or ill, and a Christian can and should seek to be salt and light for his or her team (Matthew 5:13-14). This means helping shape culture to be one that shows respect for teammates, coaches and opponents, and models the effort and attitude of a grateful, joyful servant of Christ.

A couple of years after my athletic low point of being an "unchosen one," I was selected to be one of four team captains for one of my sixth-grade volleyball teams for our physical education program, to compete in a tournament over the following month. I was tasked with drafting my team from a list of classmates in a meeting with the other captains. There was a competitive spirit that bordered on brutality as the other captains expressed value or distain for certain students based on their athletic abilities—with one small and clumsy girl taking the brunt of the ire—but I was determined not to allow someone else to experience the humiliation that I had gone through, so I drafted her on my team, along with her best friend.

In the end, my efforts were rewarded with success. The girl had a wonderful experience playing on our team, as she learned and laughed and grew as a valued team member. Not only did I have the satisfaction of pleasing the Lord in that instance, but I felt a sense of secondary vindication as well. We never lost a single game.

Choosing sides mean not only the selection of teammates in the context of play and competition. It means choosing to protect the purity of sports by not allowing ulterior motives to hijack the game for fleshly purposes. And, as the intensity of playing and level of performance increases, the role of the Christian participant is to constantly remember the balance of God's priorities, even as one strives to play with a joyful self-forgetfulness. Choosing sides means employing grace to play with a grateful heart and with a spirit of celebration as a member of God's created order.

In a sinful world, it is only through the grace of God that we can admit the realities of pain and suffering, while shrugging it off and playing joyfully. As humans, we can handle neither the one nor the other extreme, but through the reconciliation made through Christ's sacrifice, we are free to rest in his righteousness, excuse ourselves from the burden of fixing all that is wrong in the world and joyfully play.

Dr. Bill Pubols
Director, Biblical Studies Center
Boise, Idaho

Contributed by Dr. Bill Pubols. © Kendall Hunt Publishing Company

 Check out the Chapter 8 video at this link: https://www.grtep.com/

Vocabulary

Absolute Poverty	The Elderly	Social Access
Activity Theory	Elderly Employment	Social Inequality
Ageism	Ethics of Sports	Social Mobility
Age Discrimination	Living by the Flesh	Social Stratification
Benefits of Aging	Living by the Spirit	Split Labor Market
Caste System	Future Earnings	Theology of Sports
Choosing Sides	Gerontology	Underclass
Christ's Ambassadors	Global Slavery Index	Unity in Christ
Class Rift	Lower Class	Upper Class
Class System	Middle Class	Value of Sports
Dehumanization	Myths of Aging	Youth Culture
Denominationalism	Puritan Work Ethic	
Disengagement Theory	Slavery	

CHAPTER NINE: Gender

The Basics

One of the most important facets of socialization concerns *gender*, a common reality or experience for all human beings. One's gender is not the same thing as one's *sex*, although there is evidence of traits and behaviors tied to natural biology. *Sex* refers to the biological differences between males and females; *gender* refers to the social and cultural assumptions and significances attached to these biological differences of *sex*. For instance, questions on whether men should be allowed to be nurses or preschool teachers, or if women should be allowed to be firefighters or fight alongside men in the military, have arisen in the past. The answers to the aforementioned matters rest mostly upon the natural resources that men and women possess (both intellectually and physically) and upon individual rights for equal opportunities in society.

Since the colonization of the New World and the later founding of the United States of America, huge assumptions have existed regarding gender roles in American society—for both men and women. Expectations and parameters have been proffered by all generations regarding the proper activities, behavior, attitudes, wardrobe, and so on, of men and women to abide by in society; however, many gender roles are not static. Not surprisingly, it seems with every generation that there is a cultural redefining of what people should be doing (or not).

Of course, men and women can (and do) share much of the same activities in life. Men can cook, women can be pilots, men can be nurturers, and women can be protectors even though sexual traits such as physical strength and emotional awareness frequently lead to normative social assignments. One could argue that although men and women can do most of the same activities, they have "go-to" areas where their sex and physiology make them better suited to perform the tasks associated with particular activities (Goldman, 2017, online).

For instance, one rarely sees a female worker at a building site; most construction workers are men because physical prowess and endurance are needed for that job (according to the U.S. Bureau of Labor Statistics, less than 10% of construction workers are women); alternatively, more women are involved in daycare and nursery programs because of the deep and personal nurturing skills required to meet infant and children's emotional needs (according to the U.S. Bureau of Labor Statistics, 93.8% of daycare workers are women).

This can lead to stereotyping or restricting people according to preconceived notions of their sex limitations or abilities—rather than being meritoriously egalitarian at an individual level. Thus, *sex typing* is a common cultural reality for both men and women across the globe, with an association of some activities being "female" and others "male." Still, interculturally and internationally, *sex typing* for many activities is more fluid than static, although greater prestige is still given to "male activities" (Miller, 2017, online).

This relates to *gender stratification*, which is the presumption than men and women have unequal access to power, prestige, and property on the basis of their sex. A big item of debate is the gender wage gap, with men making more money in their jobs than women. This has been blamed on unfair pay practices and a conspiracy to oppress women; however, according to Danielle Paquette (2016), "Since 2003, when government researchers started collecting the data, men have reported devoting more life to paid labor than their female counterparts. In 2015, employed men recorded working an average 42 minutes per day longer than employed women. Women, meanwhile, said they spent more time on housework: 2.6 hours, compared to the men's 2.1 hours" (online). Typically, the presumption is social abuse from men to women; however, in postmodernity, with many societies shifting from a patriarchal to matriarchal culture, social problems can be more about social choices than mere social injustice.

In America, many men choose the trades over upper management jobs, formerly a male-centered area, with women filling up the ranks instead. Even further, there are many other vocational fields in America and across the globe, where sex and gender are irrelevant to one's job performance and personal resources and abilities are more important to vocational functionality and success. There has been a huge sociological shift regarding the genders and work opportunities since the Victorian Era (1837–1901).

Traditionally, *gender-role socialization* is predominantly fashioned and formed from within the family, with other important influences coming from friends, schools, church, and mass media. Parents, however, are their children's main and most important teachers regarding social parameters and etiquette. They teach the children what it means to be a man or woman, a father or mother, a son or daughter, and what children can expect (or hope) to do in greater society. They provide both rewards and sanctions for following or deviating from traditional or religious norms, with greater or lesser objectivity, at times.

In the past, females have felt an obligation to be more passive and restrained in social settings and opinions. Many people (feminists and egalitarians, alike) have suggested a social conspiracy at work to oppress women, with women being portrayed on television, the movies, and books as being helpless, passive, incompetent, and always needful of male protection. The 19th century popular *cult of true womanhood* portrayed just this notion with the "ideal woman" being morally superior, pious, pure, domestic, and submissive. Not surprisingly, many women objected to this two-dimensional summary of womanhood, and they became more involved in public politics (such as the Abolitionist Movement). Before and during the Civil War, women like Maria Stewart (1803–1879), Maria Chapman (1806–1885), and Prudence Crandall (1803–1890) circulated anti-slavery petitions and pamphlets, organized boycotts of slavery-made products, ran fundraisers, supported or taught in schools for Black children, and so on.

This activism in the public sphere led to many other freedoms and rights for women in America, including legally gaining personal control over their earnings and inheritances, the establishment of more equitable divorce laws, laxer clothing standards and city ordinances, legally being able to decide whom they wanted to marry, and deciding if they wanted to be a mother (before their pregnancy). It also helped women win the right to vote in U.S. elections (also called *women's suffrage*, which was enacted in the *19th Amendment* in 1920), due much to the sustained efforts of women such as Susan B. Anthony (1847–1919), Elizabeth Stanton (1815–1902), Lucretia Mott (1793–1880), Esther Morris (1814–1902), Anna Howard Shaw (1847–1919), and Sojourner Truth (1797–1883).

The reality of gender socialization for men and women is far more complex and more contextual than most people realize. In demonstration, one of my favorite activities and assignments in my residential Intro to Sociology class is to show them the blockbuster movie,

"Wonder Woman" (Roven, 2017) after several weeks of study. We watch the entire movie, stopping occasionally for them to discuss the sociological significance of the scenes that they are viewing. Finally, I then have them write a paper on the movie's sociological elements and their overall response to the movie. The students' views speak to both the sociological agenda of the movie and the students' own gender/sex socialization received up until college.

In *Wonder Woman*, it is clear that "Sex vs. Gender" is a major factor that the producers wish to explore throughout the movie. The script often brings up questions regarding biological differences between men and women (traits, behavior tied to natural human biology), but they often push back against gender assumptions and the cultural significances attached to biological differences between the sexes. For instance, typically men are the protectors, but Wonder Woman frequently takes on that role, physically.

Wonder Woman both affirms and challenges historical and cultural understandings of *gender stratification*, where men and women have unequal access to power, prestige, and property on the basis of their sex on the Island of Themyscira (women in charge), in England (men in charge), and in Europe (men in charge). So, it acknowledges that men have been the main rulers and warriors, historically; however, the behavior and history of the Amazons on the Island of Themyscira suggests that life does not necessarily have to embrace the typical patriarchal pattern. Also, it shows that a dark side can also exist in matriarchal cultures, too.

One of the clearer sociological discussions throughout the movie concerned *sex typing*. Time and time again, Diana violated the typical norms for women and "male activities." Although her compatriots tried to get her to assimilate into modern culture as Steve's "secretary," Diana would pragmatically perform some duty or activity normally associated with (or set aside for) men. For instance, she often spearheaded the battles instead of taking on a supportive role. It was interesting to see her try to "doll up" in a dress at the German High Command party; especially considering her desire to kill Ludendorff at the party, that form of feminization seemed incongruous.

Another dramatic discussion concerned the *gender-role socialization* of Diana while on the Island of Themyscira. Her mother was keen on protecting Diana from becoming a woman warrior like the rest of the Amazons. In fact, she received shame from her mom for trying to learn warrior skills rather than remaining a passive princess—aligning with a traditional gender-role pattern in greater humanity. As such, the movie portrayed Diana's mom as caring but an obstacle to Diana's true destiny and potential in life (which can be expounded to all men and women who try to pigeonhole their daughters to more delicate lifestyles).

Regarding *gender differences*, Wonder Woman showed both strong aggression (her ferocious military prowess in all battles) and nurturing characteristics (her maternal response to the baby in England). Mostly though, Diana is shown to be quite aggressive and not very tender; she comes across as somewhat asexual or androgynous, which was probably the intent of the director/writer for marketing (and gender politics) reasons.

Finally, regarding the movie's presentation and discussion of "leadership," *Wonder Woman* seems to suggest a more complementarian notion of leadership with both men and women doing what they need to do, pragmatically, because of personal resources. In some ways, Diana could be seen to be the instrumental leader as she sweeps victoriously through military task after task, focusing on the goal of defeating the evil forces and schemes of Ares. In other ways, Steve seems like the expressive leader who inspires both Diana and his cadre of friends in their mission to stop the nefarious plans of Ludendorff and Doctor Poison.

In the end, the movie displays both men and women at their best and at their worst. Diana's triumph over the hateful Ares comes not from her physical strength, but from the power of her love for Steve and humanity; Steve's triumph over Nazi evil and terrorism is the direct result of his bravery and self-sacrificial actions for Diana and his friends. Feminists may dislike this ending because it affirms traditional ideas about common female and male characteristics; yet, the emotional power of women is to be lauded, as is the logical power of men.

Speaking of men, they also receive active socialization from parents, schools, friends, and the mass media. They have felt just as much social pressure as women to conform to an unrealistic male archetype who excels in sports, can remain perfectly objective in stressful moments, and whose main identity is wrapped in what he does, vocationally. Men also face similar castigation if they try to enter "female" jobs like being a nurse, a preschool worker, or a ballet star. In many ways, they are supposed to be a man of steel with a giant, tender heart of gold.

In fact, one of the best examples of what men face regarding social expectations of masculinity is delivered by Andie MacDowell (Rita) to Bill Murray (Phil) in Ground Hog Day (Colombia Pictures, 1993):

Phil: "What are you looking for? Who is your perfect guy?"
Rita: "Well first of all, he's too humble to know he's perfect."
Phil: "That's me."
Rita: "He's intelligent, supportive, funny."
Phil: "Intelligent, supportive, funny. Me, me, me."
Rita: "He's got a good body, but he doesn't have to look in the mirror every two minutes."

Phil: "I have a great body and sometimes I go months . . . without looking."
Rita: "He's kind, sensitive and gentle. He's not afraid to cry in front of me."
Phil: "This is a man we're talking about, right??"
Rita: "He's like animals and children and he'll change poopy diapers."
Phil: "Does he have to use the word 'poopy'?"
Phil: "I am REALLY close on this one. Really, really close."

For men and for women, gender expectations are tricky to maneuver through—especially when personal agency gets challenged by social convention. Both men and women share a desire for personal empowerment, intellectual fulfillment, and captivating distractions; both men and women face regular and sustained institutional or cultural barriers that may or may not affirm their autonomy or personal wishes; and both men and women have expectations of the other gender that may not seem fair or kind. This is evident in the *feminism movement*, which promotes female social empowerment, and in the *masculinist movement*, which promotes male social empowerment.

Historically, men have been the dominant leaders, socially, but this is not to say that women were not working side by side with the men "in the trenches." Still, few societies existed before modernity where women, as a group, had the decision-making power over men. There are many potential reasons for this reality, the main one being men's natural dominance when it comes to strength and aggression—although that could also lead to *toxic masculinity*, an idea that is being challenged for being more politically driven than scientifically accurate (Salter, 2019, online).

Biologically, the hormone *testosterone* is significant in social interactions and provides biological predispositions different than for women whose main hormone is *estrogen*—an equally important substance in the human body. Additionally, because of estrogen (and other important pregnancy hormones), women are the only ones who can become pregnant, with which comes enormous opportunities and limitations. Although men in Western society are more engaged with their children's day-to-day rearing than before in history, women are still the primary child caretakers, with men focusing more on other social aspects such as protection and supply.

Ultimately, as mentioned earlier, men and women can and do many of the same activities, and often cultural restrictions are confused with biological restrictions. Still, there are common "go-to" areas of social life associated with men and women's biology and/or gender. Few people would argue that men are better with babies than women, in general; nor would people argue that women are better construction workers than women, in general—because of male/female natural abilities.

A meritoriously egalitarian or complementarian approach to family leadership, though, begins and exists in respect and appreciation for both the husband and the wife, knowing that each person has different personal resources that can be utilized to make life better for the whole family. Additionally, most families have one parent or the other typically being the *instrumental leader*, the person who bears responsibility for the completion of tasks, focuses on distant goals, and manages family relationships with social groups and social institutions. Either parent can also be the *expressive leader*, the person in the family who bears responsibility for the maintenance of familial harmony and emotional stability. Furthermore, parents often trade positions of leadership for various reasons and at various times for practical purposes.

Gender and biological sex are fascinating social realities that everyone on earth has, does, and will have to contend with in life. The important concept to remember is that differences do not necessarily indicate weaknesses or inferiority. In other words, anyone who has ever broken a bone comes to realize just how crucial that bone was to function properly and efficiently in life—be it a rib, a thumb, a hip, or the pinkie-toe.

Each sex, each gender is important; each sex, each gender is socially influential; each sex, each gender opens and closes some social doors; and each sex, each gender needs to be honored for the gifts to humanity that they bestow. As John Gray, the author of *Men are from Mars, women are from Venus* (1992), concludes, "When men and women are able to respect and accept their differences, then love has a chance to blossom" (p. 7). Thus, appreciation and understanding—and not animosity and dismissal—need to be foremost in any application of sociological theory or thought regarding the sexes.

Sociology from Above

Three Influential Female Theologians of the Medieval Church

Despite recent propositions within the academy that authentic feminine theology is a postmodern invention, many ancient writings exist demonstrating that women frequently played an important role in both defining and promoting theology (and praxis) within the church and in greater society. Three key women within the monastic movement—Mechthild of Magdeburg (1210-1282 CE), Catherine of Siena (1347-1380 CE), and Julian of Norwich (1342-1416 CE)—made their mark in expressing what it means to follow Jesus Christ in Western society.

In the thirteenth century, Mechthild of Magdeburg, a Beguine in Germany, through her poetic prose and pious lifestyle, enlightened her readers regarding the relationship of God and the soul. In the fourteenth century, Catherine of Siena, a Dominican tertiary nun, presented an intelligent analysis of the ideal of perfection in man (in God) and tried to enkindle the Holy See of Peter returned to Rome—its original (and rightful) establishment. During that same time, Julian of Norwich, an English anchoress in her tiny cell, offered an alternative perspective on the persona of God by focusing on His motherly aspects. Roberts (2009) points out, "The women are holy because they are humble, and their humility authorizes them to speak. The consistent marriage of contemplation, humility rhetoric, and medieval women's spiritual authority suggests lessons for contemporary women" (p. 53).

Mechthild of Magdeburg's writings, such as "The Flowing Light of Divinity," stir the soulful fires by pointing to the loss of humanity and the even more important gain of God's loving relationship. The sympathetic reader cannot help but be touched by the gifts of God's love despite what is left behind by the relationship. Mechthild's words put into perspective that although worldly things like the vanity of youth, the enabling of family ties, wealth, worldly honor are important, a relationship with the Creator is priceless. God's love is invaluable because of its sustaining and nurturing powers. She states, "Dear love of God, always embrace this soul of mine. For it pains me above all things When I am separated from you . . . you sweeten both suffering and need; you teach and console the true children of God." Moreover, Mechthild's poetry demonstrates that to her, all the worldly treasures of life are meaningless compared to God's love.

Catherine of Siena, in writings such as "The Dialog of Catherine of Siena," focused on what perfection meant to humanity regarding one's relationship with God. For her, union with the perfect deity is achieved through "infinite love and infinite grief." Humanity must first acknowledge its trespasses against God and its fellowmen and then God through his perfect love will attribute to them "infinite merit" and salvation—this is the perfect way. However, Catherine points to the fact that "spiritual self-love" is the way of imperfection and the devil.

Thus, perfection is a matter of obedience—obedience to love God and all people with integrity and truthfulness. It is an admittance of humanity's failings and God's perfect loving power. As Muto (2014) suggests,

> In summary, Catherine's teaching, seen through the lens of form reception, involves a deepening awareness of our being created in God's image and likeness; we discover God's presence in ourselves and ours in God. The more we come to know ourselves, the more we realize that our selfish sensuality has disfigured the reflection of the Divine Beauty in our souls. This discovery, painful as it may be, motivates us to grow over a lifetime in union with God (p. 244).

Julian of Norwich also offered a unique and useful theological approach to Christianity. Her writings, such as "Revelations of Divine Love" (also known as "The Short Text") and "The Long Text," added depth and nuance to the understanding of God in the patriarchal culture of fourteenth-century England.

Previously, God was expressed mainly through masculine terms, but Julian's approach showed that God has a softer, gentler side that can be attributed to his "mothering" nature. She begins by pointing out that "God is the Creator and the lover and the protector." Through the Trinity (and specifically through Jesus Christ), God's motherhood can be appreciated as He is working "in mercy on all His beloved children who are docile and obedient to Him." God the Father created us, but Jesus the Son reforms and restores us much like human natural mothers. As Heffernan (2013) notes, "For Julian, Christ's motherhood is unique for his children remaining enclosed within him, a gestation that lasts into eternity" (p. 53).

All three of these women presented personal poignant analyses of their relationships with God—not only showing their deep devotion and appreciation to their creator and redeemer, but also in discussing the nature of God while often using unmasculine terminology. Too often, the caricature of Medieval Christianity is replete with masculine domination and devoid of any feminine accolades. As Roberts (2009) notes, "Medieval theologians used contemporary science to justify women's subordinate status; and women's range of activity was severely limited to the extent that they were denied education, ordination, and other means of equal participation in culture" (p. 59).

Catherine of Siena, Julian of Norwich, and Mechthild of Magdeburg challenged these social barriers through their lives, their writings, and their ministries. As Bovey (2015) concludes, "It is clear that Medieval women were resilient, resourceful and skilled. Moreover, in exceptional instances, they were capable of exercising political power, learning and creativity outside the domestic sphere" (online).

In an age of male-dominated social systems, these women successfully and persuasively shared their understanding of God regardless of typical cultural gender restrictions. More importantly, unlike the self-serving focus of current postmodern thinking on personal and political empowerment, all three of these exceptional women—Mechthild, Catherine, and Julian—selflessly and single-mindedly sought to fan the flames of pious devotion toward God, Jesus, and the Holy Spirit, which they themselves experienced, firsthand.

Ironically, although abdicating gender rights/comforts so celebrated today in postmodernity, these women's commitment (some might say obsession) to love and speak of God in all his persons, in all his power and expanse, had a profound social influence upon the patriarchal church institution of the Medieval era that transcends into the politicalization of the present.

The Sage from the Stage

Women in the Bible: Voices of Agency

Societies become healthier, vibrant, and more creative when each of its members participates and offers their voices to be heard. Unfortunately, not every voice has been given an equal platform to speak throughout history. In particular, women's voices have been silenced in diverse areas of society and religious institutions. Women could not vote before 1920. Before 1978, a woman could lose her job for conceiving a child. Prior to 1980, there was not a clear description of sexual harassment, contributing to the difficulty of the protection of women in their professions (Cole, 2019, p. 8). Blame is often shifted to the biblical story for these origins, but when one listens closely, a surprising message of the significance and value of women's voices is rightly ascertained.

Being praised for being "meek and mild," religious groups have often contributed to the silencing of women, perpetuating messages that women's voices are not validated and important. Did these messages originate within the biblical narratives? A quick survey will reveal that women have had powerful voices throughout the Bible. In fact, on the eve of major theological and political cruxes, a woman's voice has contributed to a new trajectory in some of the darkest moments in both testaments.

Women in the Bible have powerful voices of agency throughout the Old Testament and New Testament. Immediately in the book of Genesis, the foundation is constructed that women are valued. "So, God created man in his own image, in the image of God he created him; male and female he created them" (Genesis 1:26-28). As image-bearers, the Bible values and supports women. Culturally and historically, women in patriarchal societies have been undervalued and silenced, but the biblical narratives reveal the creative agency and intervention of women as undermining the belief that their voices are not valued. A brief survey will highlight the prominence of these voices.

In the Old Testament, Zipporah, a Midianite woman, powerfully intervenes on the eve of the Exodus (Exodus 4:24-26). Moses had married Zipporah when he was a fugitive in the desert, and during the period of Moses' commissioning by YHWH to lead Israel out of Egypt (Exodus 3:1-21). Upon their return to Egypt, YHWH is angry at Moses. Zipporah responds by circumcising their son. Zipporah's voice and agency arbitrate in a powerful way at this critical juncture before Moses carries out YHWH's divine plans. On the eve of Israel entering the promise land, Rahab, a Canaanite prostitute, saves the Israelite spies from being discovered by the men of Jericho (Joshua 2:1-24). Rahab negotiates through her words and actions, risking her life. Ultimately, the Israelite spies and Rahab's entire family are saved through her agency.

A final example reveals the formidable moment of a risk at night that inaugurated the lineage of kings. Ruth, a Moabite widow, asks for redemption and marriage (Ruth 3). This is the only example in the Old Testament that highlights a request for an individual to fulfill the role of redeemer and a marriage. Boaz will respond positively to Ruth. In a place of emptiness, this woman will alter the trajectory of her life and her mother-in-law, Naomi. This story, which begins with death and hopelessness, will end in a genealogy of royalty.

The New Testament reveals several supportive passages of the voices of women. Most notably, the first persons to witness and proclaim the resurrection of Jesus were women. Mary Magdalene announces, "I have seen the Lord!" (John 20:18). Thomas Aquinas described Mary Magdalene as the "Apostle to the Apostles" for her announcement of the resurrected Christ.

After Pentecost, several examples of women reveal their vital voices and leadership roles in the planting of churches and establishment of structure within these new communities of worship. In Romans 16:1, Phoebe is acknowledged as a deacon (*diaknos*) of the church of Cenchrae. Paul uses this same descriptor of himself and others in several passages (1 Corinthians 3:5; 2 Corinthians 6:4; Philippians 1:1). Junia is named as one of the apostles (Romans 16:7) and suffered persecution for her gospel work alongside Paul. Her voice and agency in the labor of the early church were instrumental in proclaiming the gospel in church history. The New Testament examples of women reveal that their voices were instrumental as full participants in the work of the church.

The powerful message of Galatians 3:28-29 illuminates the continued importance of women's voices within the church and society. "In Christ's family there can be no division into Jew and non-Jew, slave and free, male and female. Among us you are all equal. That is, we are all in a common relationship with Jesus Christ. Also, since you are Christ's family, then you are Abraham's famous 'descendant,' heirs according to the covenant promises" (MSG).

This telos of unity crosses borders of gender, ethnicity, and socioeconomic status. All are one in Christ Jesus. If this truth can apply within society and the Church, communities will become healthier, vibrant, and creative. Celebrating diversity and valuing every voice will begin to paint a portrait of the true body of Christ (Revelation 7:9).

Dr. Jennifer M. Matheny
Assistant Professor of Old Testament
Nazarene Theological Seminary

Contributed by Dr. Jennifer M. Matheny. © Kendall Hunt Publishing Company

 Check out the Chapter 9 video at this link: https://www.grtep.com/

Vocabulary

Aggression
Biological Differences
Biological Sex
Complementarianism
Cult of True Womanhood
Deaconship
Egalitarianism
Emotionality
Estrogen
Expressive Leader
Female Role Socialization
Feminist Movement
Gender

Gender Archetypes
Gender Expectations
Gender Stratification
Gender Wage Gap
God the Father
God as Mother
Historical Realities
Image-Bearers of God
Instrumental Leader
Male Domination
Male Role Socialization
Masculinist Movement
Medieval Women

Pregnancy
Protection
Sex Typing
Stereotyping
Telos of Unity
Testosterone
The Victorian Era
Women in the Bible
Women in Monasticism
Women's Suffrage
Women's Voices
19th Amendment

CHAPTER TEN: Race and Ethnicity

The Basics

Regarding race and ethnicity, I have taught U.S. History to Chinese nationals in summers long past. In my lectures, I made sure to focus on our common humanity and the class was geared to foster my goal of racial and ethnic respect. I firmly believe that people have more things in common than they know. Interestingly, when I mentioned this notion in class one term, a student said that he disagreed with me, and then went on to say how Chinese people are better than Americans; however, another Chinese student in the class quickly challenged his views and she reiterated our similar human traits.

Sadly, many people (internationally) choose to ignore sociological evidence fairly presented to them. Instead, they choose to believe what they want to believe—most likely because they feel threatened or have been culturally programmed to resist egalitarian notions. I actually wonder if some people in American society would have labeled me a traitor because of my "citizen-of-the-world" approach and thereafter shunned me. That notwithstanding, as Witt (2009) remarks, "Sociologists seek to understand and explain why prejudice and discrimination develop and persist and what might be done to address them" (p. 300).

Racial and ethnic differences have been part of the human condition since the beginnings of time. Be it Cro-Magnon man, Neanderthals, Denisovans, or modern humans, all racial formations are the product of a bio-socio-historical process in which categories are created, established, inhibited, transformed, and destroyed. Thus, although current racial types include the Asian, African, Caucasian, and Indigenous peoples of the world, the racial mixture was quite dissimilar thousands of years ago.

According to the U.S. Office of Management and Budget (1997), America's population is made up of the following *racial groups*: American Indian (or Alaska Native) Asian, Black (or African American), Caucasian (or White), and Pacific Islander (or Native Hawaiian). There are other ethnic categories such as Hispanic or Latino, which include people of Central or South America or any other Spanish culture or origin (online).

Within the countries of the world, people in these categories fall into either the majority or minority categories. *Majority groups* may be larger in population, but more importantly, they dominate societies in regard to cultural standards, political control, and economic stability. *Minority groups* are those whose members have less control or power over their own lives than people within the dominate group. The terms, majority and minority, refer not as much about population size, though, as about political power and access to resources.

As a subset, *racial groups* exist that are set apart because of physical differences that have taken on social significance within the culture over time. *Ethnic groups* are set apart because of national origins or distinctive cultural patterns. Historically, all races have received fear responses from another people group because of an unusual appearance—an otherness that is perceived as threat, and presumptions that looking different can and should be equated with being "uncivilized."

Much of this assumption of inferiority and/or threat is based on projection, transference, and political posturing. This can lead to negative attitudes and responses to people of other races including stereotypes, prejudice, discrimination, and racism. *Racism* is the fallacious belief that all members of each race possess characteristics or abilities specific to that people-group so as to distinguish it as superior or inferior to another race.

Thus, some racist accusations have been made over the centuries that are not backed up with any scientific evidence or research. The following aphorisms can be considered to be myths based upon irrational perceptions:

"American Indians are the most environmentally friendly."
"Asians are the best at math."
"Black men are naturally the best athletes."
"Jewish people are the shrewdest with money."
"White men are automatically born privileged."
"Hispanics cannot rule themselves well."
"Middle Eastern people are all unreasonable."

None of these statements can be considered scientifically true or valid. They are opinions based on limited perspectives and personal opinions. Much of this comes from *stereotypes*, which are widely held but fixed and oversimplified ideas or images of a particular racial or ethnic group or person. For example, all American women are not vain, not all gay men dress well, and not all Italian women are feisty or fierce. These are just shallow accusations that have been used, historically, to justify political attacks, defend against shifts in cultural power, or just because of personal character flaws and/or neuroses.

Nevertheless, attitudes like those earlier can lead to prejudice and discrimination. *Prejudice* is the negative attitude toward an entire category of people for irrational reasons (and not a reasonable, fair judgment). Prejudice can be individual or communal, and not necessarily acted out despite having the opinion. *Discrimination* is the denial of social opportunities and equal rights to individuals and groups because of prejudice, bigotry, or other arbitrary reasons. Discrimination typically starts with petty, greedy, and self-serving assumptions and ends with unfair, mean, and destructive behaviors and judgments.

Racial bias is not limited to or concentrated with one racial group. Historically, all racial groups have employed bias, bigotry, and discrimination against other groups within and outside their societies. Still, no one likes to receive or perceive negative treatment regarding their race, gender, and economic backgrounds, which appears to close or restrict the professional doors more open to their (majority) counterparts (Glenn, 2012, pp. 133–134).

Sometimes, this is more of a pretentious attitude, as with *ethnocentrism*, which conveys the message that "our culture is better than your culture." While this can be true (cannibalism, female circumcision, and infant sacrifice are hard to defend, culturally), most of the time, it is the result of cultural myopia and obtuse reasonings.

Other forms of racial bias are more apparent and socially damaging such as racial profiling, institutional discrimination, and hate crimes. *Racial profiling* occurs when a person in authority presumes assumption of guilt or evil solely because of a person's personal appearance (while ignoring clear evidence or observational realities). *Institutional discrimination* has occurred often throughout history, with a systematic denial of opportunities of normal social benefits or operations because of one's race or ethnicity. Perhaps the worst concerns *hate crimes*, which combine bigotry with violence, typically because of a person's race, religion, gender, or socioeconomic class.

Sociologists have noted six general patterns of intergroup relations when racial or ethnic tensions are high within a society or between cultures. Regarding negative responses, *segregation* is employed, which is the physical separation of groups in terms of residence, workplace, or social events. *Expulsion* sometimes happens, which is the forced removal of a hated people group in society. The worst is *genocide*, which is the deliberate, systematic killing of entire people or nation.

Critical Race Theory attempts to address this social issue through the advancement of social justice and cultural awareness in the public forum and in governmental policies at the city, state, and federal level. It examines the intersections of people (particularly those affecting and involving minorities) regarding race, ethnicity, gender, and sexual orientation. It seeks to understand the social forces at play that benefit or hinder traditionally oppressed social groups. It approaches the problem solely from the perspective of the minority—regardless of counter-evidence from the majority perspective. Additionally, it focuses on how mass media has influenced the popular perception of minorities in the past (leading to unequal distribution of social and economic power), and how it can be utilized to socially engineer a more equitable or politically advantageous position for minorities.

Concerning positive responses to intergroup relations, an *amalgamation* often occurs, which is the combining of a majority or minority group to form a whole new group. At the individual level, *assimilation* is quite common, when a person forsakes his or her own culture to become part of another one. Last, *pluralism* can occur, which had been a hallmark of American society up until the last decade, which previously aided racial and ethnic relations through mutual respect for another's culture despite significant philosophical differences.

Speaking of differences, within the American population, while Whites make up 72.4% of the American population, several minority groups stand out. The Latinos (or Hispanics) is the largest minority group in United States (16.3%), with 43.2 million people claiming Latino ethnicity (from both legal and illegal immigration). Few people realize that America is one of the largest Spanish-speaking nations in the world. It is not a race but an ethnic group with origin roots in Mexico, Puerto Rico, Cuba, the Dominican Republic, and Central and South America. Many refer to Mexican Americans as *Chicanos*, which carries with it both positive and negative associations.

The second largest minority group is that of Blacks or African Americans. Although most Black people live in the American South, other centers of Black population include the Chicago area and the central Eastern seaboard. In 2010, Blacks made up 42 million people in the United States (13.6%). Despite experiencing huge civil rights gains since the 1960s, Blacks still lag behind in political power, economic prosperity, and personal education although those trends are shifting. In 2008, some 3.2 million Blacks were enrolled in college, and 80% of African Americans had high school diplomas.

Asian Americans may be the fastest growing minority group in the United States, making up 4.8% of American society. Their origins are from China, Japan, Korea, and Vietnam (among others). They have the highest incomes, and they have experienced a more stable family life regarding divorce and two-parent families than any other minority group.

Native American Indians make up the smallest minority group at 1% (besides Pacific Islanders at 0.2%). Called the "invisible minority," they have the highest educational dropout rate of any minority group, as well as cultural issues with alcoholism and suicide. There is no clear consensus on how many Native Americans (also called First Nations People) were in America when the colonists arrived. Based on cursory evidence, their population could have been as high as 1.5 million, but by 1776, that number had dropped to 200,000 because of disease and warfare. They do have the largest number of dialects with over 500 tribes.

To combat against what is perceived as minority oppression, political progressive activists have pushed for affirmative action programs to be implemented in educational institutions, federal organizations, and big businesses. *Affirmative action* is the policy favoring people groups who tend to suffer from discrimination especially in relation to employment or education. Also called by some, positive discrimination, it is a controversial and somewhat philosophically contradictory program that calls for artificially selecting some people groups over others in society because it was wrong for the majorities to select some people groups over others in society for jobs and appointments, regardless of personal qualifications.

Affirmative action is also sometimes connected to the *glass ceiling*, which is the presumption that the minorities (including women) encounter a behind-the-scenes cultural barrier blocking their promotions of qualified people in a work environment based on their gender, race, or ethnicity. Although there is some historical evidence to back up the glass ceiling theory, current studies suggest more nuanced, gender-specific reasons for salary differences and hiring practices, which is covered in Chapter 9.

Wagley and Harris (1958) called out several key responses to minorities that have been observed, sociologically. Minorities have been the targets of unequal treatment by the dominant group, which is discrimination. They are demeaned because of some physical or cultural trait of low regard by the dominant group, causing prejudice. The minority groups find group solidarity because of their physical or cultural traits. They usually marry within their own people group (endogamy) finding cultural resistance to intermarriage with the majority group (racism). Finally, they experience a form of a caste system being born with an ascribed status connected to their race or ethnicity.

Many people in America are unaware as to the extent that their race opens or closes social opportunities to them. Moreover, many have never personally experienced institutional discrimination or overt racism (although most have observed ethnocentrism—ever been to a sports event?). The question remains on how people can actually overcome racism and prejudice.

Sociological studies have shown that the best way to end racism and prejudice is to bring divergent racial groups together. Dialoguing often breaks down the walls, soothes fears, and generates utilitarian brotherhood and an awareness of our shared humanity. Education also reduces stereotypes and bigotry, bringing mysterious culturalism into context and connection.

Considering how "small" our world is becoming (check out Chapter 13 for more information on globalism), fostering better personal relations, compassion, and brother/sisterhood between the races and countries seems like the wisest and most beneficial of paths to take for all people on our beautiful planet.

Sociology from Above

Slavery, Politics, and Hermeneutical Dilemmas

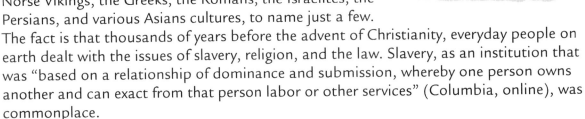

For centuries, the existence of slavery has been a reality to countless countries and cultures. Evidence of slavery exists in the ancient history of Native American Indians, the Norse Vikings, the Greeks, the Romans, the Israelites, the Persians, and various Asians cultures, to name just a few. The fact is that thousands of years before the advent of Christianity, everyday people on earth dealt with the issues of slavery, religion, and the law. Slavery, as an institution that was "based on a relationship of dominance and submission, whereby one person owns another and can exact from that person labor or other services" (Columbia, online), was commonplace.

This often led to the creation of rules and regulations on the management of slavery; often, though, slavery was legally prohibited as an immoral practice. As history and cultures progressed along, a growing dichotomy of thought developed on this issue and many countries began to question the validity of slavery in civilized society. This was especially true of Christianized countries that sought to incorporate ethical, intellectual, and moral excellence into their lives.

In the 17th and 18th centuries, a variety of hermeneutical practices were used to examine what the Bible had to say on slavery. The Deists in America and England used historical-critical methods to study the Bible and declared that "the Bible was internally inconsistent as well as intrinsically unbelievable in places" (Harrill, 2000, p. 149). Later on, the Unitarians took a systematic approach, raising questions about "biblical literalism" (p. 149). Furthermore, American literary studies began "moving toward a critical hermeneutics . . . that not only aimed at recovery of the author's intended meaning as a norm for validating conflicted readings of a text but also aimed to complete and develop what the author had only sketched and suggested" (p. 150). These factors, though well-intentioned, only confused the debate.

Politically, in the 19th century, English parliament member William Wilberforce advocated for the abolition of slavery in England and succeeded in 1806. Later in that same century, the United States of America would take up the battle over slavery and eventually end up in a Civil War wherein the pro-abolition northern states fought against the proslavery southern states. As any American history book will recount, the war was passionate and bloody for each side.

Both the North and the South felt they had a legitimate right to take a stand on the existence of slavery, and both sides used the Bible to support their cause and to disqualify their opponent.

Although ending slavery was initially a side issue for the North in the beginning of the Civil War compared to preserving the Union, with Lincoln's Emancipation Proclamation in 1863, the character of the war changed to one where the North predominantly agreed that "God had thus signaled that the oppressed should go free" (Moorhead, 2000, p. 39). With the President's endorsement and a plenitude of ministers proclaiming the virtues of ending the evil of slavery, the battle became less about military victory and more about moral triumph.

The North read the same Bible that the South did and yet came to dramatically different judgments. They "concluded certain biblical truths were decisively hostile to slavery, no matter what one made of the Bible's specific teaching on slavery." Ministers, theologians, and scholars like Albert Barnes, Theodore Weld, George Bourne, and other important debaters suggested that slavery should be abolished because "(1) slavery reduces human life to property . . . and (2) the cruel and unjust evils of slavery cannot be countenanced as in any way compatible with Christian moral teaching and conduct" (Thompson, 1996, p. 342). These men believed that the South's use of Scripture was unfounded, ill conceived, and improper.

Instead, they suggested that "biblical interpretation must look beyond the flat reading of the text" (Harrill, 2000, p. 153). The truth of Scripture lay deep within the Bible and not superficially as proslavery advocates were promoting. Furthermore, even if the antislavery sentiment in the Bible was subtle, the spirit of Jesus and His mission in the New Testament inevitably led to a cultivation of higher morality as Christianity progressed. The abolitionists "believed that Jesus and the apostles planted the original seed of the gospel in the New Testament, expecting it to grow in secret throughout church history until its flowering in the present, nineteenth-century abolitionist Christianity" (Harrill, 2000, p. 154). To be obedient to God, Jesus, and the Scriptures, the just Christian had to look beyond the words of the Bible to the spirit it embodied. Christianity was about freedom, not slavery.

The South, however, did not agree with the North's interpretation of Scripture. As they examined the Bible and contemplated its examples of the institution of slavery, Southerners saw a different side of the issue. In fact, "With a few notable exceptions, southern ministers believed that preserving slavery was an integral part of their nation's mission" (Moorhead, 2000, p. 39). Ministers and scholars like John Hopkins, Albert Bledsoe, Thorton Stringfellow, Charles Hodge, and George Armstrong held that "the Bible says nothing to condemn slavery as sinful and some of us maintain that the Bible in fact commands slavery" (Swartley, 1983, p. 32). They found, in the institution of slavery, various good and healthy aspects for society and read little, if any, condemnation of slavery in the Bible on its existence.

Instead, they claimed the omission of Jesus, the outspokenness of Paul, and the Old Testament acceptance of this subject, clearly legitimized slavery as a part of good social order. This approach, which was basically an "anti-intellectual argument, straight-forward and simple" (Harrill, 2000, p. 151), took a literal approach to interpretation, relied greatly upon an argument from silence, and dismissed the opposition interpretations as unbiblical, liberal, and biased.

The traditional understanding of slavery was that "God ordained the institution as the most humane means of relating labor to capital, of protecting an inferior race, and of introducing that race to the blessings of Christianity" (Moorhead, 2000, p. 39). To divert from this course was unwarranted and unwise. Thus, they fought a sacred battle to maintain slavery for the good of the nation and for society.

The irony of this conflict was that both sides used the same techniques to examine Scripture and yet, each came out with different conclusions. They both read the Scriptures and ignored the "canonical tension" (Thompson, 1996, p. 344) that clearly existed and instead focused on what would support their position. Their "attempts to move directly from exegesis/interpretation to application, in essence denying the larger hermeneutical issue, almost inevitably produce[d] eisegesis" (p. 349). In other words, they read into the text what they wanted to make of it.

Mark Noll (1992), in *A History of Christianity in the United States of America*, states, "The sectional strife presented a nearly irresistible temptation to express Christianity in terms of a particular region and its principles" (p. 330). The Northern states disliked the notion of slavery and so focused on the antislavery messages in the Bible; the Southern states felt slavery a good institution and so, read differently in the Bible. Either way, both parties engaged in civil religion wherein their particular regional values influenced their religious beliefs. They exploited the Bible to meet their own agendas—the results of which can still be felt today.

The Bible has much to say about slavery, but it neither overtly condemns or approves of it. However, there is a clear message of liberation in the Bible that suggests a grander desire of God in society and for its members. The use of Scriptures in the Civil War demonstrates that reading and interpreting Scripture are dangerous if a holistic approach to the Bible is not taken. The "literalism and moral intuition" that the South and North both used created animosity for biblical interpretation and the Bible in many people's eyes. The rigidity and myopia that the North and the South utilized in their battles over slavery, in a sense, tainted biblical interpretation for a long time. It took biblical hermeneutics out of a religious setting and forced American politics onto it—a risky precedent to take.

In the postmodern world, the institution of slavery is an abominable idea and its presence is still a sad part of human existence, currently (Modern slavery, 2018). Its precepts are anachronistic considering the higher value of human life and culture that exist, presently. Slavery in the past, though, was not as culturally rejected. Though the controversy over slavery in the United States seems absurd considering the modern position of social standing and moral responsibilities, it is important to remember that such modern conveniences were not as available to the participants in this debate. Even on the cross, Jesus pleaded with God, "Father, forgive them, for they know not what they are doing" (Luke 23:34). Likewise, we need to maintain a spirit of compassion and mercy when considering the misdeeds of our forefathers, for they—like we do today—lived in a mirror, dimly lit (1 Corinthians 13:12), and were prone to mistakes.

The Sage from the Stage

A Child of God in Greece and in America

I am a child of Greek refugees. Both of my parents returned back home to Greece in the early 1900s, during exchange of population agreement with the Ottoman Turkish Empire. Both families lived on the Black Sea. My father's family is from the coastal city of Burgas, Bulgaria, and my mother's family is from the coastal region of Samsun, in the Pontus region of Northern Turkey.

Due to the refugee status, education was not a priority. They taught us the basics of reading and math so that we could be able to know enough to work the land that they gave us as farmers. During our time getting established in the village of Sevasti, in Northern Greece (in the valley between Mounts Olympus and Mount Pieria), we experienced two major and destructive military conflicts. WWII and the Civil War that followed, at which time our part of Greece was occupied by Communists leaders under the support and influence of the Soviet Block.

This occupation created many financial, religious, and educational difficulties. My parents wanted a better life and more opportunities for my brother and me. I was passionate about school, and my brother was very gifted and interested in anything technical. So, we started our paper work, and after several difficult and discouraging years, we received our documents to come to the United States. We saw this as a gift from God through the generosity of the people of America. Still, we experienced a time of transition in learning a new language, adjusting to a new culture, and making a new life for us in Boston, Massachusetts.

While at Newton North High School, we were assigned to read Shakespeare's *Macbeth*, and I was devastated. I had a very hard time with regular English, and reading *Macbeth* felt like the end of my education. My teacher did not allow me to only read the *Cliffs Notes on Macbeth*, but she found me a Greek copy. This forced me to learn the discipline of using reference books and dictionaries, which was extremely helpful for the rest of my life. From that time on, I always had a Greek dictionary, an English dictionary, and Greek-English dictionary on my desk and my briefcase. This discipline helped me throughout my academic life—both as a student and now as a professor.

During that same year, I was the only 10th grader who made the varsity soccer team and led our team in scoring. Our stadium was being built and we had to bus to another park for our practices; however, since I was on the varsity team, I either had to be late for practice or skip my last period to be at practice on time. The class was typing, and the teacher was the JV coach, who told me that I should go to practice and not worry about the class. I did, and still got an A in the class. At that time, I thought skipping typing class was great, but I am still suffering from this experience in my career, today.

In Boston, I learned that everyone could be educated, and that everyone could go to college. Also, during my high school years, I discovered that higher grades got students into schools, and that sports could pay the bills. So, I worked hard at both school and soccer, and I was able to get a very good education, graduating without any debt. After high school, I attended schools such as Barrington College, Gordon-Conwell Theological Seminary, Boston College, and did medical research at the Massachusetts General Hospital/Harvard Medical School's Gastrointestinal unit.

Another problematic cultural transition for me concerned shopping. We did not have supermarkets in Greece, so American grocery shopping was a unique experience. During our first year, I remember a time when our family went shopping, and we did some impulse shopping. In one aisle, we saw cans of veggies, fruits, and meats. So, we got several vegetables we liked, some fruits, and some cans with pictures of meat and fish.

Soon thereafter, my mom decided to cook some of the meat, so she chopped the onions, garlic, and other items with it. When she opened the can of meat, it had a very "different" smell. We decided that if the Americans eat this, we should also, so she spiced it up, and served it with salad. It tasted awful. I then decided to get my dictionary and see what we were eating. To our surprise, and with both frustration and laughter, we learned that it was a can of dog food! So, we learned to be more careful and informed before we bought things on the fly.

The most important institution in my adjustment in my new life of a first-generation immigrant was getting involved in the church. I discovered a far different religious experience in the American church. In the local parish, I was welcomed, supported, cared for, and felt loved by the pastors and members. They asked how they can help make our adjustment easier and walked along side me.

This kind of Christian discipleship was a very strong foundation of my spiritual growth. I saw that their love for God, His Word, and love for their neighbor was, and still is, the foundation of the community of faith. The church had very strong Sunday School and adult education programs, as well as excellent biblical preaching, which helped my faith development and love for Scripture. Eventually, I felt God's calling on my life to trust the Bible, to study it, and to spend my life teaching it. Now, I see how that church nurtured and prepared me for my current position of professor of the Bible, and as a missionary to the postmodern American church.

I came from a very poor country to live in the most advanced country in the world. In this transition, I learned that God's Word is true, and His message is transformational. As the Apostle Paul says, we are all equals in the eyes of God; "There is neither Jew or Greek, male or female, slave or free, for we are one in Christ" (Galatians 3:28). And if we seek to know the gifts and calling of God for our lives and follow the doors or windows that He opens for us, we can become His instruments of love and ministry to the world—and God is glorified.

Tim Tsohantaridis
Professor of Biblical Studies
George Fox University

Contributed by Tim Tsohantaridis. © Kendall Hunt Publishing Company

 Check out the Chapter 10 video at this link: https://www.grtep.com/

Vocabulary

Abolitionism	Chicanos	Genocide
Affirmative Action	Civil Religion	Glass Ceiling
African American	Critical Race Theory	Hate Crimes
Amalgamation	Discrimination	Hispanic
Asian	Emotional Projection	Immigration
Assimilation	Endogamy	Institutional Racism
Bias	Ethnic Groups	Invisible Minority
Biblical Community	Ethnocentrism	Latinos
Bigotry	Exogamy	Majority Groups
Bio-socio-historical Process	Expulsion	Minority Groups
Caucasian	Fear Responses	Native Americans

Pacific Islanders
Pluralism
"Positive" Discrimination
Prejudice
Quota Systems
Race

Racial Bias
Racial Groups
Racial Profiling
Racial Types
Racism
Refugees

Segregation
Socio-Economic Class
Solidarity
Stereotypes
White Privilege

CHAPTER ELEVEN: Social Problems

The Basics

To a lesser or greater degree, everyone who has lived on the earth has experienced or observed a social problem in effect sometime during their lives. Some social problems are objectively based and are subsequently experiential and empirical. Other social problems are subjectively based and involved more of an emotional or moral understanding. Regardless, social problems exist in direct opposition to people's worldviews, values, and perspectives of how life should transpire. This reality is universal and timeless.

Awareness of social problems comes from various sources: personal exposure, accounts from friends and acquaintances, the church, news sites, social media, and so on. This recognition does not make people feel at peace; rather, it troubles them deeply. All people seem to have an innate understanding about "how the world should be," and it bothers them to see the world operating otherwise.

C. Wright Mills, wrote, "The more we understand what is happening in the world, the more frustrated we often become, for our knowledge leads to feelings of powerlessness. We feel that we are living in a world in which the citizen has become a mere spectator or forced actor, and that our personal experience is politically useless and our political will a minor illusion" (Mills & Mills, 2000, p. 184).

This is when and where sociologists can help to pinpoint and hopefully alleviate avoidable suffering stemming from the social problem(s). Social conditions are carefully measured, providing relevant and crucial data, and public opinion is then probed to determine general attitudes about the social problem. The social imagination is scientifically applied, putting the social problem in context and into proper consideration. Possible social policies are then formulated, suggesting public and private courses of action. Finally, these approaches are scientifically evaluated, with an estimation of social effects accompanying the proposed solutions.

Defining social problems typically starts by determining the cause(s), which can be man-made or biological. In nature, social strife can occur with grand global manifestations such as plagues, pestilence, or disease. Regarding human beings, social problems can be either purposefully or mistakenly created such as a deviation from group values, a decline in the effectiveness of social institutions, or an abuse of political power.

Once a social problem has been identified, four key steps are typically embraced by politicians, activists, and civic/church leaders to find and implement a solution for the issue. First, they comprehend the pressures in play demanding change. The problem gets defined and parameters become set. Leaders then emerge who formulate a plan of action and organize a movement or group to address the problem.

Second, an official response concerning the social problem is offered, mirroring the public concern over the social plight. Third, political accommodations and reprisals are made, which instigates both positive and negative responses from the various factions taking sides over the matter. Finally, the interested parties come together, suggesting alternative strategies to the continuing social problem if not solved.

Historically, two general approaches to dealing with social problems have been utilized. The older mindset (and less accepted in postmodernity) is the *medical model*, which asserts that social problems are linked to bad people or groups. This presumes a universal criterion for health and normality, making all deviances or shortcomings "abnormal or harmful," socially. Thus, social problems occur because of mental deficiency or disorder, a lack of education, or a poor or incomplete socialization.

The *absolutist approach* suggests that a specific condition in society fosters particular social problems. This model presumes a causal or catalytical effect of social relationships and social problems. For instance, one could make the case that unmarried, recreational sex in college leads to higher levels of sexually transmitted diseases within that college community. With this approach, sociologists look for pockets of social disorganization or dysfunction to study and remedy.

More specific theories have been offered over the decades regarding deviance and social problems. In 1938, Robert Merton came up with *social strain theory*. This theory asserted that social deviance occurs when a gap exists between cultural goals and personal achievements. More specifically, four components make up *strain theory*: (a) *innovation*, which occurs when a person accepts cultural goals, but then uses illegal methods to achieve them; (b) *ritualism*, which occurs when a person rejects cultural goals, but then uses legitimate methods to achieve what he or she wants in society; (c) *retreatism*, which occurs when a person rejects cultural goals and legitimate methods altogether; and (d) *rebellion*, when a person rejects cultural goals and legitimate methods, creating new goals and methods, instead.

Another theory was offered by Howard Beckner in 1963 called, *labeling theory*, which proposes that rather than holding a preexisting condition of deviance, being labeled as a "deviant" actually leads to a person being more likely to engage in deviant behavior. Moreover, the *labelers*, the ones calling out other individuals for deviant behaviors (who can be individuals, organizations, or whole social movements), are the moral entrepreneurs of the community or society. For instance, a person, "Joe," might be walking down a school path when he sees a lit cigarette on the ground. Picking it up in curiosity, Joe may be seen by another person who finds smoking a socially dangerous pastime and spreads the word that Joe is a smoker and should be shunned. When Joe is confronted, falsely accused, and publicly belittled, he may begin to smoke in defiance, accepting his new social role, as a deviant "bad boy."

Culture, which was discussed in Chapter 4, also plays a part in defining and determining deviance, as it concerns beliefs, values, norms, sanctions, and social symbols. Beliefs are definitions and explanations about what is assumed to be true. *Values* are social agreements about what is considered to be good/bad behavior and attitudes. *Norms* are socially defined rules of behavior. *Sanctions* are consequences for not conforming to accepted norms. *Symbols* concern the language, gestures, and objects whose meanings are commonly understood by members of a society.

There are many different social constructs concerning social norms although situations involving norms can change according to the varying contexts of any given situation. *Folkways* are the general customs and manners embraced in society. *Mores* are social norms with a moral basis or character. *Laws* are formal norms of behavior backed by police and judicial authorities. These typically originate with various social institutions such as family, church, government, the economy, and the educational system.

Social Problems Examples

History offers much testimony to the social problems of past eras (and over the millennia). Sociologists are not shy, though, in speculating about future social problems that could appear in Western society and other parts of the globe. In postmodernity, however, there are several social problems that are typically focused upon in sociological studies (theoretical and applied).

Prostitution

Often called "the oldest profession," *prostitution* is an oft-investigated social problem quite active all over the globe (including America). Although various types of prostitution exist (call girls, escorts, street walkers, gigolos, fleabag, brothel, child), they all share the same definition: a person (male or female) who engages in normal or deviant sexual intercourse, with no emotional or personal attachment, for a monetary (or other) reward as a regular part of their vocational profession, possibly under the management (or exploitational abuse) of a pimp.

Just how many prostitutes exist, worldwide, is impossible to ascertain (due to the illicit/criminal nature of the activity). A study from the *Fondation Scelles* (2012) indicated that at that time, there were 40–42 million prostitutes worldwide, with one million prostitutes potentially living and working in the United States. Another study from the 1990s suggested there were 25 prostitutes per 100,000 Americans and that a typical prostitute services 690 customers in their lifetime. Still, due to the murky nature of prostitution, valid and reliable data is near impossible to gather, but what is known is that the sex trade is a multibillion-dollar business.

The catalyst for becoming a prostitute can be complex. Men and women may be predisposed to get into the sex business because of a sexual addiction, promiscuous nature, or because of sociopathy. There may be economic factors such as poverty, limited jobs, unwed motherhood, and so on, forcing them into prostitution. They might feel a compulsion to "hook" out of a psychological need for power, control, or attachment. Other forces might be at play including social pressures, media promotion, a family pattern, or a religious obligation (in some parts of the world).

Historically, three main factors tend to be part of the initiation process. First, the person might know another prostitute or pimp who beckons them to try out the profession. Second, the person has experienced younger sexual activity or promiscuity. Third, the person likely grew up in a home environment of poverty, drugs, and emotional or sexual abuse.

This is followed by three subsequent stages: (a) drift, where the person's promiscuity leads to the first prostitution job; (b) transitional deviance, where the person's role ambivalence turns into a normalization or rationalization of the act; and (c) professionalization, where person surrenders to the deviant, sexual service lifestyle (Davis, 1993, pp. 1-14).

Despite the dangers and damages prostitution inflicts upon men, women, and children, there is still some debate as to its merit. Arguing for its existence, some (incorrectly) claim that it is a victimless crime, that regulation of prostitution prevents sexually transmitted diseases, and pregnancies, provides access to social programs that women otherwise would not have, and that it removes social taboo temptations, leading to a decrease in activity. Additionally, some extremists (including some feminists) assert that women should have the right to do whatever they want with their bodies, and prohibiting prostitution is both a violation of their civil rights and a stumbling block to women's financial autonomy and prosperity.

Countering this (and with stronger evidence), the argument against prostitution asserts that it creates more victims, creates more health and crime problems, that it is a gateway to worse illegal activities, that it destroys families, and objectifies and enslaves women and children. Therefore, instead of obtusely affirming the practice, cities should work to provide easier access for rescue homes and shelters for prostitutes seeking to flee the business. There should be an increase of federal, state, and city laws to protect women and prohibit sex trade and trafficking. Additionally, while licensing and regulation should be in place to shield women from harmful environments and physical illness, it would be prudent to help would-be prostitutes escape the social cycle they are caught in through welfare measures for the prostitutes and their families.

Drug and Alcohol Abuse

By definition, *drug and alcohol abuse* concerns the ingestion or injection of any substance that alters bodily function in some way, which when habitualized, hurts the individual, his or her family, or general society in a real and prolonged destructive way. For both, the abuse begins with an irrational, illogical, or unrealistic presupposition about the immediate and long-term consequences of the alcohol or drug usage. The abuse ends with a psychological and/or physiological need for the drug to maintain a sense of well-being or an avoidance of withdrawal symptoms.

Regarding drug abuse, a myriad of drugs is available within the United States including marijuana, benzodiazepines, cocaine, and heroin. People also abuse prescription medicines (the average family has around 30 different drugs in their medicine cabinet or drawer). According to the latest statistics from the 2016 illegal drug report from the Centers for Disease Control and Prevention (CDC), nearly 11% of Americans over the age of 12 have used illicit drugs in the past month and 2.3% have taken nonprescribed psychotherapeutic or physio-corrective drugs in the past month.

According to the CDC, in 1999, some 104,000 people began using *heroin*, one of the most abused and rapidly active opiates, for the first time; of those, 87,000 were 12–25 years old. Since then, there have been at least 80,000 new addicts every year, and 20% of all alcohol and drug-related suicides involved heroin dealers. From 1999 to 2017, in three waves (1990s, 2010, 2013), some 400,000 people have died from opioid overdoses. Not surprisingly, most doctors, researchers, and sociologists consider heroin to be one of the greatest evils in American history.

Alcohol is often played off as an innocuous drink, but although its immediate effects appear unremarkable compared to heroin or cocaine, its long-term effects are equally devastating. The average individual American consumes 2.5 gal. of wine, 32 gal. of beer, and 1.8 gal. of liquor per year. Alcohol acts as a depressant, suppressing the central nervous system, and, with habitual or unmoderated use, can damage brain and other vital organ functions.

Long-term drinking patterns include *social drinkers*, who imbibe occasionally at social events; *heavy drinkers*, who frequently imbibe and are often intoxicated; *acute drinkers*, who plan activities around their drinking and have trouble controlling their personal alcohol consumption; and *chronic drinkers*, who compulsively, secretively, and wantonly imbibe, leading to social dysfunction and physical impairment.

For both drug and alcohol abusers, numerous treatment plans and programs are available, including self-help groups, in-patient/out-patient programs, cognitive behavioral programs, group–family counseling, and addiction medication regiments. These plans and programs have experienced mixed results with very few people stopping their addictions on their own, a larger percentage with minimal help, but for the worst cases of drug or alcohol abuse, sustained and intense addiction therapy is required for any hope of rescue to be achieved.

Crime

Although *crime* is simply the violation of civil authoritative laws that reflect current legal opinions of what is socially acceptable or despicable behavior, its reality is far more complex and socially overarching. The causation, intent, concurrence, and the criminal act itself all carry with them great social significance and obstacles for social functionality and peaceful coexistence. Moreover, the etiology of crime is no small or trivial matter for some crimes are consensus, wherein members of society generally agree about the seriousness of the deviant act; however, other crimes are conflict, where one group passes a law over which there is profound disagreement or that disadvantages a particular social demographic group.

Adding to the complication, what is deviant may not be a crime, fundamentally. Some acts are criminal and deviant, such as killing an elderly defenseless woman, but some acts are

deviant but not criminal, such as a dog wearing a dress or talking loudly during a movie showing. Additionally, some acts are criminal but not necessarily deviant as the vast majority of the public violates the law, regularly, such as speeding in your car or jaywalking across the street.

Somewhere between the social sciences and law studies is criminology, the study of crime. *Criminologists* are concerned with how deviant acts become crimes and vice versa (and so are sociologists). They study when deviant behavior should be outlawed and when formal crimes should be decriminalized. Generally, criminologists are concerned with the impact of law on human behavior and the institution of criminal labels.

Speaking of which, there are numerous official types of crime including predatory or street crime, hate crime, organized crime, cybercrime, white-collar crime, global crime, and so on. Crimes are also classified according to their severity. *Felonies* are more serious offenses, which carry with them longer imprisonment time in a federal prison and with the possibility of capital punishment (execution). *Misdemeanors* are less serious offenses, which carry with them shorter imprisonment time (less than a year) in a local or county jail, and which sometimes give people celebrity status (especially for Hollywood stars, apparently).

People can also get in trouble for *larceny*, which includes *grand theft or petty theft* (depending upon the monetary value of the stolen goods), *burglary* (unlawful entry) and *robbery* (personal theft), *embezzlement or fraud* (stealing company money), *extortion* (a.k.a., "blackmail"), and knowingly receiving stolen property. *White-collar* crime is sometimes part of larceny, but is less publicized than other crimes; however, it is still quite damaging to the company, fellow employees, customers, and the general public.

The more serious of crimes involve the taking of another's life (also called homicide). This can be classified as a *first-degree murder*, which is premeditated killing; *second-degree murder*, which is a non-premeditated, passion-of-the-moment killing; *felony murder*, which is killing someone while committing another felony; *voluntary manslaughter*, which is the intentional killing of a person without malice aforethought; and *involuntary manslaughter*, which is the unintentional killing during a nonfelony crime.

There are several responses to crime carried out by the criminal justice system: the police, the courts, the prisons. Within this system (and sometimes outside of it), there are various responses to crime including *social protection*, which incapacitates and removes the criminal from social interaction; *deterrence*, which is meant to instill enough fear within the criminal that they abandon future deviant acts; *rehabilitation*, which is meant to resocialize and reform the criminal; and *retribution*, which is non-sanctioned vengeance against the criminal (and a crime, in itself). Ultimately, prisons and jails utilize total institutional control over prisoner's lives in order to remove dangerous individuals from society and to deter others from repeating the criminal behavior in the future.

There are alternatives to prison, though, including *shock probation*, which uses shorter prison times and intense therapy sessions to shock the prisoner out of his or her criminal habit.

Additionally, *day treatment and halfway houses* are utilized for many of the nonviolent crimes to help rehabilitate criminals and help them rebuild social networks or find healthier people to associate with in general society. *Restitution* is also sometimes employed to allow the criminal to work off or pay back what they have stolen or taken from others. This provides an opportunity for healing and balance to be regained for both the criminal and the victim. It also creates great social capital for the criminal, perhaps leading to resocialization, empathy, and self-pride that might keep him or her out of trouble in the future.

Illness and Disability

Physical illness and disability have more than just a biological impact upon the people within society. There is a context in meaning of being ill, of being disabled, that is relative to culture. For some, being sick or having a disability brings public disdain or shame in some regions of the world; for others; it brings a sense of pride and/or personal identity. For instance, in many deaf communities, the members resist being thought of as disabled, insisting that nothing is wrong with them—"Don't fix us!" they demand.

In postmodernity, however, becoming ill or disabled is far easier than before in American society. With more leisure time on their hands and with more modern conveniences, people fall prey to maladies such as alcoholism, drug abuse, sexually transmitted diseases, heart disease, diabetes, and so on. Obesity is at an all-time high and is often blamed on poor diets and an inadequate exercise regimen.

Others find themselves in a disabled capacity due to no fault of their own. A *disability* is a physical or mental impairment that substantially limits one or more "normal" major life activities. Disabilities can involve walking, seeing, hearing, speaking, breathing, learning, working, and autonomous living. People with disabilities (PWDs) experience *impairment*, which is the disruption at a system level of bodily organ or physical/mental function; and/ or *handicaps*, which are physical or social environmental obstacles that disadvantage the disabled person.

Besides their physical challenges, PWDs also face unfair cultural stumbling blocks. Several myths are promulgated regarding PWDs that have no basis in reality. First, everyone with severe autism is a bizarre genius. Second, the disabled are merely takers and not givers, being only "useless eaters" in society. Third, disabled people are always powerless and perpetual victims. Fourth, most disabled people should only be pitied and placated. Finally, most disabled people are bitter and argumentative warriors with emotional hang-ups regarding life.

All of these myths are absurd reductionisms and steal away the humanity and social value of PWDs. According to most rehabilitation counselors, all PWDs deserve respect and encouragement, the severity of a person's disability can be increased or reduced by adjusting environmental conditions, coping or adjusting to disability is dependent upon understanding environmental problems, each PWD has their own set of personal resources (to a lesser or greater degree), and the social significance of a disability is influenced by individual feelings about the person's self and social situation (Wright, 1983).

With a growing frequency, there is a mislabeling of normal human functions. In many schools, children are diagnosed as being hyperactive or ADHD and given prescription drugs to "calm them down," but boisterous behavior is not necessarily deviant or socially dangerous. Having testosterone or having estrogen is a normal state of physiology, not a disease. Drugs are supposed to be utilized for pain management, disease treatment, or for curative purposes, and not predominantly for behavioral control or suppression.

Even the medical community can contribute to social problems, though. Many deaths are caused from the medical errors of doctors, nurses, and labs. Both with and without the medical community, however, bad philosophies are often offered on what constitutes good, healthy standards, leading to arbitrary or dangerous practices—an example of this being the anti-vaxxers or the pro-marijuana faction.

Other social problems come from how people think about practitioners in the medical field, in general. Ostensibly, doctors and nurses are not gods, but many, if not most, healthcare providers are more than efficient at their jobs and deserve commendation for their skills and their services rendered, faithfully. There are many doctors in the United States, with some regions having greater resources than others. For example, Idaho has 171 doctors per 100,000 people; Massachusetts has the most with 474 per 100,000 people; and Virginia has 278 doctors per 100,000 residents.

Sometimes, though, physicians and nurses misdiagnose patients. Sometimes, they prescribe the wrong medication or in the wrong dosage. Sometimes, they get promoted despite their personal incompetence. This creates problems in a social institution whose main purpose in existing is to do the opposite—to solve problems.

There are multiple reasons for the problems dogging healthcare, overall. No one factor is to blame. Healthcare has transformed from a health service institution into a big, moneymaking business built upon diagnoses, complicated treatment plans, expensive medical procedures, assorted fees, high insurance costs, and so on. So, it is no wonder that the healthcare field has added to the social problems facing people in America and across the globe. Take into account that in 1962, the annual healthcare cost in America was $28 billion. By 2012, the annual healthcare cost had risen to $3 trillion. Part of this is due to the resumption of excess of healthcare spending and increased middle-class taxation in the past decade.

One of the ways that the American government tried to deal with the rising costs and obligations of medicine under President Obama was through the *Affordable Care Act* of 2010 (ACA), also called "Obamacare." The President and Democratic majority controlling congress promised to slow down or reverse rising healthcare costs through the ACA. It covered 10 essential health benefits (including OB/GYN service for men and prostate services for women, contrary to scientific facts or need). It permitted (or mandated) insurance coverage for preexisting medical conditions. Children were allowed to stay on their parents' insurance policies until they were 26 years old. It was supposed to lower out-of-pocket costs by $2,500 per year and guarantee that no one would lose their existing insurance coverage (as President Obama promised on television, officially). Although ACA did help some people in the lower classes, for most people in the middle class, if they did not have employer-provided insurance, it was a costly and frustrating law.

Some of the problems included the presumption that younger people would voluntarily shoulder the costs of elderly patients; they did not, choosing to take the IRS penalty for not purchasing personal medical insurance. Second, there were innumerable managerial failures in the ACA exchanges, unanticipated economic consequences, and massive exchange closures. Third, many Americans resented the *individual mandate* of the ACA, being forced out of better, former policies and into worse, new policies that crippled them, financially.

Many middle-class families discovered that their reasonable $400 per month policy (for a family of four) with a $1,000 deductible was no longer available, that they were ineligible for any federal subsidy to assist with costs and would be forced to pay $1,300 a month for a policy with a $9,500 deductible (which was my family's experience in 2014). Instead of saving $2,500, it more than quadrupled medical costs for many people. Not surprisingly, since 2010, every single one of the exchanges lost money, and very few exchanges, if any, remain open, currently.

Unfortunately, there is a growing number of elderly people in America who still need medical assistance. Plus, the burden of illegal immigrants who seek medical treatment in America has substantially increased in the past five years. Medical technologies and research are experiencing great financial challenges to fund and to develop. Medical care has turned into an industry with treatment turning into yet another commodity to sell to willing or able buyers in the public (if they can get access to care). The social problems surrounding medical care still exist and abound, needing to be carefully and wisely solved by future legislative ranks—and the sooner, the better.

Sociology from Above

Mad about Adultery

One of my older memories of the 1990s was watching "Mad About You" (starring Paul Reiser and Helen Hunt) with my wife, regularly. Being a childless couple at the time, we connected with the comedic pair and enjoyed their matrimonial craziness, which made us feel better about our own foibles, and often cheered our hearts—that is, until "the cheating episode" ("The Finale," 1996).

I remember getting more and more uncomfortable watching the show as characters Paul and Jamie edged closer and closer to adulterous affairs, feeling lonely and stressed out by their careers and hectic schedules. To be brief, neither character has a full-on sexual liaison with another person in the finale, but Paul takes an "unsanctioned" walk with a temptress who he grudgingly leaves to go home to be with his wife, and Jamie kisses her boss in an opportunistic moment, which she admits to Paul, later.

This was hard news to take, emotionally. We really loved this couple, but my dread soon turned to anger when the scene was orchestrated in such a way that Jamie's make-out session with her boss somehow became the fault of her husband, Paul, who she thought was "not there for her," enough.

While that may or may not be true, I remember thinking to myself, "Biblically, it doesn't matter." Adultery, according to Scripture, is a terrific sin in the eyes of God. Exodus 20:14 states, "You shall not commit adultery." Additionally, sociologically, as Jamie was a full-fledged adult with personal agency, she was responsible for her actions and choices. Blaming it on her husband seemed more of a statement about her neuroses and lack of character than his neglectfulness.

In the decades that followed this show, it seemed that more and more television shows were happy to include adulterous storylines, with a variety of rationalizations for the dubious acts. A permissive, self-seeking philosophy of life appears to be governing people's attitudes about adultery, currently. We are socialized through romance novels, magazines, television, and cinema that when a couple has a poor marriage where one partner ignores, neglects, or mistreats the other, it is understandable—even promoted—for the other partner to seek consolation or vengeance in other people's beds.

It is no wonder that it is hard to find a late-night drama that does not eventually succumb to the excitement of matrimonial betrayal; yet, the popular acceptance of adultery fails to take in account important social concepts and consequences about the practice. Adultery is more than just "fooling around." It affects society as a whole, it attacks the whole purpose of marriage, and hurts all parties involved.

In his book, *The New Immorality*, Walker (1968) writes, "By this time, it may seem as though we believe that the affairs are an unmitigated evil . . . Not necessarily!" (p. 106). The author goes on to provide a list of situations wherein adultery is a good, healthy, beneficial response to the stresses and speed bumps of marriage. In his adulterous apologetic, moral reductionism and logical fallacies abound.

Walker's problem begins with his misunderstanding of the purpose of marriage. In the New Testament, discussing marriage, Jesus explains,

> Have you not read that He who created them from the beginning made them male and female, and said, "Therefore, a man shall leave his father and his mother and hold fast to his wife, and the two shall become one flesh"? So, they are no longer two, but one flesh. What therefore God has joined together, let not man separate (Matthew 19:4-6, ESV).

In postmodernity, where radical individualism reigns, popular culture embraces the notion that each partner's separate satisfaction is to be emphasized high above their partner's (and regardless of the damage done to the marriage union). As White (2012) defends, "It is no contradiction to say that adultery is wrong in general, but there may be extraordinary circumstances that justify it" (online). This violates the traditional, long-standing tenet of marriage, which is to provide permanent, loving support for each other throughout all situations and circumstances.

The Apostle Paul addresses this matter with great relevance in his epistle. He writes, "But since sexual immorality is occurring . . . The husband should fulfill his marital duty to his wife, and likewise the wife to her husband. The wife does not have authority over her own body but yields it to her husband. In the same way, the husband does not have authority over his own body but yields it to his wife" (1 Corinthians 7:2-4). Paul goes on to reinforce this idea later in the letter: "Nevertheless, in the Lord, woman is not independent of man, nor is man independent of woman. For as woman came from man, so also man is born of woman. But everything comes from God" (1 Corinthians 11:11-12).

Christians are to consider others better than themselves and to effort in only responding in love and mercy to each other (1 Peter 3:9). There never is a time or situation where Christians can think of themselves over others and be morally correct. Thus, not only is adultery harmful to both marriage partners, it also causes harm to the adulterer's sexual partner. Where marriage gives each partner deserved loving treatment and respect, adultery lacks any of the deep characteristics of love.

A true loving relationship is based on trust, loyalty, stability, compassion, mercy, and deep connection. Without these qualities, any relationship would be weak, at best. Perhaps this is why God despises adultery so much and proclaims it loudly in Scripture. Hebrews 13:4 states, "Marriage should be honored by all, and the marriage bed kept pure, for God will judge the adulterer and all the sexually immoral." Proverbs 6:32 warns, "But a man who commits adultery has no sense; whoever does so, destroys himself."

Jesus also specifically spoke of the evil of adultery and its associations—"Whatever comes out of a person is what defiles them. For it is from within, out of a person's heart, that evil thoughts come—sexual immorality, theft, murder, *adultery*, greed, malice, deceit, lewdness, envy, slander, arrogance, and folly. All these evils come from inside and defile a person."

Fundamentally, adultery is clearly a harmful practice regardless of one's circumstances. Although human relationships are complex and many people have unmet emotional needs, adultery, being based on temporary lustful self-centeredness, risks hurting everyone involved and spreads like a disease, socially, if not diagnosed and dealt with, in love and purity.

Voices from the Street

The Spirit and Disability

Disability is not confined to being visible. It lurks in both light and dark. Those who have a disability often find themselves marginalized and pitied. Veli-Matti Kärkkäinen (2016) writes that it "may come as a surprise to many that people with disabilities [make up] the largest and most diverse minority group in the United States' and, roughly speaking, in the rest of the world" (p. 384).

While this is astonishing, there has been no real push to welcome or address those with disabilities in the church. The disabled have been silent for years because unlike the blind Bartimaeus (Mark 10:46-52) who ignored the people telling him to be quiet when calling out for Jesus, they believe they have no voice or they have no advocate.

Nancy Eiesland (1994) writes, "Differences among persons with disabilities are often so profound that few areas of community exists" (p. 23). Christ instructs believers to welcome all into community. And yet, the church falls short. Eiesland distinguishes that disability theology is a part of the larger liberation theology that recognizes the struggle to be recognized for both our "unique experiences" (p. 29) and by a community that was founded on inclusion and acceptance (p. 29).

In liberating us all from the death of sins, Christ asked us to share His message, one of freedom and mercy, to all—Jesus did not instruct us to only be in fellowship with the unbroken—we are all broken. Therefore, the Triune God is disabled—symbolically speaking; the Creator of all things saw our brokenness even as He fashioned us in His image. Being called a "disabled" God does not mean He is less than powerful or unable to function; it simply means that He loves us as we are. To strive and celebrate perfection is worldly; God is beyond our understanding—He reaches out to our fragmented hearts with a promise to embrace all of us, even the parts that do not work, normally.

Burton Cooper believes there are three theological problems for believers who have a disability. First, there is the problematic language of perfection found in the Bible and the church. Second, theodicy and its attempt to explain away suffering. Third, questioning how the theology of salvation and hope varies with those who have a disability (Cooper, 1992, pp. 173-174). Cooper believes that each of us should study what the Bible says about God's perfection versus our understanding of human perfection (p. 174). When one undertakes this task, he or she will find that none of us can be perfect because we are not God.

For example, there is a misnomer regarding what God looks like because we are told that we are created in His image—this means a face, arms, and legs—when, in fact, these images are merely metaphors. Humans project their experiences onto God because they wrestle with trying to comprehend that which is not mean to be known. The hiddenness of God scares a lot of people.

Regarding the suffering of others, God is not silent. He is not absent; the Spirit is with us. The Bible gives us examples of a Creator who understands suffering. He does not wish pain upon His creation. The Spirit of God uses those moments to reach out and connect with us. She is not a quiet bystander but a Mother full of empathy. Cooper (1992) writes:

> Without compassion toward a suffering other, we neither communicate love nor become a vehicle of redemptive power toward the sufferer . . . Whitehead calls God "the suffering companion who understands," meaning, among other things, that even (or especially) divine understanding presupposes suffering with the other. God could not be God without suffering because those who do not experience the suffering of the other do not understand the reality of the other. The converse is also true: Those who suffer the suffering of the other confirm the reality of the world of the other (p. 179).

Compassion pushes us to step outside ourselves and be there for others. However, if the church focuses on theodicy instead of accepting the fact that suffering is part of life, those who have disabilities are fodder for theologians and academics to explain theodicy.

The theology of hope and salvation creates a problem for those with disabilities because it talks about being made whole. The Bible has verses that speak about the sin of the father being the reason for a child being disabled as well as the bent being made straight in heaven. These moments are used to marginalize those who are not seen as whole. Even the hemorrhaging woman was seen as unclean. What hope did she have? The answer, Jesus. Is her salvation different from those who were "clean"? The answer is no. And yet, the church still considers the only hope for those with disabilities is that they will be healed.

Another misnomer about salvation for those who live with a disability is that if they are not healed, they do not have enough faith. This is where having pneumatology comes into play. Theodore Runyon (1998) writes, "What [the Spirit] demands is orthopraxy, action that addresses the ills of society and strives to right them" (p. 147).

With the Spirit as their guide, the church can begin to rectify their approach and treatment of those with disabilities. The church needs to realize that a person who is disabled longs to have people who will support and love them. Philip Hefner (2012) writes that he lives

> . . . within a network that is very personal and intimate while at the same time vast and multi-dimensional, with aspects that are by nature impersonal. I am now a dependent person in ways that I could not have imagined for most of my life. This means that I am entwined in relationships—relationships that I must be willing and daring enough to call upon every day if I am to live my life (p. 198).

Hefner finds that freedom for those with disabilities comes with medical treatment, therapy, and by others who choose to support them. This assistance does not mean solely asking for someone to be healed. Instead, support requires fellowship, listening, and inclusion. If those offering to be a brother or sister to one who has a disability utilizes his or her pneumatology, they will revolutionize the concept of unconditional love because they would be following the Holy Spirit's direction while employing the Paraclete to advocate on everyone's behalf.

With the Spirit as everyone's advocate "peace will come through dialogue, through trust and respect for others who are different, through inner strength and a spirituality of love, patience, humility, and forgiveness" (Vanier, 1998, p. 4). Believers are called to help one another. This begins with conversation, study, and a desire to serve others.

There is a stigma that comes with being disabled. Amos Yong (2011) admits to having normative biases when he writes:

> By this, I mean the unexamined prejudices that non-disabled people have towards disability and toward people who have them. These assumptions function normatively so that the inferior status of people with disabilities is inscribed into our consciousness. Note, for example, how the rhetoric functions to describe people with impairments as *dis*-abled, *in*-capacitated, *in*-capable, *ab*-normal, and so on. In other words, non-disabled people take their experiences of the world as normal, thereby marginalizing and excluding the experiences of people with disabilities as not normal (pp. 10–11).

While the American with Disabilities Act helped move business and retailers to address issues that kept those who lived with a disability at a disadvantage, the church has yet to find a way to offer something that dismisses presuppositions of "who, what, where, why, and how" of someone who lives with a disability. Too often, Philippians 4:6 is used to diminish the reality of dealing with anxiety caused by a misfire of the brain. Other verses are used as "quick fixes" to help fear, doubt, brokenness. Furthermore, while the Bible is a gift inspired by the Spirit, it does not mean that one can use a verse as the end all be all of the explanation of the unknown. The concept of perfection and a quick fix must end.

As disability theology continues to push forward, it will continue to rely on the help and guidance of the Holy Spirit. The church needs to develop an orthodoxy, orthopathy, and orthopraxy of the disabled God which echoes that of the Holy Spirit. The truth is that those who live with a disability are functioning members of the Body of Christ. The passion of the disabled is unconditional love and fellowship with others. The church must put into practice the inclusion and awareness of the disabled. Conversations need to begin before change can happen. By relying on the Spirit to right our hearts, minds, and actions, the church will be able to navigate disability theology.

Stories drive us. Each narrative shapes our thinking, actions, and dreams. Fairy tales, those not mired by Disney's happily ever after motif, reveal the darkness in our world. They serve as guideposts and warnings, but most people cannot face that kind of reality, which is why Disney's retellings have taken hold. Hefner (2012) writes that "disability is mundane" (p. 197).

The Western church treats the Spirit as one whose function is commonplace. Neither the Spirit nor the disabled get invited to the ball; they are ignored for who they are and what they offer. Both belong at the dance, to be seen, and to be loved. The Triune God fashioned us to help each other because He helps us. The Paraclete is continually working on our behalf. The disabled are forever longing to be included. Both are woven together.

And while pneumatology and disability theology require time, passion, and work, they are both worthy of the effort. The narrative can be changed; it must. By identifying the orthodoxy, orthopathy, and orthopraxy within pneumatology and disability theology, the church will be able to reflect the mission of Christ.

Heather R. Harney
MAT Seminarian
Fuller Theological Seminary

Contributed by Heather R. Harney. © Kendall Hunt Publishing Company

 Check out the Chapter 11 video at this link: https://www.grtep.com/

Vocabulary

Absolutist Approach
Acute Drinker
ADHD
Adultery
Alcoholism
Awareness of Social Probs.
Biblical View of Suffering
Burglary
Causes of Social Probs.
CDC
Chronic Drinker
Cocaine
Criminology
Decriminalization
Deterrence
Deviant Behaviors
Disability
Drift
Drug Abuse
Embezzlement
Extortion
Felonies

Gateway Activities
Grand/Petty Theft
Handicap
Healthcare Costs
Heavy Drinker
Heroin
Impairment
In/Out Patient Programs
Labeling Theory
Larceny
Laws
Manslaughter
Marijuana
Misdemeanors
Natural Disasters
Obamacare
Overdose
Plan of Action
Political Abuses
Political Accommodations
Problems Defined
Professionalization

Prostitution
PWDs
Rehabilitation
Restitution
Retribution
Shock Probation
Social Drinker
Social Policies
Social Problem
Social Strain Theory
Theology of Hope
Transitional Deviance
Treatment Plans
Victims
White Collar Crime
1st-2nd-3rd Degree Murder

CHAPTER TWELVE: Warfare

The Basics

The (in)famous Union general, William Tecumseh Sherman, once concluded, "War is hell," and it usually is. The Confederate general, Robert E. Lee, said something quite similar: "It is well that war is so terrible—otherwise we could grow too fond of it." And Winston Churchill, the Prime Minister of England, warned his countrymen,

> Never, never, never believe any war will be smooth and easy, or that anyone who embarks on the strange voyage can measure the tides and hurricanes he will encounter. The statesman who yields to war fever must realize that once the signal is given, he is no longer the master of the policy but the slave of unforeseeable and uncontrollable events.

Generally, two main opinions persist regarding warfare: war is bad, or war is good. If one takes the former position, then war should be avoided at all costs. Sometimes, though, not going to war is the lesser evil of other bad choices. If one takes the latter position, that war is good, the initiation of it will hopefully end up righting a serious wrong or punishing the wicked. Yet, as President Teddy Roosevelt admitted, "Wars are, of course, as a rule to be avoided; but they are far better than certain kinds of peace."

Choices, judgments whether to go to war or not are complex and confusing. This is why it is important to have a general agreement between battling social groups on the ethics of warfare to help protect the goals and mission of any war. These *war ethics* help leaders decide what is right or wrong, they help contribute to debates over public policy, they help direct government and individual action, they can lead to the creation of formal codes of war, they can regulate the drafting of soldiers and limit what they do as soldiers, and they can help determine appropriate punishment for war crimes.

War ethics start with three questions:

- Is it ever right to go to war?
- When is it right to wage war?
- What is the moral way to conduct a war?

As mentioned earlier, not everyone thinks war is good. In fact, some people think war is so bad that they refuse to ever sanction or participate in one. This mindset is called *pacifism*, and it rests on the notion that war and violence are never justifiable. Succinctly, all conflicts need to be peacefully settled. Pacifists might base this upon religious convictions, an appreciation for the sanctity of life, or an awareness of the tragic loss of soldiers (who tend to generally be young men in their teens and 20s).

There are several different expressions of pacifism. *Absolute pacifists* believe there should be no war, even in self-defense. In times of warfare, these people are often labeled as *conscientious objectors*. *Conditional pacifists* believe that war is bad in principle, but in some circumstances, it is a necessity. *Selective pacifists* believe that some wars are okay while others are taboo (based on individual or arbitrary standards). *Active pacifists* will participate in some war activities (such as driving an ambulance or being a medic or doctor), but they refuse to fight.

Some people are advocates for the *doctrine of double effect*, which states that the act of war must be good in itself (or at least indifferent) and the direct effect of the war must be morally acceptable. Wars should not be begun for petty personal gain, or as a means to selfish ends. The good effect of the war must be sufficient to compensate for the evil consequences of the warfare. Moreover, the agent of war seeks to minimize the evil effect, accepting the cost to himself.

One of the greatest warfare commentaries of the early Middle Ages was written by a bishop named St. Augustine. He is credited for setting up most of the theological categories that are still used in today's Christian seminaries. Known by his contemporaries as "The Knowledgeable One," this great theologian came up with some warfare advice for the Roman rulers of his day.

For Augustine, a *just war* had to follow certain requirements. First, the war must be for a just cause. The war must be officially declared by a lawful authority. The intention behind the war must be goodness. All other reasonable ways of resolving the problem should have been tried first. They must be a reasonable chance of success. Finally, there must be proportionality in response to any military attacks.

Ultimately, in a just war, only appropriate force should be used, innocent people and noncombatants needed to be protected and unharmed, and internationally agreed-upon war regulations had to be obeyed. As Pope John Paul II wrote,

Peace, as taught by Sacred Scripture and the experience of men itself, is more than just the absence of war. And the Christian is aware that on earth, a human society that is completely and always peaceful is unfortunately a utopia, and that the ideologies which present it as easily attainable only nourish vain hopes. The cause of peace will not go forward by denying the possibility and the obligation to defend it.

Wartime conduct is a tricky affair. Just because a war is just in its cause does not automatically guarantee that it has been fought in a just manner (or vice versa). Thus, soldiers were/are taught *jus in bello* (Just Conduct in War Standards) through various methods. This answers difficult questions for them like, who can you fight in a war? How much force is ethical to use? What is a proportionate response to a military attack? Is the use of certain weapons always wrong? What about chemical, biological, or nuclear weapons, or the size of them? What is the role and authority of international conventions in wartime? What is an appropriate punishment for genocide, mass rape, or torture?

In modernity, the international communities came together (in times of peace) to create diplomatic bodies and agreements to settle such questions. One of the first ones was *The Hague Convention of 1907*, which discussed an attempt at disarmament, the creation of laws of war and war crimes, the banning of poisonous weapons, banning the killing or wounding treacherously, banning the killing of surrendering soldiers, banning the declaration of "no mercy" for defeated opponents, and banning using arms, projectiles, or material calculated to cause unnecessary suffering by the enemy.

With many of those agreements in place, 40 years later, the *Genocide Convention of 1948* dealt with how each side would treat the wounded and the sick, the shipwrecked, prisoners of war, and civilians. It also addressed treaties: how they were to be established (by signature and ratification), who they were binding upon and on what terms, and it wrestled with customary law and its implications upon warfare.

Despite these meetings and measures, some nefarious war crimes still occurred. Specifically, the Japanese pushed the ethical limits of warfare with the *Bataan Death March*, where 76,000 American and Filipino POWs suffered brutal treatment as they were forced to march through the jungle with no food or water.

Though some people try to deny its occurrence, Hitler's genocide of the Jews (also known as *the Holocaust*) in WWII was, to that date, one of the worst atrocities against humanity in the history of mankind. Also, although the final figures are impossible to know, in the German concentration camps, it can be assumed that up to 11 million people could have died—including the Jews, Poles, Gypsies, and other ". . . undesirables like the mentally ill, political dissidents, and homosexuals" (Friedman, 1990).

After Germany and Japan lost in WWII, the *Nuremburg Trials* were held in Switzerland, with multiple Nazi leaders being convicted and executed for war crimes. Although many tried to defend or rationalize their actions, saying that they were only "obeying orders," they were still held responsible for their monstrous warfare actions and punished.

Interestingly (and sadly), WWII also lead to the creation of Japanese Internment camps in America after the bombing of Pearl Harbor in Hawaii. Roosevelt and his war panel decided it was best to take a precautionary action just in case Japanese spies had already made it to the continental United States and were about to aid the enemy with similar ambushes as in Hawaii. However, this really only amounted to innocent and loyal Japanese Americans being imprisoned for crimes that they never committed, and increased racism and prejudice against the Japanese on the West coast of America for years to follow.

Since WWII, most American governments have presumed that most democracies, even those far away, overseas, do not want to go to war against other democracies. This is called the *democratic peace theory*. This has led to the creation of various coalitions in warfare, with mutual oaths of defense and protection in warfare, and mutual support of similar goals and principles in times of peace. Thus, since the 1960s, America, France, England, and Germany have not directly fought against each other in military combat. Support from this is not only at an institutional level; due to globalism (check out the next chapter), most citizens of the countries of the world do not want to go to war unless attacked, because of the terrible consequences that inevitably follow warfare.

Poverty

Simply defined, poverty is the lack of basic necessities in life needed to survive, but poverty is not a simple social reality. With poverty comes a crippling lack of food, water, shelter, education, medical care, social security, and so on. Truly, it is a multidimensional issue that transcends all social, economic, and political boundaries.

The solution for poverty rests on a variety of factors. Sociological studies have shown that the causes and forces of poverty defy reductionism. Just throwing money at an impoverished people group will not necessarily lift them out of poverty (at least, for long). Poverty is complex, cyclical, and in desperate need of a thoughtful and effective global remedy.

Regarding global poverty statistics, currently, 4.5 billion people live in developing countries. Of these people, 60% lack basic sanitation. Some 33% have no access to clean water, 25% do not have adequate housing, and 20% do not have access to modern health or medical services.

The poverty line is the lowest income level needed to survive in society and procure the basic necessities in society. The percentage under the poverty line is vastly different between first and third world countries. For example, in America, some 13.5% of people live below the poverty line, and in Europe, the number of people is 14%. In Africa, 42.6% of people live below the poverty line and in South Asia, the number is 45%—nearly half the population.

There are many causes of poverty. War or civil conflict can interrupt or disrupt basic services and nominal social life. People can have too much debt, which cripples their ability to escape from their economic circumstances. There might be a lack of land to build a company or establish a farm. Finally, low (or a lack of) education definitely hurts people's chances of improving their financial circumstances as it sets up a sorrowful chain of events that perpetuates the poverty circle.

The three main types of poverty are biological, relative, and that based on the official U.S. poverty line. *Biological poverty* refers to starvation, malnutrition, and a severe lack of safe housing options. *Relative poverty*, which is more common, refers to people living below the average economic standards of their society or social group. *Official poverty* refers to people who lack in resources to meet their basic needs, as determined by the U.S. government. Federal studies first determine the lowest cost for a survivable food budget. Then, the government makes the poverty line three times that amount. So, although it is not a large amount, it still is better poverty than other parts of the world (specifically, in third world countries).

Sociology from Above

Breaking the Cycle of Poverty

One of the more powerful teaching tools that I use in my *social problems* class is to show them a cycle of poverty chart created from information gleaned and combined from other sources collected over the years. The top of the chart begins with "Born into poverty," and

it is one of the most significant factors for why people live in poverty. Much less a matter of the will or industriousness, poverty stems from one's location or environment.

The next box on the chart states, "Malnourished & Ill Health in Family," which many people can relate to as they have had to take off "sick days" to recover. Once better, they return, but what if they could not? What if the disease or sickness never left their home? That is what it is like for many people in the world, today.

Other boxes follow such as "Children help with work" (because their parents might be too sick to work or even dead), "Children miss school" (because the family cannot afford for them not to work), and "Children less qualified," which pushes them to the bottom of the hiring pool behind others with parents well enough to afford for their children to learn and play and socialize, upping their chances for a brighter future.

Without much money, the child turns into an adult, but finds only "closed social avenues," which creates a sense of "desperation and hopelessness," leading them into risky, criminal environments to survive yet another day. Perhaps they fall in love but they cannot afford condoms or other contraceptives, so they become "very young parents"—too immature to know how to parent well.

Their children grow up in the same sort of environment that they did, and the whole cycle begins again—year after year, generation after generation. This is how poverty gets perpetuated and even how caste systems ensnare their social prisoners. Questions abound: how can people break this vicious cycle? What can people do to remedy this sad reality for nearly half the world's population? What should people's attitudes in first world countries be concerning the impoverished in the third world countries?

Personally, I find John Wesley's maxims on the ethical use of our incomes to help poor, sick, and the sinners in the world (1872) rather commendable. Presumed to have been adapted from one of his earliest sermons, Wesley was reported to have recommended,

> Do all the good you can, by all the means you can,
> In all the ways you can, in all the places you can,
> At all the times you can, to all the people you can,
> As long as ever you can.

This seems like a daunting task, but it was meant to be a lifelong habit—not just a quick fix or a comfortable rescue. Wesley was all about full commitment, and taking care of the poor and sick demands just that. In another sermon, Wesley advised his congregation, "Is it not strange, that this important truth should be so little understood, or, at least, should so little influence the practice of them that fear God? Suppose this representation be true, suppose the Judge of all the earth speaks right, those, and those only, that feed the hungry, give drink to the thirsty, clothe the naked, relieve the stranger, visit those that are in prison, according to their power and opportunity, shall "inherit the everlasting kingdom" (Emory, 1853, p. 330).

Wesley was a man of one book (the Bible), so it is not surprising that one can find similar sentiments in the passages of the Old and New Testaments. For instance, Exodus 22 commands, "Do not mistreat or oppress a foreigner, for you were foreigners in Egypt. Do not take advantage of the widow or the fatherless . . . If you lend money to one of my people among you who is needy, do not treat it like a business deal; charge no interest." Proverbs 31:8-9 states, "Speak up for those who cannot speak for themselves, for the rights of all who are destitute. Speak up and judge fairly; defend the rights of the poor and needy." Psalm 109:30-31 affirms, "I know that the Lord secures justice for the poor and upholds the cause of the needy."

The New Testament has its share of the Good News. Luke 6:20–21 recounts, "Looking at his disciples, [Jesus] said: 'Blessed are you who are poor, for yours is the kingdom of God. Blessed are you who hunger now, for you will be satisfied. Blessed are you who weep now, for you will laugh.'" Romans 12:11–13 admonishes, "Never be lacking in zeal, but keep your spiritual fervor, serving the Lord. Be joyful in hope, patient in affliction, faithful in prayer. Share with the Lord's people who are in need. Practice hospitality." Finally, 1 John 3:17–18 exhorts, "If anyone has material possessions and sees his brother in need but has no pity on him, how can the love of God be in him? Dear children, let us not love with words or tongue but with actions and in truth."

So, then the questions just turn to the when and the how. We are not God, so there is only so much that we can do. We can hope to change the world, to end global poverty, to recreate our world into a Christian utopia, but such dreams fly high for time before the winds of reality die and the kite of kindness plummets. After all, Jesus himself told his disciples that the poor would always be among us (Matthew 26:11); yet, he also told his disciples to go and feed and clothe the poor, like John Wesley echoed—all the time with all they had for as many as they could while on earth.

We may not be able to go to Africa, but we can certainly help those around us in need. Ever see a homeless person sleeping on the ground? Help him. Ever see a homeless woman pushing a shopping cart around with all her belongings? Help her. And if you can travel abroad, try to be a balm, a salve, for just one hurting and needy person waiting for Jesus to help them, because, as Stearns and Sterns point out in their book, *He walks among us*, "You just might be the only Jesus they will ever see" (2013).

The Sage from the Stage

War: Boots on the Ground and Heart in the Word

So much of what we think we "know" about complex concepts come from popular culture. Looking back on why I joined the military, I can now see how much popular culture greatly influenced what I thought about the military and warfare. For complete disclosure, I enlisted in the U.S. Army in the mid-1990s. I grew up on action movies, the westerns my father watched on Saturdays, and the early morning cartoons like G.I. Joe. My heroes were not sports figures, but rather John Matrix, Colonel Mike Kirby, Major John Reisman, Ripley, Dutch, and a host of other action characters that kept boys and men entertained for only the cost of a video rental. I, like so many young men, wanted action and adventure. I expected to get it as I boarded the bus to boot camp.

Boot camp, where you learn everything you need to know about basic soldering, was not as you may have seen in such popular movies such as *Full Metal Jacket*. Boot camp serves two primary functions, to teach the basic skills required to be a soldier and to strip away the basic inhibition to kill another person. Since the entire purpose of the soldier is to kill people and break things, both functions are necessary and must be accomplished in the most expedient manner possible.

After graduation, the soldier then moves to the next training station to learn a particular job. For some, this is advanced soldiering, such as infantry or armor. For others, it is a support role, such as communications or mechanics. However, no matter what the job a soldier performs, he or she is a soldier, first. If any additional training is required, the soldier will complete it before moving on to their first duty station. I went to parachute school at Fort Benning, GA.

It was January mid-1990s when the commander for the 3rd Battalion 75th Ranger Regiment stepped onto the parade grounds for the first class of the year for the parachute school. The commander proceeded to tell the approximately 300 soldiers gathered on the brutally cold day of the history of military parachuting and our connection to that history that stretched back to World War II and that parade field.

It was at that moment that each soldier looked to his or her left and right and realized that they were not alone. Each soldier would be connected to those who shared a foxhole or similar experience with him (or her)—whether current or in the past. The connection to those real (not fictitious) men and women who fought so that others could live in peace and free of oppression was powerful. At graduation, we became part of that lineage as we moved on to our duty station.

Fast forward two years, I was a specialist about to be deployed to Africa as part of the 82nd Airborne Divisions Long Range Surveillance Company. Gear inspected. Equipment packed. Weapon issued. Everyone doing their job. Check and recheck everything. Leave nothing to chance. Everyone had questions, but no one had answers. If we were going to be deployed, it would be ahead of the main force.

It is at this point that every person begins to process what is about to happen. Some question themselves. Others question what will happen. Others seek answers collectively. Some even begin to find religion. The reality is that if called, as Gunnery Sergeant Tom Highway stated in *Heartbreak Ridge* (1986), "If you got your boots on your walking into combat." It is a sobering reality, you might kill or even die. What are you dying for?

To be honest, you are not dying for a few yards of ground, barrels of oil, cash, or college, but rather you are dying to protect the person next to you, your friends, coworkers, and all of those that are relying on you to do your job. They are your family, friends, brothers, sisters, and so on. Every deployment is like this. Some will return; others will not. We will remember those that do not come home. This is every soldier's story, no matter what side they fight. This is the reality of war.

So then, is war necessary? The pacifist would argue that violence is never the solution to any problem. The pacifist would say that the cost of lives and money is a waste of resources when everything can be solved through nonviolent means, such as diplomacy. However, the fundamental problem with pacifism is it is only effective if the opposition plays by the same rules.

Some even use the Bible to support their argument, "You have heard that it was said, 'An eye for an eye and a tooth for a tooth.' But I tell you not to resist an evil person. But whoever slaps you on your right cheek, turn the other to him also" (Matthew 5:38–39, NKJV, 1982).

Do we think that the Nazis in World War II stopped with one cheek? What about other conflicts? Ask the protesters of Tiananmen Square (1989), as they were crushed by tanks and shot for just protesting.

In contrast, war cannot solve all problems. Violence cannot erase cultural conflicts, it only escalates them. We can observe firsthand the cultural clashes in the Middle East as evidence that violence cannot resolve all issues (1900s to present).

So then, if war is sometimes necessary, when is it right to wage war? Theologians, politicians, and experts have debated the concept of a just war for centuries. Simply put, war may not always be the worst choice when potential outcomes are examined. For example, the Civil War was necessary, even though it was one of the costliest wars ever fought in terms of lives alone, as it ended the practice of slavery while preserving the Union (what happened afterward is another tragedy).

In other cases, war may be necessary to protect the things that we, as a society, steadfastly value, such as life or liberty (World War I and World War II). Pragmatically, war is necessary when all other options have been exhausted or the consequences of inaction are in conflict with our values.

As the world exists, we will have war and strife until we let go of our pride and embrace Jesus. James asks,

Where do wars and fights *come* from among you? Do *they* not *come* from your *desires for* pleasure that war in your members? You lust and do not have. You murder and covet and cannot obtain. You fight and war (James 4:1–2, NKJV).

Are we, as a society, guilty of pride in our rush to war? Have we exhausted all the other opportunities available before we march to war? Even in the deepest parts of our heart, we still struggle with our sinful nature. Isaiah tells us,

He shall judge between the nations and rebuke many people; They shall beat their swords into plowshares, and their spears into pruning hooks; Nation shall not lift up sword against nation, neither shall they learn war anymore (Isaiah 2:4, NKJV).

That will truly be a glorious day. Until then, we have a duty and responsibility to remember the costs of our beliefs and the price that was paid for our freedom.

Craig Brigman
Entrepreneur
Central Virginia

Contributed by Craig Brigman. © Kendall Hunt Publishing Company

 Check out the Chapter 12 video at this link: https://www.grtep.com/

Vocabulary

Absolute Pacifists	Biological Poverty	Conscientious Objectors
Active Pacifists	Boot Camp	Cycle of Poverty
Bataan Death March	Causes of Poverty	Democratic Peace Theory
Biblical View of Warfare	Conditional Pacifists	Doctrine of Double Effect

Genocide Convention 1948
Global Poverty
Hague Convention of 1907
The Holocaust
International Conventions
Japanese Internment Camp
Jus in Bello

Just War Theory
The Knowledgeable One
Nuremburg Trials
Pacifism
Peace
Proportionate Response
Official Poverty

Relative Poverty
Selective Pacifists
War Ethics
Warfare
War-time Conduct

CHAPTER THIRTEEN: Globalism and Technology

The Basics

The *globalization movement* is ubiquitous, and it has been a social force for centuries. Although slow in its beginnings, globalization, since the 1950s and 1960s, has caused a social explosion of trade, people, investments, technological advancements, cultural awareness and influences, as well a blending of ideas between foreign countries previously separated by long distances. It is not an understatement to say that globalization has created a more integrated and dependent world community.

Historically, scholars have evidence of globalization as far back as the fifteenth century CE, with European explorers and colonists being credited for starting the globalization movement. Yet, there are archeological hints that ancient maritime activities connected distant countries together long before previously thought in the historical timeline. Rather than living in isolated regions, speculations and suspicions abound on whether the Egyptians visited Central and South America (or vice versa) or if the ancient Chinese explorers made it to North America.

As most Western civilization scholars will attest, after the thousands of years of hunter-gatherer existence, the rise of organized agriculture communities aided in the development and building of nation-states and empires, who frequently reached out into the known world to accumulate more goods and ideas to profit the state. Although the movement saw its share of inactivity, after the Dark Ages (459–1350 CE), the emergence of the *Renaissance* (1350–1600 CE) saw an incredible increase of new thought and investigation. Ultimately, this led to new, better technologies and economic options, which in turn boosted international trade and financing exploration into the New World by countries like England, France, and Spain, who sought to increase and protect their global reach. While their goals may have been fundamentally political in nature, these countries' empire-building efforts helped to spread new ideas, products, and communication across the globe via the resources and forces of *imperialism*.

The driving force of globalization in the twentieth century began with the decline of socioeconomic barriers after World War II. Before the second great war, most countries had innumerable international trade and foreign investment restrictions. Many countries, in order to thrive or even remain in existence, adopted less isolationist, friendlier international policies to avoid future wars and to reap the benefits of globalization. The threat of a Communist takeover was real, and joining the Western global community helped in political protection and economic provision.

Additionally, the technological advancements after WWII positively influenced globalization. New inventions and new technologies assisted in worldwide production (commercial and agriculture), better health and medical options, an easier shipping of goods, and the facilitation of faster communication between the nations of the world. Decade after decade, globalization, with the powers of technology, brought the traditional spheres of social influence (economics, politics, culture) into greater and more unified alignment than ever before in human history.

The majority of sociologists today would agree that the most influential factor in the globalization movement, currently, is technology. Very few people would have known how deep, how far, and how wide the World Wide Web (WWW) would affect human society. The Internet provides immediate access to financial data and immediate communication abilities, making transactions that formally took hours, days, or years to complete, done in minutes—if not seconds.

The speed of technological advancements is staggering as the world launches into the twenty-first century. Many sociologists do a reasonable job in summing up the connection between technology and social change. Ogburn (1947) is astute in his assessment of the influence of technology upon society in regard to social desires and needs for increased production, an accompanying infectious usage of technological products, and these products' overall influence upon social activity and norms—both productively or destructively (pp. 81, 86). Shipp et al. (2012) additionally affirm that the relationship between technological products and social change is intertwined and catalytic in many ways (p. 72).

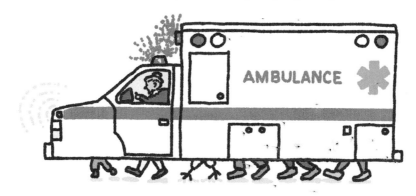

One can envision society and technology "leapfrogging" over each other, with human needs creating opportunities for advancements, which in turn lead to new needs or wants, in an endless cycle—for better or worse. As such, Ogburn (1947) suggests that a population reduction could influence both technology and social change (p. 84), and Shipp et al. (2012) suggest that the social changes brought on by technological advancements and offers will require new rules, regulations, and guidelines to protect moral and safety standards in society (p. 79).

Also, few if any companies can exist without computers anymore. In fact, the functional nature of computers has become a social force of its own, with speed and hard drive size being quintessential components for an efficient, productive company. However, with the advent and development of the virtual world, some technologies (like hard drive size) have been supplanted through virtual hard drives, making the old technology obsolete. Still, computers are the equivalent of financial capital, with Silicon Valley in California becoming the one of largest economies in the world (Segarra, 2018, online).

All global societies utilize technology and all global societies pay millions (or billions) of dollars to develop the best technology. Thus, in many ways, globalism and technology are integrally joined, with each pushing the other onward into new frontiers. This prompts the questions of how far human society will change and what will follow the current postmodern era. The old central narratives that surrounded vocations no longer exist in postmodernity. Currently, personal choice and diversity are a nominal part of work life.

With industrialization and the facilitation of production being more automated and inexpensive than ever before, knowledge and service for workers/owners have become primary economic products. Most people have more than one job and expect to do more than one duty while at work. Furthermore, the work that people do often reaches far beyond the confines of their office or business. One can write a book and get it published in Eugene, OR, and then discover it advertised online in England, China, and Australia.

Presently, one can easily find the evidence of globalization in the media outlets, television and movies, in music and literature, and in day-to-day living. Of course, not everybody appreciates globalization, but everyone benefits from it to a greater or lesser degree. The evaluation of this grand social change is a complex and hotly debated topic, which Kellner (2002) discusses in his article (pp. 287–290); however, the social "tendrils" of globalization affect all aspects of human existence—from continent to continent, and culture to culture—and thus challenge blanket statements of condemnation or commendation.

Certainly, there are profound benefits to globalization, not least of which is the increased availability of goods and services for third world countries that formerly were available only to select first world countries in Europe and North America. Presently, globalization has brought advanced technology, communication, goods, comforts, and cultural freedoms to areas of Asia and Africa that previously were shut out or ignored. New markets have opened, new international connections have been established, and new channels of sociological exchanges have been created. This is a definite benefit of globalization.

That being said, as Satterthwaite (2009), Caldwell (2004), and Westley et al. (2011) point out in their articles, not everything about globalism is positive when it comes to the realities of such intense global exchange, integration, and interdependence. In the past five years, a countercultural, anti-globalization movement has arisen, pushing back against the homogenization of national identity and distinctives. Examples of this can be seen in England's "Brexit" from the European Union as well as the handful of countries resisting the mass Islamic immigration/invasion into European lands and, in the opposite direction, the introduction of any Western progressive culturalisms in more radically Muslim Middle East countries. Eschle remarks, "Clearly, 'the anti-globalisation movement' does not operate outside globalized economic, gendered, racialized and geopolitical power relations but is bound up within them and reflects them" (Eschle, 2004, p. 68)

Satterthwaite (2009) suggests that globalization, with its encouragement of consumerism, carries with it a dangerous threat of damaging the climate even more than it already has been since the Industrial Era (p. 564). Caldwell (2004) questions what will ultimately transpire in the world by 2050—economically, educationally, and environmentally—because of the increase in world population and the limitation of planetary resources (p. 313). Finally, Westley et al. (2011) point out that technological advancements accompanying globalization have a great potential to harm natural environments across the globe (pp. 763-764).

Effectively, globalization is a two-edged sword (Westley et al., 2011, p. 763); yet, contrary to some Utopian dream of humanity living in perfect harmony with nature and each other, human existence before globalization had its pros and cons, humanity during globalization will have its own share of benefits and detriments, and people after globalization will no doubt have its own slides and speed bumps to contend with in life (as we move out into the cosmos, perhaps).

Regarding global inequality, I can think of nothing more important in the future of our planet. So much fighting, bloodshed, and conflict come from people perpetually suffering because of their social circumstances. As Witt (2009) states, "One of the things we learn from sociology is that we are embedded in larger networks in which decisions and events that happen far away, and about which we may know little or nothing, shape our daily life experiences" (p. 261). This is such a powerful, unrecognized notion in the world today. People live in what they think are disconnected social bubbles, but in truth, we are all fighting the same battle to stay alive or to live our lives well. My life does affect people in Africa and China, and their lives affect me, too. With such sociological awareness, I can make good choices so that I contribute positively to the world society.

Sociology from Above

Contending for the Faith

We have entered an age of "Mediapostasy" (a word of my own creation). Because of my great passion for church history and the Bible, I frequently find myself pulled into watching a Bible or church history documentary on the *History Channel* or *Discovery* (see your local listings). They always have such awesome titles: "UFOs in the Bible," "The Real Jesus," "Banned from the Bible," and "The Pagan Christ." They offer an interesting-but-perverted view of the Scriptures, Savior, and followers, and they pander to the masses with no biblical or church history understanding.

Watching these movies becomes a lesson in patience and self-control. It is a good thing that no bricks are laying about in arm's reach. I must look like a zombie with my eyes perpetually rolled up into my head with all the false deconstructionist proclamations being spewed out like promises from a politician.

"The Bible writers never believed in the One God," they overstate. "Most scholars think David was mythic figure," they bloviate. "No historical evidence exists for Pilate," they obfuscate. "At no point do the resurrection narratives in the four Gospels say, 'Jesus has been raised, therefore we are all going to heaven,'" they misstate (Wright, 2019, online). "None of the Gospels were actually written by their purported authors," they perpetuate. Their deviances from traditional understanding go on and on.

Departing from truth accepted for nearly 2,000 years, they are the false teachers as Paul warns about in 1 Timothy 6, "If anyone teaches otherwise and does not agree to the sound instruction of our Lord Jesus Christ and to godly teaching, they are conceited and understand nothing. They have an unhealthy interest in controversies and quarrels about words that result in envy, strife, malicious talk, evil suspicions and constant friction between people of corrupt mind, who have been robbed of the truth and who think that godliness is a means to financial gain." Their perspective is limited and darkened, and they want others to join in with them in ignorance.

For the early Christians, the biblical message of God's plan of salvation through Jesus was the "Good News" because it offered a truthful, dependable, refreshing take on life with God and each other. It allowed them to be human, affirmed God's love despite their faults, and promoted a positive but realistic outlook on life that benefitted everyone. As McGiffert (1909) wrote, "Christian brotherhood was to manifest itself in mutual kindness, forgiveness, forbearance, and charity" (p. 32).

For them, it was not just another way to the divine; it was the *only* way. John 17:3 states, "Now this is eternal life: that they may know you, the only true God, and Jesus Christ, whom you have sent." Orthodoxy was not a political position. Something was "orthodox" because it was right thinking, not artificial or fraudulent, and it had to be a powerful truth. As the ancient Church Father Polycarp proclaimed before his martyrdom, "It is unthinkable for me to repent from what is good to turn to what is evil. I will be glad though to be changed from evil to righteousness" (Lightfoot, 1989, pp. 137–138).

The media outlets suggest something quite different. They offer modern society an unassertive, watered-down version of Jesus, a mythic/fairy tale view of Yahweh, and a convoluted, corrupt composition of the Bible. This is not unexpected considering key biblical prophecies. Paul says in 2 Timothy 4:3, "For the time will come when people will not put up with sound doctrine. Instead, to suit their own desires, they will gather around them a great number of teachers to say what their itching ears want to hear. They will turn their ears away from the truth and turn aside to myths."

The media's version is not "Good News" and hardly something that people would turn their lives upside down for (or die) if it meant as little as media makes it out to be. The Way would not have caught on as an international, inclusive, indelible faith and spread like wildfire through a withered, self-centered society consumed with its own greatness, and lacking in mercy, truth, and love. In the darkness, people are drawn to the light.

The Bible (including the New Testament) calls people to live godly, holy lives fighting against their destructive human instincts. It requires Christians to take the righteous path and bravely suggest that others do likewise for a better, healthier relationship with each other and God. It suggests that each believer "contend for the faith that was once for all entrusted to God's holy people" (Jude 1:3).

Why? Because the accounts are true. Because there really is a God. Because Jesus really died for the sins of the world. Because this really is one story worth fighting for in life.

Voices from the Street

Sweaty in Africa: Globalism and Contextualization

My wife and I live in a central African country on the edge of the Sahara Desert with our two children (ages one and three) to work as teachers and live among an unreached people group of 400,000 that has little or no exposure to the Gospel and no known believers living among them. Although the country is over 50% Muslim and the rest Christian (at least, nominally), the northern half of the country has very few believers, and hundreds of years of animosity between tribes has made it difficult to expect the southern "Christian" tribes to do much evangelism outside of their own tribal regions.

With very little literacy in their second languages and no written or audio Bible in their heart language, it becomes an interesting dynamic when trying to reach our neighbors with the Gospel. In this context, it becomes very important to literally "practice what you preach" and live out your faith. When you are one of two Western families within 200 miles, you gain a lot of attention. You are on display all the time. Everyone watches you everywhere you go. Many are very suspicious of you. Not only do you learn the language, but you are constantly learning culture to be able to better fit in (as best I can as a white man in a turban) and be honoring to your neighbors in a way that would open doors for the gospel.

If my wife chooses to walk around town in shorts and a tank top, she will be seen as dishonoring her husband and acting scandalously. You cannot exactly be a feminist in this culture. Her witness and credibility would be destroyed. If I wear a T-shirt outside of my own house, as a married man, it is seen as very inappropriate. We as a family have chosen to dress in a way that honors our neighbors and their culture, even though it is not the most comfortable when it is 120° F outside (and inside). When living in an international context for the sake of the Gospel, you have to ask yourself if you are willing to give up some of your freedoms that you usually have as an American in order to not be a stumbling block to those around you.

Another way that we choose to love our neighbors and communicate what we believe is by celebrating Easter and Christmas in a way that is culturally appropriate. Yes, we sometimes get together with our teammates and celebrate in American ways also, but holidays here are always celebrated in particular ways. For instance, Tabaski (Eid al-Adha) is the most holy holiday for Muslims in most of the world. It is the holiday celebrating God providing a ram so that

Abraham would not have to sacrifice his son (Ishmael for Muslims). Here, they celebrate it by borrowing money from whomever they can in order to be able to afford a ram and slaughter it in a halal manner (praying to thank God for providing it while slitting its throat). Then, they throw a huge party with their neighbors and give out pieces of meat to everyone they know. This caught us off guard our first time because we have a very tiny solar refrigerator and ended up with three sheep legs and a lot of internal organs (nothing is wasted).

For both Christmas and Easter this year, we slaughtered a ram and gave most of the meat to our neighbors. This, of course, was very odd to them because they do not consider it to be a holiday. With Christmas, they understood it, because even the Qur'an speaks of the Virgin Birth of Christ and they hold him in high regard (sadly, as just a Prophet). But with Easter, giving all our friends and neighbors meat meant that we drove around town to different places and had spiritual discussions with them on a very touchy topic. They do not believe Jesus died. They believe God rescued him and Judas took his place. How could God subject such an honorable Prophet to such a humiliating death?

So, as best we can, by celebrating our own holidays in a way that is contextualized to where we live, we communicated the Gospel. This past Easter, I did as best I could in my broken French and little mastery of the tribal language to explain to my language helper, Mohammed, that their celebration of Tabaski in the Qur'an and Old Testament was symbolic of Christ dying on the cross for our sins. Of course, this becomes controversial very quickly with people who are more educated within Islam, but most people who know us personally know that we love them and are here to serve them and shrug off the fact that we have different beliefs than they have.

When you live in a way that is contextualized to the culture and people you want to reach, it opens doors and relationships and conversations that otherwise would not be possible. I have had locals thank me for being here, dressing appropriately, and honoring them by trying to learn their language. The Gospel transcends any cultural and geopolitical boundaries, and we want to do our best to not cause any hindrances to this people group entering the Kingdom. We try to follow the example of Paul in 1 Corinthians:

> For though I am free from all, I have made myself a servant to all, that I might win more of them. To the Jews I became as a Jew, in order to win Jews. To those under the law I became as one under the law (though not being myself under the law) that I might win those under the law. To those outside the law I became as one outside the law (not being outside the law of God but under the law of Christ) that I might win those outside the law. To the weak I became weak, that I might win the weak. I have become all things to all people, that by all means I might save some. I do it all for the sake of the gospel, that I may share with them in its blessings (1 Corinthians 9:19–23, ESV).

Joshua Nunn
Language and Computer Trainer
Central Africa

Contributed by Joshua Nunn. © Kendall Hunt Publishing Company

Check out the Chapter 13 video at this link: https://www.grtep.com/

Vocabulary

Anti-globalization Movement
Brexit
Christian Brotherhood
Colonialization
Communication Advances
Computers
Consumerism
Cultural Contextualization
Environmental Concerns
European Exploration

Exploitation of Resources
Geopolitical Boundaries
Global Citizens
Global Community
Global Inequality
Globalization Benefits
Globalization Movement
Great Commission
Imperialism
Internet

"Mediapostasy"
Orthodoxy
Postmodern Media Agenda
Postmodernity
Social Change
Tabaski (Eid al-Adha)
Technological Advances
A Transcendent Gospel
World Community
World Trade

REFERENCES

Albert, T., Ramis, H. (Producers), & Ramis, H. (Director). (1993). *Groundhog day*. Culver City, CA: Colombia Pictures.

Anonymous. (2012). Prostitutions: Exploitations, persecutions, repressions. *Fondation Scelles*. Retrieved from http://www.fondationscelles.org/pdf/RM4/Prostitutions_Exploitations_Persecutions_Repressions_Fondation%20Scelles_FR.pdf

Anonymous. (2018). Modern slavery: A hidden, everyday problem. *The Global Slavery Index*. Retrieved from https://www.globalslaveryindex.org

Bentley, D., & McCallum, A. (2019). Rise and fall: The shift in household growth rates since the 1990s. *CIVITAS*. Retrieved from http://www.civitas.org.uk/content/files/riseandfalltheshiftinhouseholdgrowthratessincethe1990s.pdf

Berger, P. (1969). *The social reality of religion*. London, England: Penguin.

Berlinksi, D. (2009). *The Devil's delusion: Atheism and its scientific pretensions*. New York, NY: Basic Books.

Bloch, M. (1953). *The historian's craft* (P. Putnam, Trans.). New York, NY: Vintage.

Bonacich, E. (1972). A theory of ethnic antagonism: The split labor market. *American Sociological Review, 37*(5), 547–559.

Bovey, A. (2015). Women in Medieval society. *The British Library: The Middle Ages*. Retrieved from https://www.bl.uk/the-middle-ages/articles/women-in-medieval-society

Bruce, S. (2002). *God is dead: Secularization in the West*. Boston, MA: Blackwell.

Bruun, H. H., & Whimster, S. (2012). Introduction. In Bruun, H. & Whimster, S. (Eds.) *Max Weber: Collected methodological writings*. London, England: Routledge.

Burke, P. *The Italian Renaissance: Culture & society in Italy* (3rd ed.). Princeton, NJ: Princeton.

Burton, N. (2105). When homosexuality stopped being a mental disorder. *Psychology Today*. Retrieved from https://www.psychologytoday.com/us/blog/hide-and-seek/201509/when-homosexuality-stopped-being-mental-disorder

Butler, R. N. (1969). Age-ism: Another form of bigotry. *The Gerontologist, 9*(4), 243–246.

Caldwell, J. (2004). Demographic theory: A long view. *Population and Development Review, 30*(2), 297–316.

Chaiklin, H. (2011). Attitudes, behavior, and social practice. *Journal of Sociology & Social Welfare, 38*(1), 31–54.

Chambliss, R. (1954). *Social thought from Hammurabi to Comte*. New York, NY: Dryden.

Christiano, K., Swatos, W., Jr., & Kivisto, P. (2016). *Sociology of religion: Contemporary developments*. New York, NY: Rowman & Littlefield.

Cole, K. (2019). *Developing female leaders*. Nashville, TN: Thomas Nelson.

Collins, P. H. (2007). Going public: Doing the sociology that had no name. In Clawson, D., Zussman, R., Misra, J., Gerstel, N., Stokes, R., Anderton, D., & Burawoy, M. (Eds.) *Public sociology: Fifteen eminent sociologists debate politics and the profession in the twenty-first century*. Berkeley and Los Angeles, CA: University of California.

Cooper, B. (1992). "The disabled God." *Theology Today, 49*(2), 173–182. doi:10.1177/004057369204900204

Crosby, R. G., III, & Smith, E. I. (2015). Church support as a predictor of children's spirituality and prosocial behavior. *Journal of Psychology and Theology, 43*(4), 243–254.

Crouch, A. (2013). *Culture making: Recovering our creative calling*. Downers Grover, IL: Intervarsity.

Davis, N. (Ed.). (1993). *Prostitution: An international handbook on trends, problems, and policies*. Westport, CT: Greenwood.

Dawkins, R. (2006). *The God delusion*. Boston, MA: Houghton Mifflin Harcourt.

Dough, W. (1994). *Sayings of E. Stanley Jones: A treasury of wisdom and wit*. Franklin, TN: Providence House.

Dowling, P., & Brown, A. (2010). *Doing research/reading research: Re-interrogating education*. New York, NY: Routledge.

Drescher, J. (2012). The removal of homosexuality from the DSM: Its impact on today's marriage equality debate. *Journal of Gay & Lesbian Mental Health, 16*(20), 124–135.

Eastwood, C. (Director). (1986). *Heartbreak ridge* [Video file]. Los Angeles, CA: Malpaso/Jay Weston.

Eiesland, N. L. (1994). *The disabled God: Toward a liberatory theology of disability*. Nashville, TN: Abingdon.

Emanuel, E., Onwuteaka-Philipsen, B., Urwin, J., & Cohen, J. (2016). Attitudes and practices of euthanasia and physician-assisted suicide in the United States, Canada, and Europe. *JAMA, 316*(1), 79–90. doi:10.1001/jama.2016.8499

Emory, J. (Ed.). (1853). *The works of the Rev. John Wesley, A.M.* New York, NY: Carlton & Phillips.

Eschle, C. (2004). Constructing "the Anti-Globalisation Movement." *International Journal of Peace Studies, 9*(1), 61–84.

Finke, R., & Stark, R. (1992). *The churching of America, 1776-1990: Winners and losers in our religious economy.* New Brunswick, NJ: Rutgers University.

Flory, R., & Miller, D. (2007). *Gen X religion.* New York, NY: Routledge.

Foster, R. (2009). *Celebration of discipline: The path to spiritual growth.* New York: NY: HarperCollins.

Franklin, S., Lury, C., & Stacey, J. (2000). *Global nature, global culture.* London, England: Sage.

Friedman, I. (1990). *The other victims: First person stories of non-Jews persecuted by the Nazis.* Boston, MA: Houghton Mifflin.

Fuller, R. (2001). *Spiritual but not religious: Understanding unchurched America.* New York, NY: Oxford University.

Furseth, I., & Repstad, P. (2006). *An introduction to the sociology of religion: Classical and contemporary perspectives.* Aldershot: Ashgate.

Gadoua, S. P. (2013). Three reasons why you shouldn't marry for love: By raising the bar, have we weakened the institution? *Psychology Today.* Retrieved from https://www.psychologytoday.com/us/blog/contemplating-divorce/201311/3-reasons-why-you-shouldnt-marry-love-alone

Gerrish, B. A. (1984). *A prince of the church: Schleiermacher and the beginnings of modern theology.* Philadelphia, PA: Fortress Press.

Gill, R. (2003). The "empty" church revisited. Aldershot, England.

Glenn, C. L. (2012). Stepping in and stepping out: Examining the way anticipatory career socialization impacts identity negotiation of African American women in academia. In Gutiérrez y Muhs, G., Niemann, Y., Gonzalez, C., & Harris, A. (Eds.) *Presumed incompetent: The intersections of race and class for women in academia* (pp. 133–141). Logan, UT: Utah State University.

Goldman, B. (2017). Two minds: The cognitive differences between men and women. *Stanford Medicine: Sex, Gender and Medicine.* Retrieved from https://stanmed.stanford.edu/2017spring/how-mens-and-womens-brains-are-different.html

Gonzalez, J. (1985). *The history of Christianity,* Vol 1 and Vol. 2. San Francisco, CA: HarperSanFrancisco.

Gray, J. (1992). *Men are from Mars, women are from Venus: The classic guide to understanding the opposite sex.* New York, NY: HarperCollins.

Gregory, B. (2012). *The unintended reformation: How a religious revolution secularized society.* Cambridge, England: Belknap.

Harrill, J. A. (2000). The use of the New Testament in the American slave controversy: A case history in the hermeneutical tension between biblical interpretation and Christian moral debate. *Religion and American Culture, 10*(2), 149–186.

Hatcher, D. (2002). Saved by grace V—Election, free will, fairness, and evangelism. *Trinitykirk. org.* Retrieved from http://www.eefweb.org/sermons/topical/Saved%20By%20Grace/Election%20Free%20Will%20Fairness%20and%20Evangelism.htm

Heelas, P., Woodhead, L., Seel, B., Szerszynski, B., & Tusting, K. (Eds.). (2005). *The spiritual revolution: Why religion is giving way to spirituality*. Malden, MA: Blackwell.

Heffernan, C. (2013). Intimate with God: Julian of Norwich. *Magistra: A Journal of Women's Spirituality in History, 19*(1), 40–57.

Hefner, P. (2012). Mobility: Disability and life in the Spirit. *Dialog: A Journal of Theology, 51*(3): 195–201. doi:10.1111/j.1540-6385.2012.00685.x

Heidemann, B., Sukhomlinova, O. & O' Rand, A. M. (1998). Economic independence, economic status, and empty nest in midlife marital disruption. *Journal of Marriage and the Family, 60*(1), 219–231.

Hitchens, R. (2007). *God is not great: How religion poisons everything*. New York, NY: Hatchett Book Group.

Hollander, P. (2018). Explaining the counterculture. *Academic Questions, 31*, 23–32.

Kant, I. (1970). An answer to the question: What is enlightenment? In T. Humphrey (Tr.) *Kant's political writings* (pp. 54–60). Cambridge, England.

Kärkkäinen, V. (2016). *Spirit and salvation*. Grand Rapids, MI: Wm. B. Eerdmanns.

Kellner, D. (2002). Globalization. *Sociological Theory, 20*(3), 285–305.

Kennedy, J. W. (2004). The 4-14 window. *Christianity Today, 48*(7), 53.

Kinnaman, D., & Hawkins, A. (2016). *You lost me: Why young Christians are leaving church . . . and rethinking faith*. Ada, MI: Baker Books.

Klesse, C. (2006). Polyamory and its "others": Contesting the terms of non-monagamy. *Sexualities, 9*(5), 565–583.

Kline, M. (2019). Suzerain treaties & the covenant documents in the Bible. *The reading room*. Retrieved from https://www.fivesolas.com/suzerain.htm

Knox, J. (2016). *Sacro-Egoism: The rise of religious individualism in the West*. Eugene, OR: Wipf & Stock.

Kohls, L. R. (1984). *The values Americans live by*. Washington, DC: Meridian House International.

Laluddin, H. (2016). A review of three major sociological theories and an Islamic perspective. *International Journal of Islamic Thought, 10*, 8–26.

Lehman, J. (2019). *Your child is not your equal: Why you have to be the boss*. Retrieved from https://www.empoweringparents.com/article/your-child-is-not-your-equal-why-you-have-to-be-the-boss/

Lightfoot, J. B. (Trans.). (1989). *The Apostolic Fathers* (2nd ed.). Grand Rapids, MI: Baker.

Loannidis, J. P. A. (2018). Meta-research: Why research on research matters. *PLOS Biology, 16*(3), e2005468.

Márquez, G. G. (2004). *Memories of my melancholy whores*. New York, NY: Vintage.

Mascolo, M. (2016). Is radical individualism destroying our moral compass? *Psychology Today*. Retrieved from https://www.psychologytoday.com/us/blog/values-matter/201612/is-radical-individualism-destroying-our-moral-compass?collection=1097070

May, S. (2005). *Children matter: Celebrating their place in the church, family, and community*. Grand Rapids, MI: William B. Eerdmans.

McCloud, S. (2007). Liminal subjectivities and religious change: Circumscribing Giddens for the study of contemporary American religion. *Journal of Contemporary Religion, 22*(3), 296.

McGiffert, A. C. (1909). The influence of Christianity upon the Roman Empire. *The Harvard Theological Review, 2*(1), 28–49.

McGrath, A. E. (1997). *An Introduction to Christianity*. Malden, MA: Blackwell.

McGrath, A. E. (1998). *Historical theology: An introduction to the history of Christian thought*. Malden, MA: Blackwell.

Mead, G. H. (1997). *Mind, self, and society*. Pleven, Bulgaria: EA.

Miller, C. (2017). Why men don't want the jobs done mostly by women. *The New York Times*. Retrieved from https://www.nytimes.com/2017/01/04/upshot/why-men-dont-want-the-jobs-done-mostly-by-women.html

Miller, W. W. (1996). *Durkheim, morals and modernity*. London, England: UCL.

Mills, K., & Mills, P. (Eds.). (2000). *C. Wright Mills: Letters and autobiography*. Berkeley, CA: University of California.

Moorhead, J. (2000). Preaching the Holy War. *Christian History, 11*(1), 39.

Muto, S. (2014). Catherine of Siena. *The Catholic Library World, 84*(4), 244.

Noll, M. (1992). *A history of Christianity in the United States and Canada*. Grand Rapids, MI: William B. Eerdmans.

Ogburn, W. F. (1947). How technology changes society. *The Annals of the American Academy of Political and Social Science, 249*, 81–88.

O'Hara, L., & Shue, C. (2014). A sensitive question: Asking about race in a research interview. *The Qualitative Report, 19*, 1–21.

Olson, R. E. (1999). *The story of Christian theology: Twenty centuries of tradition & reform*. Illinois, IN: InterVarsity.

Paquette, D. (2016). Men say they work more than women: Here's the truth. *The Washington Post*. Retrieved from https://www.washingtonpost.com/news/wonk/wp/2016/06/29/men-say-they-work-more-than-women-heres-the-truth/?noredirect=on&utm_term=.381fd66d016e

Philologos. (2011). Did Moses have a speech impediment? *Forward*. Retrieved from https://forward.com/culture/142439/did-moses-have-a-speech-impediment/

Richards, L. (1988). *Children's ministry: Nurturing faith within the family of God*. Grand Rapids, MI: Ministry Resources Library.

Ritzer, (2018). *The McDonaldization of society: Into the Digital Age*. London, England: Sage.

Roberts, M. (2009). Retrieving humility. *Feminist Theology, 18*(1), 53.

Roof, W. C. (1999). *Spiritual marketplace: Baby boomers and the remaking of American religion*. Princeton, NJ: Princeton University.

Rosenfeld, M., & Roesler, K. (2019). Cohabitation experience and cohabitation's association with marital dissolution. *Journal of Marriage and Family, 81*, 42–48. doi:10.1111/jomf.12530

Roven, C., Snyder, D., Snyder, Z., Suckle, R. (Producers), & Jenkins, P. (Director). (2017). *Wonder Woman*. Burbank, CA: Warner Bros.

Runyon, T. (1998). *The new creation: John Wesley's theology today*. Nashville, TN: Abingdon.

Saad, L. (2008). Americans believe religion is losing clout. *GALLUP Online*. Retrieved from http://www.gallup.com/poll/113533/Americans-Believe-Religion-Losing-Clout.aspx

Salter, M. (2019). The problem with a fight against toxic masculinity. *The Atlantic*. Retrieved from https://www.theatlantic.com/health/archive/2019/02/toxic-masculinity-history/583411/ .

Satterthwaite, D. (2009). The implications of population growth and urbanization for climate change. *International Institute for Environment and Development (IIED), 21*(2), 545–567. doi:10.1177/095624780934436

Sauer, J. (2007). *AARP Oregon poll of employers in the state on age 50+ employees*. Washington, DC: AARP: Knowledge Management.

Segarra, L. (2018). California's economy is now bigger than all of the U.K. *Fortune*. Retrieved from http://fortune.com/2018/05/05/california-fifth-biggest-economy-passes-united-kingdom/

Semuels, A. (2016). Poor at 20, poor for life. *The Atlantic*. Retrieved from https://www.theatlantic.com/business/archive/2016/07/social-mobility-america/491240/

Sherman, S. R. (1998). Film and folklore. In Brunvand, J. H. (Ed.) *American folklore: An encyclopedia*. New York, NY: Garland.

Shipp, S., Gupta, N., Scott, J., Weber, C., Finnin, M., & Lal, B. (2012). Advancing manufacturing to new frontiers: Increasing opportunities for society. *Innovations: Technology, Governance, Globalization, 7*(3), 71–81.

Sorba, R. (2007). Homosexual activists intimidate American Psychiatric Association into removing homosexuality from list of disorders. *Conservative Colloquium: An intellectual forum for all things conservative*. Retrieved from https://conservativecolloquium.wordpress.com/2007/10/01/homosexual-activists-intimidate-american-psychiatric-association-into-removing-homosexuality-from-list-of-disorders/

Starks, B., & Robinson, R. (2007). Moral cosmology, religion, and adult values for children. *Journal for the Scientific Study of Religion, 46*(1), 17–35.

Stearns, R., & Stearn, R. (2013). *He walks among us*. Nashville, TN: Thomas Nelson.

Swartley, W. (1983). *Slavery, Sabbath, war & women*. Pennsylvania, PA: Herald Press.

Taylor, C. (2002). *Varieties of religion today: William James revisited*. Boston, MA: Harvard University.

Tertullian, Q. S. F. (1885). *Prescription against heretics*. In Holmes, P. (Ed./Trans.) *Ante-Nicene fathers* (Vol. 3). Buffalo, NY: Christian Literature Publishing. Retrieved from http://www.newadvent.org/fathers/0311.htm

Thompson, D. (1996). Women, men, slaves and the Bible: Hermeneutical inquiries. *Christian Scholar's Review, 25*(3), 326–349.

Vanier, J. (1998). *Being human*. New York, NY. Paulist Press.

Vogt, W. P., Gardner, D. C., & Haeffele, L. M. (2012). *When to use what research design*. New York, NY: Guilford.

Wagley, C., & Harris, M. (1958). *Minorities in the New World: Six case studies*. New York, NY: Columbia University.

Walker, B. (1968). *The new immorality*. New York, NY: Doubleday.

Wand, A., Peisah, C., Draper, B., Jones, C., & Brodaty, H. (2016). Rational suicide, euthanasia, and the very old: Two case reports. *Case Reports in Psychiatry, 2016*, 1–5. doi:10.1155/2016/4242064

Wax, T. (2019). Is there really an "orthodox" view of sexuality? *The Gospel Coalition*. Retrieved from https://www.thegospelcoalition.org/blogs/trevin-wax/really-orthodox-view-sexuality/

Webb, R. K. (1960). *Harriet Martineau: A radical Victorian*. New York, NY: Columbia.

Weber, M. (1964). *The sociology of religion*. Boston, MA: Beacon.

Wesley, J. (1872). On visiting the sick. *Sermon 98*. Retrieved from http://wesley.nnu.edu/john-wesley/the-sermons-of-john-wesley-1872-edition/sermon-98-on-visiting-the-sick/

Wesley, J. (1766). The law established through faith. *Christian Classics Ethereal Library*. Retrieved from https://www.ccel.org/ccel/wesley/sermons.v.xxxv.html#v.xxxv-p0.3

Westley, F., Olsson, P., Folke, C., Homer-Dixon, T., Vredenburg, H., Loorbach, D., . . . van der Leeuw, S. (2011). Tipping toward sustainability: Emerging pathways of transformation. *Ambio, 40*, 762–780. doi:10.1007/s13280-011-0186-9

White, J., Klein, D., & Martin, T. (2015). *Family theories: An introduction*. Washington, DC: Sage.

White, M. (2012). Is adultery ever justified?: You be the judge! *Psychology Today*. Retrieved from https://www.psychologytoday.com/us/articles/201207/is-adultery-ever-justified

Wilson, B. (2003). Prediction and prophecy in the future of religion. In G. Davie, P. Heelas, L. Woodhead (Eds.), *Predicting religion: Christian, secular and alternative futures* (pp. 64–73). Aldershot, England: Ashgate.

Wilson, B. (1966). *Religion in secular society: A sociological comment*. Oxford, England: Clarendon.

Wilson, B. (1982). *Religion in sociological perspective*. New York, NY: Oxford University.

Wilson, B. (1979). The return of the sacred. *Journal for the Scientific Study of Religion, 18*(3), 268.

Wilson, B. (1990). *The social dimensions of sectarianism*. Oxford, England: Clarendon.

Witt, J. (2009). *SOC*. New York, NY: McGraw-Hill.

Woodhead, L., Fletcher, P., Kawanami, H., & David Smith, D. (Eds.) (2002). *Religions in the modern world*. London, England: Routledge.

Wright, B. (1983). *Physical disability: A psychosocial approach*. (2nd ed.). New York, NY: HarperCollins.

Wright, N. T. (2019). Jesus is coming: Plant a tree! *Plough Quarterly Magazine*, p. 4. Retrieved from https://www.plough.com/en/topics/justice/environment/jesus-is-coming-plant-a-tree

Yong, A. (2011). *The Bible, disability, and the church: A new vision of the people of God*. Grand Rapids, MI: Wm. B. Eerdmanns.

CONTRIBUTORS

Craig Brigman (Chapter 12) works as a financial advisor (but has also been an assistant professor of IT teaching technology), he was involved in telecommunication at AT&T, and he worked as a revenue agent for the IRS. Having served in the 82nd Airborne Division, Craig went on to multiple successful careers and is married to a wonderful woman. Together, they have four children. Craig has degrees in business, accounting, education, and currently spends his extra time mentoring and advising small businesses. Craig has helped launch more than 20 successful businesses and helped many to recover from financial distress and be successful.

Pastor Brian Cook (Chapter 7) is a graduate of Asbury Theological Seminary and has been pastor of local churches for 32 years. He has served churches in Virginia, Wisconsin, and Guayaquil, Ecuador. He is currently serving Brookhill Wesleyan Church in Forest, Virginia. Brian and his wife Martha have been married for 37 years and have four married children and six grandchildren.

Donna Davis Donald (Chapter 4) is an assistant professor in the Department of History at Liberty University. She joined the history faculty in 2001 and was honored with the Liberty University's President's Award for Teaching Excellence in 2014. Donna also serves on the Faculty Advisory Board for the Center for Academic Development, is a member of Phi Alpha Theta, the Conference on Faith and History, the National Council on Public History, and the American Association of State and Local History.

Dr. Benjamin Esswein, PhD (Chapter 3), is an assistant professor of History at Liberty University since 2014. Professor Esswein's academic focus is on Early Modern Europe, Central and Eastern Europe, and the Austro-Ottoman Borderlands in the sixteenth and early seventeenth centuries. His dissertation concerned "The Formation of Territorial Churches in the Hapsburg/Ottoman Borderlands: Primus Truber, Hans Ungand, and Peter Paul Vergerio, 1550–1565." He recently presented a paper, "Compromise for the Gospel" at the Sixteenth Century Society Conference, Continuity and Compromise: Regional Movements across the Spectrum of the Congressional Divide (2018).

Heather R. Harney (Chapter 11) is a writer and graduate student with a training and management background. She has been called to help others, find their voices, and to create a safe space for those with disabilities—both visible and invisible—to share their stories. She is currently pursuing a Master's in Theology from Fuller Theological Seminary. Heather graduated from George Fox University with a BA in Biblical Studies and a Minor in Literature in 2017. She is an *übergeek* who loves attending comic cons, traveling, reading, exploring creation, and collecting memories.

Skylar Collins (Chapter 2) is a junior at Liberty University and pursuing a degree in the biomedical sciences. He was chairman of the Florida Federation of Teenage Republicans, he has written a book on politics and activism, and he is currently researching and developing a new type of immunotherapy called "The Yahweh Technique." Additionally, Skylar works as a medical and research consultant, providing advice to patients and groups in need of solutions and direction), and he is a board member of a medical group launching a new hospital system in India.

Stephen Konyndyk (Chapter 5) is the owner of Endurance Auto Repair and Tire in Lynchburg, Virginia. He has worked in the auto business for almost two decades, and he is the fourth generation in his family to manage/own an auto and tire service business.

Dr. Jennifer M. Matheny, PhD (Chapter 9), is an assistant professor of Old Testament at Nazarene Theological Seminary in Kansas City, Missouri. She did her PhD work at the University of Kent, Canterbury. Her research focuses on gendered violence in the Hebrew Bible, and the ethical responsibility of voices within the canon, utilizing the work of Mikhail M. Bakhtin. Matheny is passionate about the church and enjoys teaching and preaching the Old Testament. This fall (2019), she has an illustrated translation of *Joshua* scheduled to be released with GlossaHouse in their Illustrated Hebrew-English Old Testament Series (GIHEOT).

Ashley Mayhew (Chapter 1) is a junior at Liberty University where she is working on a degree in social work. She is active in her church (and at various Christian camps), and she enjoys reading and volunteering in her spare time. She is a proud aunt and loves spending time with her niece, Reagan.

Joshua Nunn (Chapter 13) is a language and computer trainer specialist currently living in central Africa with his wife and children. He has a BA in Leadership and Ministry from Multnomah University in Portland, Oregon, and has worked in the computer industry and church ministry since 2010.

Dr. Bill Pubols, DMin (Chapter 8), has been the director of the Biblical Studies Center in Boise, Idaho, since 2013. He worked as a campus minister with *CRU* at the University of Oregon until 2004, when he started an Athletes in Action chapter at Boise State University. He began teaching apologetics at the Biblical Studies Center in 2009, was hired as Executive Director in 2013, and completed his Doctor of Ministry from Talbot Graduate School of Theology in 2018.

Dr. Tim Tsohantaridis, PhD (Chapter 10) teaches Greek and Biblical Studies in the College of Christian Studies at George Fox University, and has hosted multiple student groups over the years to his native Greece, as well as other Biblical sites and Europe. He is an ordained minister, passionate about soccer, and loves spending time with his children and grandchildren. Tim divides his time between New England and the Northwest with his wife, Valerie, and coauthored a Bible survey textbook in 2017, *God in the details: A biblical survey of the Hebrew and Greek scriptures* (Kendall Hunt).

Dr. Kenny Warren, DMin (Chapter 6), serves in an administrative role in the psychology department at Liberty University in the School of Behavioral Sciences. He resides in central Virginia where he enjoys spending time with his family, serving in his church, and attending collegiate sporting events. He recently coauthored a book on effective Sunday School practices, *But children matter* (Wipf and Stock), which is expected be released in fall of 2019.

Index

T